THE TEN TRILLION DOLLAR GAMBLE

THE TEN TRILLION DOLLAR GAMBLE

THE COMING DEFICIT DEBACLE AND HOW TO INVEST NOW

RUSS KOESTERICH

NEW YORK CHICAGO SAN FRANCISCO
LISBON LONDON MADRID MEXICO CITY MILAN
NEW DELHI SAN JUAN SEOUL SINGAPORE
SYDNEY TORONTO

1 2 3 4 5 6 7 8 9   DOC/DOC   1 8 7 6 5 4 3 2 1

ISBN 978-0-07-175357-9 (print book)
MHID   0-07-175357-3

ISBN 978-0-07-175404-0 (e-book)
MHID   0-07-175404-0

The interior design is by Lee Fukui and Mauna Eichner.

This publication is designed to provide accurate and authoritative information in regard to the subject matter covered. It is sold with the understanding that neither the author nor the publisher is engaged in rendering legal, accounting, securities trading, or other professional services. If legal advice or other expert assistance is required, the services of a competent professional person should be sought.

> —From a *Declaration of Principles jointly adopted by a Committee of the American Bar Association and a Committee of Publishers and Associations*

McGraw-Hill books are available at special quantity discounts to use as premiums and sales promotions or for use in corporate training programs. To contact a representative, please e-mail us at bulksales@mcgraw-hill.com.

This book is printed on acid-free paper.

To my parents, who taught me the dignity in thrift.

CONTENTS

Acknowledgments

I WOULD LIKE TO THANK a number of my colleagues at BlackRock whose guidance and assistance were instrumental in researching and writing this book: Blake Grossman, Naozer Dadachanji, Ken Kroner, Paul Harrison, Tom Parker, Fred Dopfel, Joanne Madera, Mike Rierson, Daniel Morillo, Gerry Garvey, and Dennis Stattman. I also need to acknowledge Nancy Card who was instrumental in the editing of this book. Thank you for your patience, wit, and tolerance of my creative uses of English grammar. And finally, thank you to my wife Alice and son Palmer for their understanding, support, and encouragement.

INTRODUCTION

OR THE FISCAL YEAR 2010 the U.S. budget deficit was approximately $1.3 trillion. Huge numbers can be abstractions, so let's put this one in context. Simply stated, $1.3 trillion is approximately equal to the total amount of debt the United States accumulated from its founding until 1984. In a single year the U.S. government would outspend its income by as much as it did during two entire centuries of cross-continental expansion, civil war, depression, world wars, and the implementation of the modern social welfare state.

Unfortunately, 2010 was not an aberration. In 2009 the deficit was an even larger $1.4 trillion. And going forward, things do not get much better. Between 2010 and 2019, we will add more than $900 billion a year, on average, to the national debt. This means that by the year 2020, the national debt will have more than doubled from current levels. Then, after 2020, things will start to get much worse.

Since the 1980s, economists have periodically warned that the rising U.S. national debt was going to cause big problems for the United States. But in the past when they issued these warnings, they were talking about some time in the abstract future. We are now rapidly approaching that future. The government's continuing inability to balance its budget is about to move from the abstract to the concrete. The enormous U.S. deficit will soon fundamentally change the world's economic and financial climate: taxes will begin to rise, benefit levels will start to fall, and interest rates will go up. Furthermore, unless the United States' political class begins to demonstrate far more courage and resolve than it has in the past, inflation may jump as well. In such an environment, the old strategies for financial success, even survival, that have served investors for the past three decades will no longer work. This book will explore what investors can do to weather, and to the extent possible, take advantage of, these events.

How Bad Will It Be?

According to documents issued by the Congressional Budget Office (CBO), the official scorekeeper of the U.S. budget, the federal government is in the most precarious financial state it has ever been in, outside of a major war, such as World War II or the Civil War. Adding to the problem, a number of our largest states are in dire financial condition as well. And while the official budget estimates are ominous, they are also optimistic. In other words, they make a number of assumptions that are unrealistic, bordering on fanciful.

The official federal budget numbers assume, for example, no recession during the next decade. In fact, the budget assumes that the U.S. economy will grow at roughly 4 percent between 2011 and 2014, or approximately twice the rate at which the economy has expanded over the past decade. If the economy grows more slowly, which it almost certainly will, then tax revenues will be lower, spending for benefits will be higher, and the deficits will be even larger. The budget also assumes a number of spending cuts, which in the past have consistently failed to materialize. If history is any guide, deficits over the next decade will in fact be significantly higher even than today's dire forecasts.

Why Dick Cheney Was Wrong: Deficits Matter

Many people will argue that we have been here before and don't need to worry. It is true that back in the 1980s, the country also faced large deficits. Yet, the 1980s were a prosperous decade, aside from a stock market crash or two. In 2002, former Vice President Dick Cheney famously remarked that "Reagan proved that deficits don't matter." Unfortunately, Cheney was wrong. Deficits do matter, and more importantly, they will eventually start impacting individual Americans. The fact that we've gotten away with our financial profligacy in the past does not mean that we will get away with it in the future. Compared to the 1980s, there are a few critical differences that suggest that soon the deficits will not only matter but they will matter quite a bit.

First, while the deficits of the mid-1980s were certainly large, they were comparatively small when measured against what we are facing today. Even at the peak of the budget crisis in 1985, deficits were approximately 6 percent of the gross domestic product (GDP). In 2009 and 2010, the deficits were approximately 10 percent of the GDP, the largest since World War II.

There is a second critical difference between 1985 and today: we owe more as a country. Leaving aside some of its more ambiguous obligations, such as the more than $5 trillion of mortgage debt it has recently guaranteed, the U.S. federal government currently has approximately $14 trillion in outstanding debt, equal to more than 90 percent of the gross domestic product. By comparison, back in 1985 the gross federal debt was roughly 45 percent of the GDP. This is important because there is significant evidence that higher levels of debts make deficits more dangerous. The larger the current level of debt, the more likely it is that any new borrowing to fund continuing deficits will push up interest rates.

Finally, in the mid-1980s, the United States was still in the early stages of recovering from the heightened inflation of the 1970s. As a result, short-term interest rates were falling, and bond investors were becoming more comfortable that rates would continue to fall as the Federal Reserve (Fed) seemed to have finally gotten the better of inflation. Today, we are in the opposite position. Investors expect that the Fed will soon be raising rates and inflation has nowhere to go but up. What this means is that investors are going to be reluctant to buy bonds and lock in today's low interest rates. If investors expect inflation to accelerate in the future, this will further depress bond prices and put upward pressure on interest rates.

Even Washington is starting to get religion, or at least they are talking as if they have, as it is becoming increasingly apparent that our current fiscal path is unsustainable. The policy choices for Congress are simple to articulate but notoriously difficult to implement: raise taxes and/or cut spending. Should Congress attempt the former, any meaningful tax increase—one that actually raises enough money to put a real dent in the deficit—will have to impact the middle class, not just the affluent. The simple reality is that the wealthy do not have enough money to single-handedly cover our obligations.

But tax hikes alone won't do the job, so spending cuts will also be necessary. Here, a quick examination of the budget math reveals how difficult this will be. Five-sixths of the federal budget is made up of entitlement spending (Medicare, Medicaid, and Social Security), interest payments on our outstanding debt, and defense spending. If defense spending remains sacrosanct, as it has been in the past, and we plan on meeting our obligations to existing holders of U.S. debt, serious cuts will have to be made in the major entitlement programs. Contrary to suggestions from angry radio show hosts, cosmetic cuts to the National Endowment for the Arts and eliminating "waste" won't do it.

In order to have any meaningful impact, cuts will have to be made in programs that impact lots of people. This means putting both Social Security and Medicare benefits on the chopping block. The problem with this approach was neatly illustrated in a recent *Wall Street Journal* article. The main obstacle to cutting the deficit is that so many Americans benefit from deficit spending. Nearly half of all Americans live in a household in which someone receives a government benefit, more than at any time in history. And at the same time nearly half of Americans, fully 45 percent, pay no federal income taxes.[1] Effectively, we have a growing portion of the population dependent on government spending and a dwindling portion paying for it.

Raising taxes and cutting benefits to the extent needed to really reduce the deficit would inflict serious economic pain on most Americans. Lawmakers are notoriously reluctant to vote for actions that inflict even moderate pain, so their efforts almost certainly will not go far enough. As a result, even though Americans will see higher taxes and fewer benefits, deficits will continue to rise.

So where do larger deficits leave the United States? Historically, chronically high deficits have been associated with slower economic growth, higher real interest rates, and in many cases, some amount of inflation. After three years of economic pain through 2010, that's not what most people want to hear.

One of the more noxious side effects of large deficits is higher interest rates. In order to fund the deficit, that is, to pay for the outlays that tax revenues don't cover, the federal government sells Treasury bonds. Higher deficits mean that the federal government will need to sell more bonds to pay its bills. As with most things, the greater the supply, the lower the price. Lower Treasury prices translate into higher interest rates, and because the interest rate on Treasury obligations is used to set other interest rates, this will lead to higher mortgage rates, higher student loan rates, and higher car loan rates.

When rates do start to rise, these increases will undercut the stabilization in the housing market. Rising mortgage rates mean that fewer people can afford to buy. A significant rise in rates is likely to cause another leg down in the housing prices. Even a modest rise in rates will cause prices to stagnate, which will in turn undermine the housing rebound that many have been expecting.

Large deficits are also likely to lead to slower economic growth: rising interest rates will be a further drag on the economy. Both corporations and the government will need to devote more of their income to interest payments rather than productive investments, like building new roads or factories. As productive investment declines, we are likely to see slower overall economic growth, which will in turn translate into a weaker job market and higher unemployment. Getting a job will be more difficult, especially when compared to the relatively robust labor market we enjoyed in the 1980s and 1990s.

The stock market will also be impacted, and not for the better. One of the critical factors supporting stock prices during the great bull market between 1982 and 2000 was the slow, steady decline in long-term interest rates. When rates decline, it lowers the cost of borrowing for businesses, spurs consumer activity, and makes stocks more attractive relative to fixed-income investments, that is, bonds. Relatively low interest rates are critical in supporting the stock market's overall valuation. The amount of money people are willing to pay for a dollar of earnings normally goes up when interest rates are low. As a result, when long-term interest rates are falling, as they did for nearly 30 years, the valuation of the stock market tends to rise. In that way, falling interest rates act as a tailwind for equity market returns. In contrast, rising rates are a headwind.

Finally, and most dangerous, higher deficits raise the likelihood that inflation will accelerate over the long term. Rising debt levels will create serious economic pain in the form of slower growth and rising interest rates. To avoid or mitigate that pain, the Fed, while nominally an independent branch of government, can nevertheless take the politically expedient route. This entails the direct purchase of Treasury bonds by the Federal Reserve. In other words, one branch of the government, the Fed, would buy the debt of another branch of government, the Treasury. This is known as *monetizing the debt*.

Nominally at least, the Fed has been doing this since 2009 and voted to continue the practice in late 2010. While the direct purchase of U.S. debt by the Fed has yet to stir any real inflation, if this practice continues indefinitely, it will create trillions of dollars in new money, which will raise the risk that we will see higher inflation over the long term. A significant rise in inflation will weaken the dollar. This, in turn, will further increase inflation, igniting a vicious spiral of even higher rates and even higher inflation. A long-term rise in inflation is one of the risks that investors need to account for in constructing their portfolios and managing their finances.

How to Secure Your Financial Future

Outside of voting and writing letters to their representatives in Congress, there is little that most Americans can do about the federal deficit. At this point, and in the absence of some politically unpalatable choices, it is not even clear if there is a lot that elected officials will be able to do. There are, however, many things investors can and should do to protect their financial well-being. There will definitely be opportunities to make money, but these opportunities won't be found in the same places as in the past few decades.

Investors need to adjust their portfolios to reflect the new economic realities that are coming. Whether we are in for a prolonged period of high interest rates or a vicious cycle of spiraling inflation, investors must revisit their assumptions about how to save and invest for the long term. Because the global economy is affected by so many complex factors, it is impossible to say exactly when the changes will hit. Looking out over the next 10 years, however, there are some assumptions that are relatively safe to make: interest rates and taxes will be higher, U.S. economic growth will be slower, especially relative to emerging markets, and there will be higher inflation over the longer term.

Some of the implications of the deficit, particularly a rise in inflation, may be avoided if politicians and central bankers act responsibly and govern for the long term as opposed to the short term. But, while as citizens we should hope for the best, as investors we need to prepare for the worst.

The fiscal situation has now reached a point where even if politicians behave responsibly, there are no easy choices. At best, the government

tackles the deficit head on, producing a prolonged period of slower economic growth due to lower government spending and higher taxes. Even
under this scenario, the size of the deficit suggests that it will take many
years to bring it under control. During that time, interest rates are likely
to rise to accommodate the flood of new Treasury issues. And that is the
good scenario. The bad one is that the government explicitly or implicitly resorts to higher inflation as a device for managing the national debt.

No matter what, the era of cheap money is over. Interest rates will
eventually rise. They are going to go a lot higher, and they are likely to
remain there until the U.S. government demonstrates some willingness
to curb its deficits and reduce, or at least stabilize, its debt. We are in for a
period of slow growth and tough decisions.

Welcome to the new financial world.

CHAPTER 1

WHY WORRY ABOUT THE DEFICIT?

A NOTHER FLOOD OF RED INK dismays economists, bankers, and consumers alike." A headline from yesterday's *Wall Street Journal*? Actually it came from *Time* magazine in 1982. We have been agonizing over the U.S. deficit for nearly 30 years. Economists have puzzled over it, pundits have debated it, and elections have been fought over it. And yet for most of that period the economy has expanded, interest rates have fallen, and despite a few speculative bubbles, the stock market has increased tenfold. So why is the deficit going to start to hurt us now?

It's a matter of time. Some things get better with time, but the U.S. federal deficit is not one of them. In the mid-1980s, the last time the deficit was particularly high, the Sony Walkman was introduced. If you used a 60-minute cassette—if you were born after 1990, ask your older siblings—you could maybe get about 20 songs on it. The iPod 8GB Nano holds around 2,000 songs, and, adjusted for inflation, it costs the same. We have far cooler gadgets today.

When it comes to federal deficits and our national debt, however, the picture has gotten far worse. In 1984, the federal deficit was around $200 billion. In 2010 it was approximately $1.3 trillion, and given the recent extension of the Bush tax cuts, the 2011 deficit is likely to be of a similar magnitude. In 1984 total U.S. nonfinancial debt was approximately

$5 trillion. By 2010, it was more than $35 trillion, a sevenfold increase. Between 1983 and 1984 our economy grew at over 6 percent a year. Today, most economists and politicians would be thrilled if we could grow at half that speed. In 1984 the United States had net national savings of nearly $300 billion. In 2009, our net national savings were −$300 billion. And finally, in 1984 the average age of a U.S. citizen was around 30. Today it is 37. As a country, we are more indebted, slower, and older. That is why the deficit is going to start to hurt us now.

The problem with having large, persistent deficits is that someone has to finance them. This is what investors do when they buy a country's debt. U.S. deficits have gotten so large that it now takes a considerable chunk of the world's savings just to fund our deficits. And these record deficits, the largest ever recorded during peacetime, are distinguished not only by their magnitude but also by their persistence. Except for a brief period in the late 1990s, the government has spent more money than it takes in every year since 1970. This pattern of large and consistent deficits will continue over the next decade. Then it gets even worse, with deficits growing to truly astronomical levels as the country ages and medical costs skyrocket. This means fewer working-age Americans paying the bills and more retired Americans receiving benefits.

Those economists who 30 years ago predicted a day of fiscal reckoning were not wrong, just early. Our deficits are primarily driven by runaway entitlement spending, which will only get worse over time and which cannot be repealed without huge political cost. There is no evidence that today's generation of politicians is willing to pay that cost or confront the problem in a meaningful way. The cumulative effect of this will be record national debt, which eventually will have to be repaid, repudiated, or inflated away.

Over the coming years, financial markets will start to pay attention to the approaching train wreck. Investors will demand higher interest rates to buy government bonds. Higher rates will punish both bonds and stocks. Politicians will probably offer a few token efforts to rein in the deficits, so we will see higher taxes, at least on the affluent, and probably some curtailment of benefits. But this will not be enough, so deficits will continue to rise throughout the decade, and financial markets will get increasingly nervous.

There are a few scenarios for how this all ends. From a purely economic point of view, the optimistic one includes the government making a serious effort to reduce benefits and fix the long-term problem. This is not likely to happen without a crisis that forces the government's hand. In the absence of a crisis, the political costs of real deficit reform are simply too great. If you need a visual picture of what such a crisis would look like, think of burning banks in Athens, Greece, in the spring of 2010. And if you thought Greece was scary, it is worth noting that in 2009 the United States actually had a higher ratio of government debt to revenue than Greece. In other words, by one measure our fiscal position is actually worse than that of Greece![1]

That said, the United States is not Greece. For now, the world is still happy to lend us lots of money, and there is little danger of bank burnings in the near future. The more likely scenario is that we will muddle along with higher taxes, higher interest rates, and a slower economy. But there is a worse scenario, and that is inflation. This is the real nightmare possibility. If the government, through the central bank (that is, the Federal Reserve System), continues to buy its own debt, sooner or later this will cause an increase in the nation's money supply and eventually a surge in prices. Inflation will erode the value of the debt, making it easier for the government to pay it off in inflated dollars. But this will come at a huge cost to the standard of living of virtually all Americans.

As depressing as this all sounds, there are things you can do to protect your finances. That is primarily what this book is about. But to lay the groundwork, so that you will understand what is going to happen and why, I am going to start with a couple of chapters on deficit economics. After that, I am going to describe the warning signs to look for and how to read the economic tea leaves. Then I am going to dig into what you need to do.

While I recognize that fiscal projections and charts from the Congressional Budget Office (CBO) are not most people's idea of a relaxing afternoon, there are several reasons to persevere with a little budget math. First, it will help you to appreciate the severity of the problem. Understanding the economics will also help you to recognize the warning signs that I am going to describe in Chapter 3. Finally, I think that history is instructive. These problems have been building over decades. Understanding how we got into this mess will illustrate how difficult it will be to extricate ourselves from it. That said, those of you who feel that you already get it and who have started to stockpile canned goods and gold can skip ahead to Chapter 4, which will start to focus on how to position your portfolio. But I think you are going to do a better job of managing your finances if you keep reading here—although, full disclosure, it will get a bit nasty.

Today's Deficit: Think in Trillions

What are fiscal deficits and the national debt? Why do we have them, how big are they, and why can't we get rid of them?

The U.S. federal deficit for 2009 was approximately $1.4 trillion, by far the largest in our country's history. When the current annual deficit is measured as a percentage of the gross domestic product (GDP), it is the largest since World War II (see Figure 1-1). While the deficits of 2009 and 2010 were magnified by the government's continuing efforts to stabilize the economy, deficit spending had become the norm long before the financial crisis hit, and it will be with us long after we have forgotten the miseries of 2008. As a result of perpetual deficits, today the amount of gross federal debt outstanding—that is, the sum of all previous deficits and surpluses—is approximately $14 trillion. Of that amount, roughly $9.3 trillion is publicly traded debt, while an additional $4.5 trillion is intra-government agency borrowing—that is, it is debt held by the Social

Security trust fund (it is worth remembering that as large as those numbers are, they ignore roughly $3 trillion of state and municipal debt as well as approximately $5 trillion in mortgage-related bonds guaranteed by the federal government). And the truly bad news is that, as daunting as that number sounds, it will get significantly worse from here.

Figure 1.1 **U.S. Surpluses and Deficits as a Percentage of the Nominal GDP**

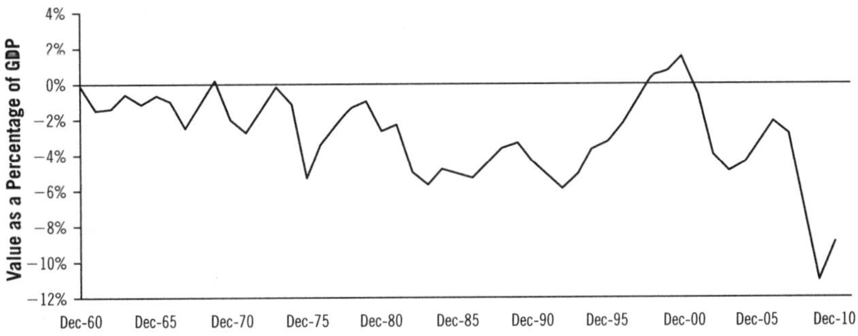

Source: Bloomberg and the Organisation for Economic Co-operation and Development, as of April 15, 2010.

Large deficits are not expected to disappear any time soon. Even under some very optimistic assumptions, the administration expects the federal deficit to average more than $900 billion per year through 2019, after which the deficits are likely to really take off under the burden of unchecked entitlement spending and an aging population. By 2019 publicly traded debt, which excludes intra-government holdings, is expected to be over $17 trillion, roughly 15 times what it was back in 1982! Much of this increase will be driven by the major entitlement programs of the New Deal and Great Society: Social Security, Medicare, and Medicaid. Together, these three programs will account for an ever-growing percentage of the federal budget. Without significant changes to these programs, the steady escalation in spending will push the government's debt and interest expense to unprecedented levels. The total costs of government, including interest expense, could more than double as a share of the economy.[2] That last point is not taken from a fringe economist or a particularly shrill blogger. It comes from the Congressional Budget Office. As the deficit grows and the government's share of the economy increases, the effects are likely to be higher interest rates, a slower economy, and potentially inflation.

ARE ALL DEFICITS BAD?

Deficits are not always bad. There are legitimate reasons for a country to spend more in a given year than it generates in taxes. It is common for governments to run deficits during a recession. When the economy is contracting, it is reasonable for a government to spend more in an effort to stabilize the economy. Deficit spending during a recession can result from various actions, including cutting taxes, providing companies more incentives to invest, or providing unemployment or other cash transfers to citizens to lessen the pain caused by the recession. Most economists agree that deficit spending aimed at mitigating an economic downturn is money well spent.

Government spending under the right conditions and if properly targeted can help spur private demand and get a country out of a recession sooner. If citizens have more money to spend due to tax cuts or transfer payments, this is likely to spur additional spending and expedite the recovery. Along with lowering interest rates, this type of deficit spending is generally regarded as a reasonable and rational response to a recession. Unfortunately, this is not the type of deficit spending that the United States has been engaged in for most of the past three decades.

The United States is running what economists call a *structural deficit*. In other words, the deficit spending is not primarily due to a temporary, or cyclical, phenomenon such as a recession. When a recession ends, the deficits should evaporate and, ideally, revenues should return to surplus levels. But with a structural deficit, the imbalance is between long-term commitments and revenue. Even if the U.S. economy were to stage a miraculous and sustained economic recovery, nobody is expecting the U.S. deficit to go away. Our deficit, while exaggerated by the recent recession, is a function of our spending more on entitlements than we are able or willing to generate in taxes. Our deficit therefore accumulates year after year. We as a nation habitually spend more than we take in.

The United States is not alone in resorting to deficit spending to fund entitlements. In recent decades, many countries around the world have seen expanding entitlements push them into chronic deficits. The practice isn't a recent development either. Consider, for example, the Roman Empire.

Most people are familiar with the phrase "bread and circuses" and realize that it dates back to ancient Rome. It refers to the efforts of Roman emperors to maintain public support by offering food subsidies and public diversions. While comparisons to the Roman Empire always run the risk of being a bit of hyperbole, this one is fairly apt. The nature and trajectory of U.S. public spending has followed a remarkably similar pattern to that of ancient Rome. The events of 2,000 years ago serve as a useful lesson on how uncontrolled growth in government programs can wreak havoc with the public finances.

In Rome, the entitlements started around 58 BC when a small group of citizens began to receive free allotments of grain. Over the years, the handouts grew to be a perk of Roman citizenship that expanded to encompass free oil, and occasionally pork and wine. Slowly the benefits began to extend beyond Rome to include other cities in the empire, including Constantinople, Alexandria, and Antioch.[3] As with today's entitlements, what began small eventually spread, both in terms of what was received and who was covered.

In another parallel to today, the Romans also began to play around with the numbers in an effort to disguise the size of the deficits and debts they were incurring. Today, we call this *off budget spending*. In the Romans' version of this practice, the state budget for AD 150 showed the free grain allotment as allocated from the emperor's personal domain in

Egypt. As a result, it was not included in the overall accounts. Had this amount been represented in the total budget, it would have accounted for 13 percent of state spending.[4]

I am not suggesting here that the barbarians are at the gate and the United States will in short order follow in Rome's footsteps, but Roman history does illustrate two very important points. First, government spending and entitlement programs tend to become entrenched over time. Once you grant a citizen a benefit, it is extremely difficult to take it away. If anything, over time you will grant more benefits to a wider range of citizens. The other critical point, illustrated by the emperor's preference for off-balance-sheet spending, is that governments will go to great lengths to disguise the true cost of entitlement spending. Whether it is overly optimistic revenue expectations, spending cuts that never materialize, or dodgy bookkeeping for Social Security, a preference for opaque accounting infects the U.S. budget debate, just as it did in ancient Rome.

MODERN-DAY BREAD AND CIRCUSES: SOCIAL SECURITY AND MEDICARE

The fact that a large portion of government spending is on autopilot is crucially important to popping one of the great myths of the budget debate—that is, the budget problem could be solved by eliminating "waste" (always remember that one person's waste is another person's benefit). And once you add all those benefits up, there is precious little left over to cut. Once you account for entitlement spending—which can be rescinded only through a massive legislative change and in any case represents benefits that people both like and expect—interest payments, and defense spending, you've removed the lion's share of the budget from discussion. This leaves only about one-sixth of the overall budget up for discussion. Even if you somehow had eliminated everything but entitlement programs, interest payments, and defense spending, there would have still been a deficit in 2010.

We have a structural deficit because, like the Romans before us, we've granted too many benefits to too many people. Budget deficits today, whether in the United States or other countries, arise from the same underlying cause as throughout history—that is, a country is spending more money than it generates in taxes and other sources of revenue. In effect, we consume more than we produce. In order to make up the difference, we borrow from future production in order to fund today's consumption.

How big a gap exists between production and consumption? For fiscal year 2009, the total federal revenues from taxes and other sources were approximately $2.1 trillion. While $2.1 trillion seems like a good deal of money, it was actually about $1.4 trillion shy of what the government spent. For fiscal 2009 the federal government's expenditures totaled more than $3.5 trillion. The list of government expenditures would consume a book in itself, but suffice it to say that an ever-growing share of its budget is composed of what is euphemistically known as *programmatic spending*. These expenses occur regardless of budgetary constraints, falling tax receipts, or anything else. They also take up an ever-growing portion of the budget. In 2009, programmatic spending was $2.28 trillion, or 65 percent of the budget.

Another large and also unavoidable expense is interest on existing bonds. This amounts to another $187 billion, or 5.3 percent, of expenses. So in aggregate, roughly 70 percent of the budget is spent before a single vote, appropriations meeting, or discussion even takes place. When you add in defense spending, technically flexible but practically fixed, it becomes quite clear that the vast majority of federal spending is politically untouchable. This is exactly why the deficits continue to pile up year after year and why they are unlikely to go away. Contrary to myth, the U.S. deficits cannot be fixed by "eliminating waste." Instead, the only way to really rein in the deficits is to dramatically reduce the benefits to which most Americans have become accustomed and for which they have developed a sense of entitlement. Neither political party appears willing to deliver that message so the deficits will keep piling up year after year.

And while we have run deficits in the past, the cumulative impact of growing entitlement spending, higher spending on health care (of which the government bears an ever-growing share), and an aging population have pushed the budget deficits toward a new level of fiscal dysfunction. Whether you look at the budget in absolute dollar terms or as a percentage of the GDP, we have never experienced deficits like this in the past, absent a major war (Figure 1.2). Government spending during times of war can reasonably be expected to cease when the war is over. In contrast, in the current case, there is no event or point on the horizon after which the situation improves (the situation is compounded by the fact that modern wars don't seem to ever end). Instead, it just keeps getting worse as Americans age and fewer people pay for benefits while more receive them.

Figure 1.2 **U.S. Department of the Treasury Federal Budget Yearly Summary, Deficit and Surplus**

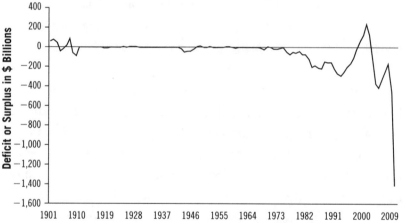

Source: Bloomberg and the U.S. Department of the Treasury, as of April 15, 2010.

WHY THE NUMBERS ARE ACTUALLY WORSE

The deficit for 2010 was approximately $1.3 trillion, a slight improvement on 2009's $1.4 trillion. For the decade as a whole, the White House's own estimates have indicated that the cumulative deficit will be slightly under $10 trillion, or a bit under $1 trillion a year on average—and that was before the recent $857 trillion tax extension and stimulus package passed in December 2010. Prior to the recent financial crisis, the government had never before run a deficit much in excess of $400 billion in a fiscal year. And as daunting as trillion-dollar deficits are, the truly bad news is that those estimates include some wildly optimistic assumptions.

Unless the government is very lucky, its deficit estimates are likely to prove too low. This is important because financial markets operate on expectations. If the deficits wind up being worse than investors were lead to believe, that will shake their confidence and likely make it even harder to sell bonds in the future. As a result, interest rates may rise even more than they would have if the original estimates had reflected the true size of the problem. So we may all end up paying the price of overly optimistic deficit estimates in the form of higher interest rates.

Every year, both the White House and the Congressional Budget Office produce budget estimates for the coming decade. In order to do this, the government planners must make a number of assumptions about the future, including those pertaining to overall economic growth, unemployment levels, tax rates, and spending levels for everything from health care to defense. The accuracy of the budget estimates will be largely a function of the accuracy of those estimates.

For example, overall economic activity has a huge impact on the budget. When the economy is growing strongly, tax revenues tend to rise as more people are working and paying taxes. A strong stock market can also influence tax revenues. Rising stocks translate into capital gains, which in turn generate government revenue when individuals sell their shares. Indeed, it was exactly this effect that contributed to the temporary budget surpluses in the late 1990s. Finally, corporate earnings will rise faster in a robust economy, in turn generating even more revenue for the federal government. In short, a strong economy will boost government revenue, while a weaker economy will reduce it.

The economy also influences government expenditures. When the economy is weak, the government will spend more on social programs, such as unemployment insurance, food stamps, and other types of transfer payments. During the recent recession, unemployment benefits were extended several times. Each time this happened, it increased the government's outlays for the year.

Given the impact on both the revenue and expenditure sides of the equation, the overall level of economic growth will have an enormous impact on the budget. For example, in 2009 federal revenue was down $400 billion, or 17 percent, due to the effects of slower economic growth, while total federal spending was up more than $500 billion, or 18 percent, due to, among other things, higher payments for benefits. Weak economies produce a drag on revenue and a pickup in spending, while strong economies have the opposite effect. This is why the government's estimates of future economic activity should not be viewed as just an economist's talking club. Accurate and realistic estimates are crucial if the budget estimates are to be meaningful.

The economic assumptions contained in the current budget are aggressive, and in some cases, very aggressive. If they are overly optimistic, which seems likely, the deficit estimates will be too low.

For 2010, the Office of Management and Budget (OMB) assumed 2.7 percent real or inflation-adjusted economic growth. This assumption was in line with the consensus among most mainstream economists, and it could even be argued that it was a bit conservative given that economies normally grow a bit faster coming out of a recession.

However, the estimates for 2011 and beyond require a bit more blind faith. For the years 2011 through 2014, the budget assumes that real GDP growth will average 4.1 percent. This will prove a tall order. First of all, this is significantly above long-term historical growth rates. Since 1947, the United States has averaged roughly 3.3 percent real economic growth per year. The current estimates are approximately 25 percent above what we've actually been able to achieve over the past 60+ years. But if you focus on the more recent past, the current estimates look even more un-realistic. Over the past decade the U.S. economy has grown at less than 2 percent per year once you adjust for inflation. The current budget as-sumes that the U.S. economy will grow at more than twice the rate at which it has grown over the past decade, despite the numerous head-winds still facing the United States. An aging workforce, increasing regu-lation, an overly indebted consumer, and a still weak financial sector are unlikely to contribute to above-average growth. Given these headwinds, growth is likely to be lower than assumed in the budget estimates, and therefore the deficits are likely to be even larger.

According to the White House's own planners, even a small overes-timation can translate into a significant change in the budget. If the real GDP is 1 percent lower per year than expected, the cumulative deficit over the next 10 years will be approximately $3 trillion higher than under the current assumptions! Even a relatively small slip in growth in the near term has enormous repercussions. If economic growth in 2010 turns out to have been 1.7 percent rather than 2.7 percent, the cumulative deficit for the next decade will rise by over $600 billion, even if economic growth is at target in all of the subsequent years.[5]

Economic growth rates are not the only place where the numbers are dodgy. The budget also implicitly assumes that the United States, un-like smaller countries such as Greece, will not pay a price for running huge deficits. While Greece and other serial budget offenders have had to contend with sharply higher borrowing costs—that is, they have had to pay higher interest rates to bondholders—there is no similar ex-pectation in the official U.S. budget estimates. Instead, the budget's es-timates on future U.S. interest rates assume that lenders, an increasing number of whom are foreigners, will continue to lend to the United States on very generous terms. This is a very odd assumption. The numbers ac-knowledge that the U.S. federal debt will continue to grow, but there is no expectation that this will have any impact on our borrowing costs, which flies in the face of basic economics. In effect, the government planners are arguing that we can indefinitely increase the supply of something without impacting its price.

A look at the numbers helps to reveal how the budget assumptions on interest rates may impact the magnitude of future deficits. A quick example: The budget assumes that between 2011 and 2013 the federal government will pay interest of between 4 and 5 percent on a 10-year Treasury note. This is well below the long-term average of around 6.5 percent. To the extent that the economy remains weak for the next three years, it is not unreasonable to expect that interest rates will remain low. However, as just described, the budget also assumes that during this same period, the economy will be growing at a brisk 4 percent clip, a rate much faster than we've managed to achieve over the past decade. In an environment of robust growth, it would be unusual to see rates remain this low for this long. Under these circumstances, investors are less likely to accept such a low interest rate to lock up their money for the next decade. They are likely to demand a higher interest rate. As rates rise, so will the amount of money the U.S. government pays in interest. Given that the United States currently has approximately $9.3 trillion of publicly traded debt, every 1 percent increase in interest that the government has to pay translates into another $90 billion more in spending. To the extent that the government is underestimating its borrowing costs, it is once again underestimating its deficit.

Beyond rosy economic forecasts there are other levers for embellishment. Unrealistic policy assumptions can have a similar impact on budget estimates. The budget makes a number of revenue assumptions that are related to particular taxes. Some of these taxes will be delayed, and some of them will be watered down or never implemented. In a similar way, when the budget assumes spending cuts that never happen or are even just delayed, the deficit will also be higher due to the unexpected spending. For that reason, it is also worth asking the question: What policy assumptions does the current budget make that are likely to change?

One particularly relevant example comes from the recently enacted health-care legislation. The legislation assumes significant cost savings in

Medicare spending over the next decade. The only problem is that Congress has habitually avoided these cuts in the past. As a result, the expected savings have never materialized. Even the CBO explicitly acknowledges this. The director of the CBO recently admitted, "The current legislation would maintain and put into effect a number of policies that might be difficult to sustain over a long period of time."[6] The English translation is that while we have just agreed to a number of new policies, that is, cost cuts, we're unlikely to stick to them. The costs associated with health-care reform in particular, and broader government spending in general, are likely to be larger than the official estimates, and so will be the deficit.

The government is trying to tell investors that the United States will spend approximately $10 trillion more than it takes in over the next decade, but as astronomical as that number is, it is probably too low. To the extent that the budget has made unrealistic assumptions about economic growth, borrowing costs, and public policy, the deficit will end up being higher than expected. Practically, this is likely to lead to the financial equivalent of a temper tantrum. Think of bond traders as cranky, tired three-year-olds being told they have to eat just another two bites of spinach, only to find that their mothers keep filling their plates. Actually that may not be a great analogy—the average three-year-old is likely to be more measured in his or her response.

Totaling the Deficits: The National Debt

In calculating the damage the deficit will do to the economy, it is important to consider the big picture. If deficits are persistent, eventually the debt becomes more difficult to sell, and interest rates need to rise in order to attract investor interest. Under this scenario, the cumulative impact of deficit spending eventually overwhelms the market's ability to absorb the new debt.

Looking at the last few years, and more broadly at the last few decades, you might think that the U.S. government has always run deficits and tried to hide the damage. This is not true. For nearly two centuries, the U.S. government lived within its means more often than not. While deficits, often large ones, were common during times of war, they were relatively rare during peacetime. Before 1930 the government ran surpluses in two out of three years, on average.[7]

More recently, the government has evidenced less self-restraint. With the exception of four years, 1998 through 2001, the United States has run a deficit in every year since 1970. And as discussed in the previous section, there is relative certainty that it will continue to do so for the next decade. The deficits probably will get even worse after that given the current demographic patterns and trends, but we are spared the pain of an exact estimate as budget forecasts only extend one decade forward.

The national debt is a different story. When you add up the cumulative deficits since the founding of the U.S. government, you have the national debt. Because the government has occasionally run deficits during the course of its history, it has had a debt balance since well before the Civil War. The last U.S. president to run a debt-free administration was Andrew Jackson.[8]

To state the obvious, the national debt has been growing of late. It took until 1982 for gross public debt to exceed $1 trillion. In the less than 30 years since then, it has grown to over $14 trillion, and it will hit over $20 trillion before the end of the decade. Rather than just looking at the total number, a better way to think about the size of the debt is to compare it to what we as a nation produce. While $10,000 in debt seemed daunting when you were in your early twenties and were just starting out in your career, a $200,000 mortgage might be very manageable 20 years later when your income is five times what it was in your youth. In a similar way, economists typically compare the debt to the GDP, which represents the sum total of the goods and services produced by the economy. As with an individual, the higher the GDP, which can be viewed as a rough proxy for the national income, the more debt we can support.

Unfortunately, even by this measure the debt levels are off the charts. *Gross public debt* now stands at roughly 90 percent of GDP, the highest level since we were repaying the debts incurred in fighting World War II. Rather than focus on gross public debt, many economists and commentators tend to reference a slightly less frightening measure, *publicly traded debt*. This measure, unlike gross public debt, does not include federal debt held by government agencies. In other words, it ignores the federal debt held by the Social Security trust fund on the argument that the government is borrowing only from itself. The United States' publicly traded debt is around $9.3 trillion, or more than 60 percent of GDP. The key point here is that both measures, gross public debt and publicly traded debt, are higher relative to GDP than they have been at any point since the immediate aftermath of World War II. (See Figure 1.3.)

Figure 1.3 **U.S. Total Publicly Traded Debt as a Percentage of the Nominal GDP**

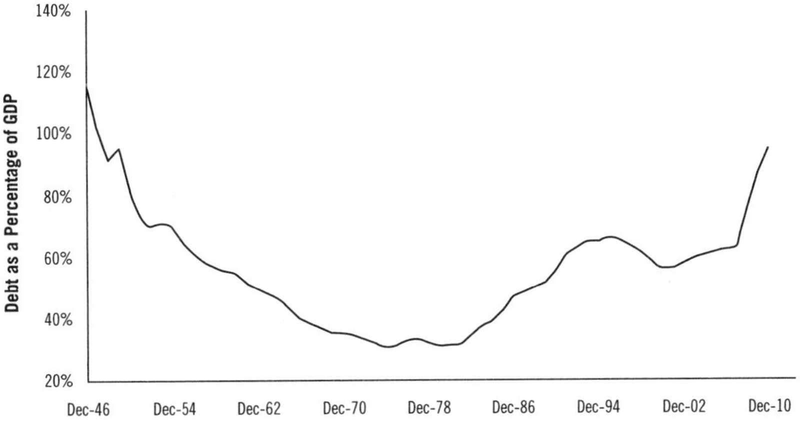

Source: Bloomberg and the U.S. Department of the Treasury Bureau of Economic Analysis, as of April 15, 2010.

Even though we have been living with a large national debt for as long as most of us can remember, the government continues to pay its obligations and to function. So why worry about the size of the debt now? For one thing, there is the moral question of burdening future generations with a crushing liability. For another, the size of the federal debt has important implications for what impact continued deficit spending is likely to have. As I'll talk about in the next chapter, the higher the debt burden, the more likely deficits are to drive interest rates higher. With the U.S. debt as a percentage of GDP being at its highest level since the 1950s, deficit spending in the coming years is more likely to push up long-term interest rates. Finally, higher deficits may encourage the government to pursue inflationary policies as higher prices mean nominally higher GDP, which would at least in theory make the debt burden easier to manage (if inflation is higher, nominal GDP grows faster, which means that there is more money to repay the debt).

WHY HEALTH-CARE SPENDING WILL ULTIMATELY BANKRUPT THE UNITED STATES

If the federal deficit is such an enormous problem, can't we simply fix it? Why do we not simply tax more, spend less, and once and for all put this problem behind us? The short answer is that the deficit can, in theory, be eliminated or a least substantially reduced, but doing so would be politically difficult. The solutions to deficit spending are well understood, but they are politically problematic: they require significant reform of entitlement programs—specifically Medicare—and a broader tax base. As a result, we are likely to muddle along making cosmetic changes to the tax codes and entitlement spending. Some people will see higher taxes, and a few might see some trimming of benefits, but these changes are likely to be at the margin.

At its root, a structural deficit is as much a political problem as an economic one. Like the Romans before us, we've granted ourselves a steadily increasing list of entitlements to which we have grown accustomed. These include, but are not limited to, medical care for the aged, medical care for the poor (with *poor* being defined in ever-broader terms), a pension in our old age, housing subsidies for the middle class (that is, interest and real estate tax deductibility), and so on. The list goes on and on. Add to this the more or less entrenched cost of maintaining a global military presence and the growing share of our national income that goes to paying interest on our debt, and it becomes obvious that the favorite political refrain of "cutting waste" is laughably inadequate to address the problem. The problem can be solved only by taking away lots of things from lots of people.

To better understand how entitlement spending has taken over the budget, it is helpful to take a quick look at the long-term budget projections. Figure 1.4 is taken from testimony given by the director of the Congressional Budget Office, Douglas Elmendorf, when he testified before Congress in the summer of 2009. The figure looks at federal spending in

Figure 1.4 **Congressional Budget Office Projections for Federal Spending on Social Security, Medicare, and Medicaid**

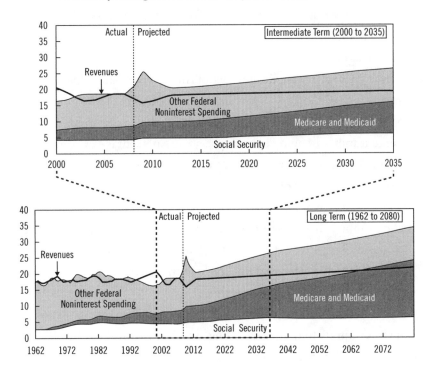

Source: Congressional Budget Office.

three broad categories: Social Security, health care (Medicare and Medicaid), and everything else. A cursory examination of the figure demonstrates that the real fiscal disaster is being driven by Medicare, which over time is on autopilot to take over an ever-greater slice of federal spending. Current projections suggest that in the absence of any change to current laws, federal spending on Medicare and Medicaid combined will grow from roughly 5 percent of the GDP today to almost 10 percent by 2035.[9]

Why is health-care spending taking over the budget? Simply put, as a country we are getting older and are spending more and more on health care due to improvements in technology that allow for more elaborate and expensive treatments. And of the two factors, aging will be the primary driver over the next several decades.[10] This is important because it suggests that absent a wholesale reform of medical spending, much of the increase in spending will be driven by demographics and therefore largely outside of our control. The only real way to address this increase would be to dramatically limit public medical spending, that is, Medicare and Medicaid.

Over the next decade the number of Americans 65 and older will increase from 40 million, or 13 percent of the population, to 54 million, or 16 percent of the population. And due to longer life expectancy as well as the large number of aging baby boomers, the percentage of Americans over 65 will continue to rise with time. By 2035 there will be 77 million Americans over the age of 65, accounting for approximately 20 percent of the population.[11] Not only do older people vote, but they also vote in far greater numbers than other demographic groups. More and more of our federal spending will be directed at a politically sensitive and powerful group that is unlikely to react positively to the government taking away benefits to which they feel they are due.

So if demographics are driving our destiny, an older population is going to doom us to higher spending. So what about the other side of the budget equation, revenue? Is it possible to tax our way to fiscal rectitude? While higher taxes can help, they will not be enough, and they may actually prove counterproductive. According to a recent CBO report, without significant adjustments to the tax code, inflation will push taxpayers into progressively higher tax brackets. This should make it easier for the government to balance the budget, as higher taxes, at least on paper, mean higher revenue. It will not be enough. Even if government revenues reach an unprecedented 26 percent of GDP, this will be insufficient over the long term. Eventually, demographics will overwhelm the government's ability to tax, and the debt will continue to climb higher.[12]

What if the government tries to raise taxes even further? History suggests that this will not work. There seems to be a practical ceiling on how much a government can tax, or at least on how much the government can tax Americans.

Since World War II, economic growth, that is, GDP, has been far more important in determining government revenue than marginal tax rates. Over the past 60 years, federal tax receipts have bumped up against an upper limit of approximately 20 percent of GDP regardless of the tax regime. In other words, regardless of the tax rate, the government has been unable to extract more than about one-fifth of the economy in tax revenue. At least historically, higher marginal tax rates have motivated high-income earners to look for loopholes and ambiguities in the tax code. The net result has been that hikes in the marginal rate have not produced the net increase in revenue that was expected.

And even if tax hikes could in theory solve the problem, they are unlikely to be implemented to the extent needed. In order to generate the necessary revenue, at the very least we would need to subject many more households to the *alternative minimum tax* (AMT). The AMT is an alternative tax system that was originally designed to prevent wealthy taxpayers from taking excessive deductions. Tax filers who fall under the AMT calculate their taxes using the ordinary schedule and then using a special AMT schedule, and then they pay the higher of the two taxes. While the AMT was originally envisioned to impact only the wealthy, it has gradually expanded to include more middle-income taxpayers. If Congress does not constantly adjust for inflation the threshold under which the AMT takes effect, it will impact more and more of the middle class.

In order to hit the type of revenue targets described above, the threshold under which the AMT takes effect would need to drift lower and lower. In other words, the AMT would need to start to impact most households, effectively constituting a major tax hike on the middle class. Without any further future fixes, as inflation rises, the AMT will apply to almost half of all households by 2035. Second, the effective marginal rate on labor income (not capital gains or dividends) would rise from 29 percent today to 34 percent by 2035.[13] In essence, the dilemma on the revenue side is the same as the problem on the expenditure side: you cannot fix the deficit without inflicting massive pain on the middle class. Whether this pain takes the form of drastically lower benefits or substantially higher taxes, there is no other way. As argued previously, this is unlikely to happen soon enough or severely enough to change the current trajectory of the deficit.

What you are left with is the inescapable conclusion that the deficit is not going away. Over the past 40 years we as a country have collectively voted ourselves more benefits than we are willing to pay for. As we age and require and demand more medical care, this will get worse, much worse. With sufficient political will, deficits can be reduced, but only at the expense of repudiating benefits and entitlements that people have come to expect. In the absence of that political will, the cautionary tale of Rome becomes more than just hyperbole. Today, there is little evidence that the United States has the stomach to adopt the necessary measures, and the longer these measures are put off, the more draconian the changes will need to be. Over the long term, the deficit will get worse, and in the not-too-distant future, it will start to push rates higher and economic growth lower, and it eventually may set off an inflationary spiral. In the next chapter we will explore what this will mean for you.

CHAPTER 2

WHY THE DEFICIT WILL MATTER TO YOU

NOTHING COULD BE DULLER to most Americans than economic statistics. Mention real interest rates, the consumer price index (CPI), or the gross domestic product (GDP), and people start to fall asleep or walk away. Change the conversation, though, to mortgage payments, gas prices, and unemployment, and those topics strike close to home.

What's the difference? In some essential ways, there isn't any. Real interest rates reflect how much everyone pays to borrow money. For individuals, higher rates mean higher payments on car loans, student loans, and mortgages. The consumer price index measures the prices that people pay for the essentials of life. When the CPI goes up, that's because the prices of the things you want and need, like gasoline and food, are going up. The gross domestic product shows economic activity. If there isn't a lot of it, jobs start to disappear, and it becomes harder to keep yours or find a new one. So when you hear that the federal government is going to be running big deficits for a long time and that this is going to boost interest rates, push up the CPI, and depress GDP, you need to take note and prepare to deal with the very real effects that you are going to feel in your own life.

There is no question that the continuing huge U.S. deficits are going to change the financial landscape for everyone. The fact that it has not happened yet does not change the likelihood that it will happen eventually. The changes will happen the way earthquakes happen. My family and I live in San Francisco. Scientists have been talking about the "Big One," the powerful earthquake that will eventually hit Northern California, for decades.

The fact that we have not seen a major quake in decades does not lower the odds that a big earthquake will occur; instead, it increases the odds. In the case of earthquakes, geological pressures build slowly over a period of years or decades. They can continue building for some time, but eventually the pressure has to be released. The longer the pressure builds without the offsetting release of smaller quakes, the larger the eventual big earthquake.

The economic shakeup heading our way is no different. In fact, it is very similar. The fact that we have avoided small quakes has set us up for a much larger one. It is impossible to predict the exact timing, but we are already feeling the foreshocks, and it will be here before the end of the decade. We are in for a long period of slower growth and higher interest rates. This is going to affect everyone's wallet and most people's living standards. There is little you as an individual can do to change what is coming, but you can prepare to live with it.

In the previous chapter we explored why the deficit is large, is not going away, and is likely to get worse over time. Now we will explore why you should care.

Before making the case for why the deficit will matter, it is worth asking why it hasn't in the past. As outlined in the previous chapter, large deficits have been the norm since the early 1970s. Yet, despite them, the U.S. economy has grown nearly tenfold (as measured by the nominal GDP), the U.S. stock market has risen by a similar amount, and both interest rates and inflation have generally been heading lower for most of the past 30 years. It is all well and good to quote academic studies and reference theoretical relationships between budget deficits and interest rates, but where's the proof? How is it that we've managed to avoid the economic consequences of our prolificacy for nearly four decades?

FORTY YEARS OF DEFICIT SPENDING AND NOT A SCRATCH: WHY?

In the past we were able to avoid the impact of chronic deficits for a number of reasons. First, both our deficit and our national debt were much smaller in both absolute terms and as a percentage of the GDP. Second, there used to be a much bigger cushion, in the form of higher real interest rates, in the bond market. And finally, many large foreign investors, such as China, have found the U.S. debt markets a convenient place to invest really large sums of money.

Start with the size of the deficit and national debt. While we've been running deficits for most of the past 40 years, they used to be smaller. Between 1970 and 2007, budget deficits averaged less than 2.5 percent of the GDP. As recently as 2007, the federal deficit was only 1.15 percent of the GDP. In 2010 it was approximately 9 percent. Larger deficits translate into larger funding needs and bigger Treasury auctions. It was easier for the bond market to absorb the supply of Treasury bonds when there were fewer of them.

Until very recently, not only was the deficit much lower, but so was the national debt. Back in the mid-1980s, the last time we had large, persistent deficits, the gross federal debt was roughly 40 percent of the GDP. Today it is around 90 percent. This is important because less debt makes it easier for countries to fund deficits at lower interest rates.

In addition to smaller deficits and less debt, we've also benefited from the fact that for a long time, real interest rates were unusually high. Put slightly differently, there was a lot of bad news already reflected in bond prices. In effect, back in the 1980s, and even through the 1990s, the bond market was prepared for bad inflation news that never came.

In 1984, the yield on the 10-year note ranged between 12 and 13 percent. With inflation running at about 4.5 percent annually, the real, or inflation-adjusted, yield was around 8 percent. That is a very large after-inflation return, much larger than most economic textbooks would suggest you can get on what is effectively a risk-free investment. Why were investors demanding such a high interest rate on bonds when inflation was modest? Basically because after their experience in the 1970s and early 1980s, investors were skeptical that the Federal Reserve would be able to contain inflation. Since 1980, inflation had been falling, but for more than a decade before that, inflation had been rising. So bond investors had become accustomed to demanding big premiums to cushion against a resurgence of inflation.

As it turned out, inflation actually peaked in early 1980, and it has been falling ever since. As inflation kept falling, investors became more comfortable that it would stay low, and both real and nominal interest rates fell despite the deficit. A big reason why the deficit has not impacted interest rates is that for a very long time the bond market was expecting bad news that never materialized.

Finally, we've gotten away with deficit spending for so long in part because the United States is the world's largest and most liquid bond market. China and other large exporting countries haven't had a lot of other options for investing their trade surpluses. Even today, the Chinese, who own roughly $1 trillion of our debt, have made it clear that while they are increasingly uncomfortable holding so much U.S. debt, they don't plan on selling. The Chinese realize that if they were to start to sell any significant portion of their holdings, it would only depress prices and create huge losses for themselves. In a way the Chinese are stuck in the same position as the banker in John Paul Getty's famous quote. As Mr. Getty quipped, "If you owe the bank $100, that's your problem. If you owe the bank $100 million, that's the bank's problem."

Smaller deficits, more modest debt, a bond market priced for an inflationary train wreck, and a convenient place for large, developing nations to park their money—this is why the United States has managed to overspend for 40 years with so little damage. Going forward we will not be so lucky. The deficit and national debt are now much higher, both in absolute terms and relative to GDP. The bond market has gone from total skepticism to an almost childlike trust in the Fed and a future without inflation. It can only be disappointed. And finally, while the Chinese and others are not looking to burn themselves, they are painfully aware of the risk of continuing to put all their eggs in one basket. They will slowly diversify away from U.S. government debt.

Going forward the deficit will matter. Not all at once, but looking out over the next decade the deficit will mean slower growth, higher interest rates, and potentially higher inflation.

Deficits and the Economy: Why Higher Deficits Mean Weaker Job Markets

Over the past four years, we've all seen firsthand why economic growth is so important. The last recession provided a dramatic illustration of the practical effects of an economic contraction. Millions of jobs were eliminated, home prices collapsed, savings evaporated, and unless you were very fortunate, your income probably stagnated. Long-term deficits will not help. As more and more government spending is diverted to paying interest on our debt, there will be fewer dollars left over for other, more productive types of government spending. In addition, to the extent that taxes are raised to punitive levels, this will be yet another obstacle to economic growth. Slower growth will translate into a less robust labor market, that is, fewer jobs, and less consumer spending.

The magnitude and persistence of the deficit spending suggest that it is likely to inflict lasting damage on the economy. To understand why, it is helpful to recall a basic economic relationship, that between savings and economic growth. Today's savings—whether from individuals, corporations, or the government—funds investment in future productive capacity, such as start-up companies or new factories and equipment for existing firms. If savings drop, there is less to invest for the future. The budget deficit cuts directly into our national savings. When the budget deficit goes up, all else being equal, the national savings go down.

With less savings, Americans accumulate fewer assets. The return generated on those assets has a significant impact on our future income. With less of an asset base, our national income suffers as there are fewer productive assets to generate future income. Take a simple example: If the deficit reduces our national savings by $5 trillion over the next decade and national savings earn a rate of return of 6 percent, that would equate to a loss of $300 billion a year in national income. This loss will manifest itself in a significantly lower GDP, but more practically and closer to home, this loss will also equate to a drop in household income of $2,600 a year on average![1] In a very real sense, the budget deficit represents current consumption over future savings. Running persistent deficits is the equivalent of borrowing from future production. We will pay for this with slower growth.

There are other ways that large, persistent deficits will slow economic growth. One is that they will eventually scare the financial markets. Deficits create additional market volatility, which in itself will harm growth (if your portfolio is plunging, you're less likely to buy a new car or television). As foreign investors now own a large portion of our national debt, their panic will have implications for the dollar. To the extent that foreign investors become less comfortable buying our debt, or even modestly reduce the rate of their purchases, this will put downward pressure on the dollar, which in turn will cause an eventual acceleration in inflation.[2]

And to the extent that the government does try to curb the deficit with spending cuts, this will further slow the economy. At $3.5 trillion, government spending is currently 25 percent of the GDP; $1 out of every $4 of economic activity in the United States is government related. At

25 percent, the government's footprint is the largest it has been in decades. While curtailing spending is certainly the right thing to do in the long term, it will be particularly painful given the large role the government now plays in the economy. Even a modest pullback in government expenditures will be felt as a drag on growth.

Even in the absence of a meaningful reduction in government spending, we are still likely to see slower growth as a result of the deficit. In the years ahead more and more of the money the government does spend will be dedicated to interest payments on the national debt, which is not productive in the same way as building a highway or providing tax incentives to small businesses.

What will slower growth feel like? The recession of 2007 to 2008 was certainly a good example of the personal pain inflicted during a recession, but even less dramatic slowdowns can hurt. The early 1990s are a good illustration of how you don't need an outright recession to feel the effects of slow growth. The United States experienced a fairly mild recession around the time of the first Gulf War. By the spring of 1991, the economy was already growing again, albeit at an anemic pace. And while the economy continued to grow throughout the rest of the decade, the first few years of the 1990s were distinguished by an unusually sluggish economy.

One place in particular in which the weak economy was felt was the labor market. Typically, when the economy is strong, it creates more jobs. You can explain more than 50 percent of the variation in labor market growth by changes in GDP. When growth is weaker, job creation lags.

A related side effect of a sluggish economy is slow growth in real income. If unemployment is relatively high and many people are looking for work, it is hard to get a raise. In the early 1990s, with unemployment around 7 to 8 percent, employees were by and large too scared to ask for more money. As a result, wage growth was so low that it was actually below the rate of inflation. Between 1991 and mid-1993, hourly wages grew by approximately 2.7 percent, about two-thirds of the long-term average and less than the rate at which inflation was rising. If your income is not keeping up with inflation, even if you are nominally earning more, you are losing purchasing power.

Over the long term, real economic growth—that is, economic growth resulting from more production rather than more inflation—raises living standards. Slower economic growth means that living standards stagnate, or worse, recede. The differences may not be perceptible over a year or two. But given the long-term drag that deficits will place on growth, they will add up over time. As a simple rule of thumb for the next decade, assume that the boom periods will be less frequent and shorter than they were during the last three decades.

Deficits and Interest Rates: Why Your Mortgage Rate Is Going Up

As the supply of government debt begins to overwhelm investor appetite, interest rates will start to rise. All else being equal, higher deficits lead to higher interest rates on government debt. As the rates on U.S. Treasuries serve as the benchmarks for many types of consumer loans, higher deficits will lead to higher payments on mortgages, credit cards, and student loans.

The theory that higher deficits lead to higher interest rates is known as the *crowding-out effect*, in which large sustained government borrowing forces out private capital and pushes real interest rates higher. The higher the number of borrowers competing for capital, including the government, the higher the interest rates need to be to attract lenders, that is, bond investors. Unless investors suddenly decide they want to buy more bonds, the excess supply of bonds will force down prices and push up interest rates.

Academic research suggests that each additional percentage point of the deficit versus GDP raises long-term interest rates by 30 to 60 basis points. For example, a sustained budget deficit of around 3.5 percent of GDP would raise long-term interest rates by approximately 1 to 2 percent compared with a balanced budget.[3] Even under the optimistic assumptions from the CBO, between 2010 and 2019 the average budget deficit as a percentage of GDP will be close to 4 percent.

While there is some variability in how much deficits impact rates, the effect this time around is likely to be toward the upper end of the range given our large national debt. Not only do deficits push up interest rates, but the impact of deficit spending is also far worse when it occurs in the context of an already elevated debt level. In a recent paper from the International Monetary Fund (IMF), economists again confirmed that higher deficits raise interest rates, but the economists added a new twist. The extent to which deficits impact interest rates is much more significant when deficits occur in countries with already elevated debt levels. In these cases, the relationship between deficits and interest rates is much stronger. When large deficits interact with already large public debts, interest rates rise 65 basis points for every 1 percent increase in the deficit relative to GDP.[4] Under this scenario, a hypothetical deficit of 3.5 percent would push interest rates up by nearly 2.5 percent. Put differently, this is the difference between a 7 percent mortgage and a 10 percent mortgage.

This is a big risk for the United States. Not only is the government too extended, but so are your neighbors. As a result of the last decade's housing boom, individuals are still carrying more debt relative to their income than has historically been the case. Mortgage debt in the United States doubled between 2001 and 2008. As a result, total consumer debt is still nearly 120 percent of after-tax income. Historically, consumer debt levels have been much lower.

The excessive debt problem in the United States is by no means limited to the government; the entire U.S. economy is struggling under a mountain of debt. As overall U.S. debt levels are considerably higher than they were in the 1980s, this time around the impact of the deficit on interest rates is likely to be significant.

Another factor that will lead to higher rates is that today's bond market, unlike 25 years ago, is priced for perfection. In the 1980s, real interest rates could drop because they were unusually high. Fast forward to 2010 and real long-term interest rates are around 1 percent, well below their long-term average of around 2.5 to 3 percent. In the recent past, investors have accepted low real yields because they wanted the safety of U.S. government bonds and believed that inflation would remain low. Either inflation has to stay low for the next decade, or bond yields are likely to rise as additional supply brushes up against excessive investor optimism. In other words, just as bond investors were too pessimistic in 1984, they are too optimistic today. This is likely to prove a bad bet.

There is a third reason why the deficit is likely to push U.S. rates higher. We have unequivocally become a nation of debtors, not savers. While other countries, notably Japan, have been running chronic deficits for years, there is a crucial difference between these other countries and the United States: they can fund their own deficits with private savings. Japan, for example, has a debt-to-GDP ratio of more than twice that of the United States, yet its long-term interest rates have remained very low, less than 2 percent. The Japanese buy virtually all of their own debt, with domestic investors owning more than 90 percent of Japanese government bonds.

In contrast, roughly half of U.S. publicly traded debt is held by foreign investors. This represents a dramatic increase in foreign dependence of capital. Our ability to maintain low interest rates is increasingly out of our control. Instead, in the future our interest rates, at least the long-term ones, will be set in Beijing and Tokyo, rather than in Washington and New York.

And to the extent that foreign appetite for U.S. assets moderates, we will no longer have the ability to fund our own deficits. In 2008, we marked the first year since 1934 that our net national savings were negative. As recently as 2006, net savings for the United States were still over $500 billion. By 2009, net national savings were −$355 billion. What this means is that as a whole, the United States must now import capital from abroad to make up for our savings shortfall.

While foreign investors will continue to buy our Treasury bonds, they are unlikely to do so on such generous terms and in sufficient quantity. It will take time and happen over a period of years, but the Chinese will and have already started to diversify their investment portfolios. I previously referred to the Chinese as our bankers, which they are in a very real sense. And while China will be very cautious in calling our loan, they are not particularly motivated to keep extending it either. The Chinese will certainly continue to buy Treasuries in large quantities, but they are unlikely to buy enough to match the flood of new supply. The problem is that this is happening at a time when we need them to buy even more. To the extent that foreigners are less inclined to fund our deficit, we will have to offer more attractive terms—that is, higher interest rates.

MORTGAGE RATES AND HOUSING

Practically, what will higher interest rates feel like? Interest rates are the cost of money, so for anyone looking to borrow, the price is going up. This will apply to every type of borrowing, from credit card balances to mortgages. Mortgage rates have been relatively low for years. Since the end of 2008, a 30-year conventional mortgage has averaged around 5 percent. The longer-term average, since 1990, is closer to 7.25 percent. Expect mortgage rates to start to head back toward these levels. With the average U.S. mortgage at around $130,000, this translates into around $250 more each month in interest payments.

Rising mortgage rates will not impact only your monthly budget but also the price of your home. Home prices are heavily influenced by mortgage rates, so higher mortgage rates mean that the housing market may not recover as fast or as far as some think.

After having just been through the worst housing crisis since the Great Depression, it probably seems somewhat pessimistic bordering on masochistic to predict a weak to stagnant housing market going forward.

After all, haven't home prices already been hammered? The short answer is yes, but probably not enough. While certain markets may do better than others, for the broader American housing market, home prices are still not particularly cheap when compared to what people earn. They will be even less cheap when interest rates start to rise.

Historically, U.S. housing prices have been determined by a number of factors, but two of the most important are incomes and interest rates. When incomes rise, people can afford to spend more for housing. But when interest rates rise, mortgage payments take a bigger bite out of people's housing budgets, and they can afford only a less expensive house.

In the coming decade, thanks in large part to the continuing federal budget deficits, affordability will get hit on both fronts: people's income growth will be slower due to a weak job market, and their monthly mortgage payments will be higher thanks to rising rates. If you're looking for a practical implication of the deficit, look no further than your house. Slower growth and higher rates will mean that your home will appreciate slower, if at all.

INFLATION: THE REAL NIGHTMARE SCENARIO

As depressing as it might sound, the conditions described above represent the best-case scenario. Because of continuing high levels of federal borrowing, interest rates will have to rise, and that will slow growth. If the government does seriously try to reduce the deficit, lower spending and higher taxes will also be a drag on growth. And if the government doesn't do much about curbing the deficit, bond investors are going to get spooked and drive up interest rates even more. Slower economic growth is already evident, and higher interest rates will eventually follow. The big question is whether we are going to get the much uglier outcome: inflation. This is a very real possibility over the longer term.

Historically, higher deficits have often led to higher inflation. Of all the potential consequences of higher deficits, this is the most serious.

Inflation robs individuals of purchasing power, erodes savings, and ultimately reduces people's living standards. This is because wages generally do not keep pace with inflation. Since 1964, hourly earnings in the United States have grown on average, by around 4.5 percent per year. This is in line with the average inflation rate, meaning that people's earnings have roughly kept pace with rising prices. However, when inflation has been above average, wages have not kept up, and real income has been approximately −1 percent. This is the equivalent of having a 1 percent salary reduction each year.

Inflation also punishes savers. As prices rise, the purchasing power of your savings also drops. Rather than being rewarded for saving, you are actually punished. Ironically for a country that just went through a crisis caused by overborrowing, a good financial strategy when inflation is rising is to save less and accumulate more debt because debt is easier to pay off with inflated dollars. While this seems perverse, it is one of the many malignant consequences of high inflation.

How Government Spending Leads to Inflation

In the absence of a corresponding increase in supply, excess demand for goods and services tends to push up prices. In thinking about excess demand, it is useful to remember that the government is a very large consumer. The government buys everything from health care for millions of citizens to billion-dollar airplanes. For fiscal 2010 the U.S. government spent approximately $3.5 trillion, 25 percent of the total GDP.

The theory that higher government spending will lead to higher inflation is borne out by the facts. A little noted statistic is that historically inflation has been much higher under Democratic administrations than Republican. Since 1871, under Democratic administrations, inflation has averaged roughly 4.5 percent. Under Republican administrations, it has been less than 1.5 percent. The apparent reason for the discrepancy is that Democratic administrations spend more money.

Looking at the data since 1914, average spending under Democratic administrations has risen by approximately 13.5 percent a year, or about 9.5 percent after adjusting for inflation. Under Republican administrations, spending has risen by only 4.9 percent a year, or 3 percent adjusted for inflation. The spending may have been justified, necessary, or the right thing for the country. Nevertheless, it increased demand and boosted inflation

Today government spending is higher than it has ever been. Arguably, it was a good thing for the government to boost spending in 2008 and 2009. The country was in the middle of a brutal recession, and increased government spending helped to offset the drop in consumer demand. So far the excess spending has not been inflationary, and that is partly because spending by consumers and corporations is still relatively weak. But private demand will eventually return, and if government spending remains at current outsized levels, inflation will be a side effect.

The risk of higher inflation will be even greater if the Fed keeps short-term interest rates low for too long. This is because low interest rates encourage people to buy houses, cars, and other items they would not normally buy if borrowing costs were higher. If the Fed provides cheap money, which encourages excess spending, at the same time the government is on its own spending spree, demand will eventually rise, supply will be unable to keep up, and inflation will start to pick up.

When Is a Default Not a Default?
Debasing the Currency

Inflation results not just from higher real demand but also from the circulation of more money in the marketplace. If real demand and output don't change but there is more money in circulation, that money is going to compete for the limited supply of goods, and that boosts prices. Deficits can also lead to too much money.

This can happen when, rather than making a good-faith effort to repay its obligations, the government chooses to repudiate them, or in other words, it defaults. Defaulting on debt can take many forms. At its simplest, it can mean refusing to pay. When most governments default, they do so by changing the terms of the debt, by paying back only a portion of the debt, or by lengthening the maturity of the bonds. Large countries, like the United States, however, have another option. Big countries enjoy the privilege of issuing debt in their own currency, so they can choose to depreciate the value of that currency and thereby lower the cost of paying off that debt. Under this method, a country repays the nominal value of its obligations, but it does so in a currency that is worth a fraction of its former value. When the value of the currency drops, prices rise.

Let's go back to our Roman example.

While ancient Rome had neither a central bank nor paper money, it did have money in the form of coins minted from precious metal. The main coin used for most commercial transactions was known as the Roman *denarius*. At the time of Nero, around AD 60, the Roman denarius consisted of 90 percent silver. Around 200 years later, the silver content was down to 0.02 percent![5] In effect, the government decreased the value of its money by substituting cheap copper for more valuable silver. The government could now nominally pay off its obligations. The only catch was that it was paying them off with money that was no longer worth very much. In effect, the Romans were defaulting on their debts because the money they used to pay their obligations was worth only a fraction of the money they borrowed. Debasing the currency, however, robs not only the nation's creditors but also its citizens because the money they now have is less valuable.

Just as the Romans could and did create more money by diluting its precious metal content, governments today can perform the same type of financial alchemy, literally creating money out of thin air. To do this, the U.S. government, however, would need the cooperation of the Federal Reserve.

MONETIZING THE DEBT AND HYPERINFLATION

Monetary conditions are under the control of the nation's central bank, the Federal Reserve. In managing monetary policy, the Fed has several tools at its disposal, including the ability to set short-term interest rates and the ability to impact the nation's money supply through the direct purchase of government securities. The Fed typically purchases short-term Treasury instruments to adjust the nation's money supply in response to changes in the demand for credit and the overall strength of the economy. But the Fed could also use these same powers in a different way.

Rather than limiting itself to the buying and selling of Treasury bills, the Fed can also purchase longer-dated Treasury instruments and leave those securities on its balance sheet. By doing this, the Fed, in effect, would be creating money, in this case electronic money in the form of excess bank reserves. The banks in turn would lend this money out, either to businesses or individuals. When a bank creates a loan, it debits the checking account of the business, which in turn increases the supply of money. By buying Treasury securities from the banks, or directly from the government, the Fed can create lots of new money.

This practice is very controversial and has already begun. The Fed started direct asset purchase back in 2008 and has continued this program under various guises ever since. Most recently, it announced in November 2010 that it was going to buy another $600 billion in intermediate-duration Treasuries. This latest incarnation has come to be known as QE2, that is, the second round of quantitative easing. The express goal of QE2 is to raise inflation expectations in an effort to stave off deflation, or a prolonged drop in prices. The danger is that the program may work too well.

So far at least, the Fed's purchase of Treasury instruments and other long-term bonds has not been inflationary as banks have not been lending. Instead, the banks are sitting on the money. Since the banks are not lending, the new money, known technically as *excess reserves*, is not finding its way into the real economy. In other words, the supply of money is not increasing at a particularly rapid rate.

What would happen if the Fed continued to buy and hold massive amounts of government debt under more normal conditions? Assuming they did not "sterilize" the operations by draining reserves from the banks, the banks would lend out the new money, and the supply of money would rise. An expansion in the money supply literally means more dollars in circulation and in checking accounts. In other words, this is money that can be used to buy things. Like any other tradable commodity, when the supply of money increases, the value tends to decrease. When the value of a dollar goes down, you need more dollars to buy the same good or service—that is, you have inflation.

I said earlier that this scenario, monetizing the debt, was much more dangerous than your average run-of-the-mill inflation. The reason is one of magnitude. When governments start monetizing their debt, they do it because the debt is a big problem, and big problems take big solutions. Therefore, efforts to monetize debt in the past have often involved a lot of new money, which has resulted in what is known as *hyperinflation*. If the Fed continues to buy Treasuries, not in an effort to prevent deflation but rather because nobody else wants them, this will significantly raise the risk of inflation over the long term.

THE DEFICIT'S IMPACT OVER THE NEXT DECADE: APOCALYPSE NOW

While some of the more painful side effects of higher deficits won't show up for another few years, others are already here. Higher taxes, at least for upper-income earners, look like a real possibility after 2012. So far, while the economy has avoided a double-dip recession, the recovery has been subpar. Given historical patterns and the magnitude of the 2007 to 2008 recession, the U.S. economy should be growing about twice as fast as it currently is. We are already living in a slow growth world. Unemployment remains close to 10 percent, a generational high. And because the federal government is effectively broke, there is no further latitude for the government spending to help jump-start the economy.

Higher interest rates will take a little longer, but they will arrive. For now, the U.S. government has the debt markets mostly to itself. It is not competing with other borrowers. This will not last indefinitely. It will take only a couple of weak government bond auctions to scare the markets and drive rates higher. When this starts to happen, all borrowing costs, including mortgages, will also rise. Many have assumed that the worst of the housing crisis is behind us. While the future drop in home prices is unlikely to be as severe as what was experienced in 2007 and 2008, no one should be expecting a big rebound either. The combination of slower income growth and higher mortgage rates means that home prices are likely to be flat for years to come. Housing, the great savings vehicle of the last decade, will continue to struggle.

And finally there is the very real prospect of higher inflation. For now, there is not much risk of inflation because the economy still has too much spare capacity, particularly in labor markets. As long as the labor market remains as weak as it is now, it is very hard for wages to grow much. And without wage hikes, overall inflation is less likely to rise. Also, because U.S. banks have been reluctant to lend since the crisis began, the supply of money has been growing unusually slowly. Without quicker money supply growth, inflation is not a near-term threat.

That said, while it is not a near-term threat, inflation is a risk investors will eventually need to contend with. In the past, U.S. inflation has been higher when government spending has been higher. The size and persistence of our current deficits further increase the risk of inflation as the government, with cooperation from the Fed, may continue to monetize the debt.

For those who question why the Fed would pursue such an irresponsible policy, inflation does have one advantage over cutting the budget and raising taxes. The Fed can induce inflation without the formality of a vote, hearing, or even public debate. Because of that, inflation may be a politically expedient if not economically wise solution. If inflation becomes our preferred method for managing our debts, it will not end well. Just ask the Romans.

CHAPTER 3

WHAT TO WATCH AND WHEN TO ACT

O N THE EVENING OF December 5, 1996, at a speech he gave to the American Enterprise Institute, Alan Greenspan uttered one of the more memorable phrases in financial lore: "irrational exuberance." The phrase was part of a rhetorical question. The Fed chairman was musing on how to tell if the stock market had become detached from reality. At the time, some investors took the Fed chairman's words as a sign that the market was set for a sharp decline, so they promptly sold their stocks. These investors were correct that a decline was coming, but their timing was off. One of the biggest bull markets in history was barely a third of the way through its eventual run. The individuals who sold their stocks in December 1996 left a lot of money on the table. The professional money managers who sold at that time lost their jobs.

Whether you are running a huge hedge fund or managing a small personal portfolio, timing is critical to your success. The investors who decided in 1996 that the market was turning into a speculative bubble were right; they were just three and half years early, a fact that even in hindsight probably produced little comfort. Gold, for example, is an excellent inflation hedge. If you think that government deficits are going to produce inflation, it makes sense to increase your allocation to gold. But gold produces no income. So when inflation is flat and stable, it is not the best asset to own. Indications are that there is little risk of inflation before 2012, so buying a large gold position today may be premature. In a similar vein, while bonds are likely to get hit over the next two to three years, selling off your bond portfolio too early will leave you with excess cash to invest at a time when money market accounts are paying 0 percent interest. Not a good trade.

The big economic risks over the next decade are slow growth in the United States and much of the developed world, rising interest rates, and potentially inflation. These conditions suggest that you should hold a portfolio with less money in U.S. equities and bonds, more in cash, and a higher allocation to commodities. But you want to move to these new allocations at the right time. You don't want to move too late, but you also don't want to anticipate conditions that may take a few years to develop. In other words, you don't want to move too early either. While slower economic growth is already the new norm, interest rates are unlikely to rise significantly before the end of 2011, and inflation will take at least another year after that to get going.

RISING RATES AND SUPPLY: WHO IS COMPETING WITH THE GOVERNMENT?

Academic literature suggests that, all else being equal, higher deficits will lead to higher real interest rates. The rub of course is that things are rarely equal. In macroeconomics, unlike the physical sciences, relationships are often imprecise. Higher deficits will push rates higher, but the extent and timing of that effect will be determined by a number of other factors. To evaluate when rates are likely to start rising, investors need to watch the supply of debt, who is looking to borrow and how much, as well as the demand for debt.

First, pay attention to supply, specifically supply from other entities beyond the government. We already know that over the next decade the

U.S. government will have a voracious appetite for money to fund the deficit. But the government is not the only entity that likes to borrow money. While the recent financial crisis was the worst of the past 70 years, the economy will eventually heal itself. As the economy grows stronger, the government will find itself increasingly competing with corporations and other private borrowers to sell its debt. This competition will start to boost rates.

To track corporate borrowing, one metric to focus on is commercial and industrial (C&I) loan demand. The C&I loan demand is the measure of commercial loans from banks. The Federal Reserve publishes data on bank loans each Friday (www.federalreserve.gov). In the summer of 2010, loan demand was just starting to stabilize after the biggest collapse in bank lending in modern history (Figure 3.1). Part of the collapse was due to stricter lending standards, but a large part of the reason was that companies were reluctant to take on additional debt. In the spring of 2010, about nine months after the recession ended, C&I loan demand was still falling.

Figure 3.1 **U.S. Demand for Commercial and Industrial Loans**

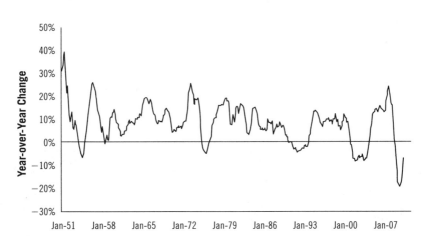

Source: Bloomberg and the Federal Reserve, as of February 18, 2010.

A sustained turnaround in bank lending would be one sign that interest rates were likely to start to experience upward pressure in the near term.

The other borrowers to watch are consumers. As the last decade demonstrated, under the right conditions the household sector is not afraid to borrow, particularly when it comes to buying a house (most consumer debt is in the form of mortgages). If household borrowing is weak, there is less demand for capital, which helps the Treasury sell its debt. If the banks are not lending to consumers, they have more left over to lend to the government, which they do by buying Treasuries. As with business lending, the rate at which consumers demand capital will impact when rates are likely to rise.

Stung by the recent recession, consumers were in a particularly penitent mood. Not only were corporations eschewing debt but so were individuals. The last decade's housing bubble was financed on top of the largest explosion of consumer debt in history. Between 2000 and 2007, household debt in the United States doubled, from $6.5 trillion to over $13 trillion. Over 80 percent of the increase in consumer debt was driven by an increase in mortgage debt. By the time the housing bubble ended in tears, consumer balance sheets were a disaster.

Following the party, came the hangover. By the end of the third quarter of 2010, household debt had declined for 10 consecutive quarters, an unprecedented contraction in consumer debt. Yet, despite all their efforts to shed debt, most individuals remained on shaky ground.

When assessing consumer debt levels, it is useful to compare them to annual income, specifically disposable or after-tax income (Figure 3.2). The more money people make, the more debt they can carry. The government tracks total consumer debt in the United States, along with personal income. In 2010, consumer debt relative to after-tax income remained well above the levels of the 1990s, and even further above its long-term average. While there is no law of nature that demands that debt levels drop, history suggests that consumers will feel the need to pay down their debts before they start borrowing again.

Figure 3.2 **The Ratio of U.S. Household Debt to Disposable Income**

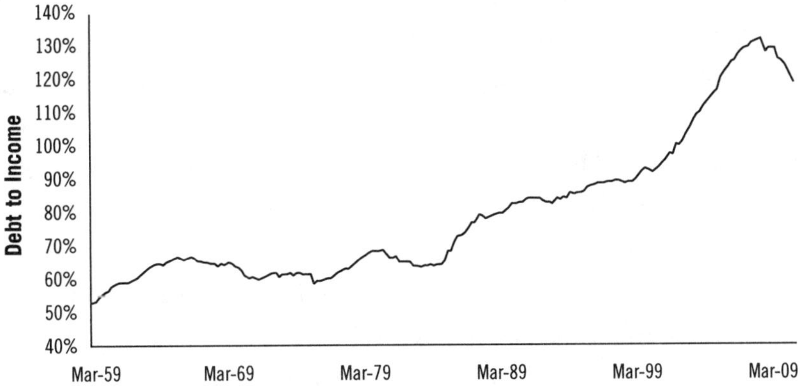

Source: Bloomberg, the Federal Reserve, and the Bureau of Economic Analysis, as of March 31, 2010.

This view is reinforced by the fact that the amount of debt people are willing to carry has traditionally been influenced by the ease with which people can get and keep a job. When jobs are more plentiful, individuals are more comfortable carrying debt. When the economy turns down and jobs become scarce, consumers traditionally pare back their borrowing. As long as U.S. unemployment continues to hover near record levels and wage growth stagnates, it is safe to assume that most people will not be ready to start increasing their debt again.

Why is this important for the future direction of interest rates? When banks lend less to consumers, they can lend more to the government. This is exactly what has happened during the recession. Banks were writing fewer mortgages and instead were buying Treasuries. In fact, the growth in bank holdings of Treasuries in 2009 and 2010 was close to its fastest pace since the early 1990s. This is not surprising. Similar to the early 1990s, banks could borrow from savers and pay little if any interest. They then could turn around and park the money in risk-free, longer-dated Treasuries. Effectively, they borrowed for nothing and got a guaranteed return of 3 percent. Even bankers couldn't lose.

So when will consumers resume their love affair with debt? Two conditions need to be met. First, the labor market needs to improve, so watch the unemployment rate. Second, households need to pay off more of the debt that they incurred during the previous housing boom. Practically, this means that consumers are unlikely to start to borrow aggressively again until the debt-to-income ratio is back to around 90 percent, right about where it was at the end of the 1990s. Neither of these conditions is likely to be met before the end of 2011, so look for interest rates to stay low at least until then. If the labor market is slow to rebound and/or consumers dawdle in their efforts to repair their balance sheet, then any significant rise in rates could easily be pushed out to 2012.

Rising Rates and Demand: Are There Enough Buyers?

In addition to watching the supply of debt, you should also pay attention to the demand for it. This may be a bit tricky to follow because when economists talk about suppliers in the debt markets, we are talking about the people who want to borrow the money. They supply the notes and bonds and other debt instruments to be sold. The demand comes from the lenders—that is, those who may be willing to buy those instruments.

Fortunately, the demand side is easy to track. The Treasury conveniently publishes on its Web site (www.treasurydirect.gov/RI/OFGateway) a number of statistics after each auction. These statistics indicate how many investors, and what type, wanted to buy government debt. By watching who turns up for the government's latest debt auction, you can obtain a clear picture of whether investors, both domestic and foreign, are still willing to fund our deficits.

New Treasury debt is auctioned on a regular basis to both financial institutions and individuals. Large institutions actually bid, and the highest bid—which means the lowest interest rate—gets the bonds. Most individuals put in what is known as a *noncompetitive bid* (you can put in a noncompetitive bid only if the amount of Treasuries you are bidding on is $5 million or less). In a noncompetitive bid, you agree to accept whatever rate or yield is determined by the auction.

Based on this system, the government actually discloses how much excess demand a Treasury auction generates. The simplest measure is to watch what is known as the *bid-to-cover ratio*, which is released immediately following each government auction. This ratio tracks the number of bids received versus the number of bids accepted. Interpreting the number is simple: the higher the bid-to-cover ratio, the greater the demand.

Figure 3.3 tracks the bid-to-cover ratio for 10-year Treasury auctions (the main benchmark for long-term interest rates) going back to 1994. For most of the past 15 years, the bid-to-cover ratio has fluctuated between approximately 1.5, indicating weak demand, to around 3, indicating strong demand. As of the end of 2010, there was still no evidence of a dropoff in demand for Treasury instruments. In fact, demand appears to have risen. A Treasury auction in the spring of 2010 produced a bid-to-cover ratio of 3.45, the highest level since 1994. The resilience in demand was a function of several factors, including concerns over the viability of

Figure 3.3 **Treasury 10-Year Auction Bid-to-Cover Ratio**

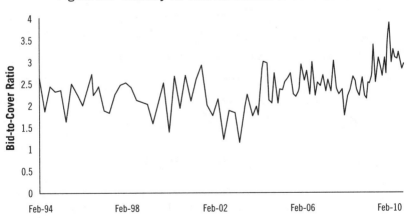

Source: Bloomberg and the Department of the Treasury, as of April 7, 2010.

the euro, lingering risk aversion among investors, and a conviction that the Fed would keep short-term rates low for the foreseeable future. All of these factors are conspiring to keep rates low for the time being. Going forward, pay attention to any signs of flagging interest in Treasuries. A consistent bid-to-cover ratio below 2.4, the 15-year average, would indicate that demand is no longer keeping up with supply.

There is another metric from the Treasury auctions that bears watching. As the United States relies on foreign buyers to help fund the deficit, it is important to pay attention to what foreign investors are doing. A simple way to track a change in the foreign appetite for debt is to look at the *indirect bidder percentage* at the Treasury auctions. Like the bid-to-cover ratio, this is a statistic that the government announces immediately following an auction of government debt. The percentage of indirect bidders represents the portion of bids that did not come from the primary dealers—that is, the large banks and other financial institutions that are required to participate in Treasury auctions. This category of investors has been used as a proxy for foreign participation in auctions. Higher percentages are interpreted as demonstrating more foreign interest.

As with the bid-to-cover ratio, there is no sign of a problem, yet. Over the past 10 years, foreign participation has fluctuated significantly from auction to auction, but it has averaged roughly 30 percent. If the indirect bidder amount fell below the 15 to 20 percent level for several consecutive auctions, this would be another warning sign for bond investors. As long as foreign investors still value the safety and liquidity of Treasury instruments, this will help to keep rates low. Unfortunately, strong foreign demand will not continue forever.

THE FED AND SHORT-TERM RATES

Finally, in evaluating the outlook for long-term interest rates, you need to also pay attention to short-term rates and what the Fed is doing.

While the Fed does not directly set long-term rates, it can influence them through its manipulation of short-term interest rates.

The difference between long- and short-term rates is known as the *yield spread* or *yield curve*. The yield curve compares bonds with similar characteristics—risk and tax treatment—but with different maturities. Typically, lenders charge higher interest rates for longer-term loans. This applies whether it is a mortgage, corporate loan, or the government borrowing in the Treasury market. If borrowers want lenders to lock up their money for a longer period of time, most of the time they will need to offer a higher rate of interest. First, there is a time premium to money. People would rather have a dollar today than a dollar in 10 years. A longer loan means that the lenders' money is locked up for a longer period of time. Also, the longer the life of the bond, the more opportunity for inflation to rise, which will erode the value of the lenders' principal. Even if inflation does not rise, the lenders are taking a risk that interest rates may go up before the loan matures. If rates rise, then the lenders are forgoing additional interest they could obtain by lending to different borrowers at higher rates. For all of these reasons, long-term rates are generally higher than short-term rates; this is known as an *upward-sloping yield curve.*

While rates are higher for longer-term loans, they are usually not that much higher. Historically, the difference between short-term interest rates and long-term interest rates in the United States has been about 2 percentage points. The spread between overnight money and 10-year loans is rarely in excess of 3 percentage points. This means that if the Fed keeps short-term interest rates close to zero, long-term rates are unlikely to rise too far. When the Fed does start to hike interest rates, it removes the "anchor" from the short end of the curve.

Interest rates will start to rise when the supply of government debt begins to overwhelm demand. This will happen when other borrowers increase their demand for capital and when bond buyers (particularly foreign investors and U.S. banks) decide they have better things to do with their money. Specifically, watch the following factors: bank lending, consumer debt, short-term interest rates, and government auction results. When the supply of other types of debt begins to rise and demand can no longer absorb the torrent of government supply, lower your allocation to bonds.

INFLATION SIGNS: LABOR MARKETS

While inflation does not necessarily follow deficits a *real* effort to curtail deficits through spending cuts would actually be deflationary— governments have often tried to use inflation as a politically expedient way to deal with excessive debt.

It takes a while for inflation to get going, so it is unlikely to accelerate before 2012, at the earliest, given the anemic state of bank lending and the slow growth in the money supply. Inflation, however, is very dangerous to your portfolio, so you should be on the alert. As the economy improves, the risk of inflation will increase. Inflation is less likely to occur when there is still significant slack in the economy in the form of high unemployment or excess manufacturing capacity.

When focusing on inflation, it makes sense to start by looking at jobs. Wages represent a large part of the economy. Personal income in the United States is approximately $12 trillion, out of a $14.5 trillion economy. People are less willing and able to pay higher prices if their wages don't rise as well. And their wages are unlikely to rise when there are a lot of unemployed people who would be willing to do their jobs for the current wage, or less. Therefore, job creation is a useful indicator of inflation risk. Rising inflation follows rising job growth with about a year's lag.

Historically, inflation has remained contained, defined here as 3 percent or below, when job growth was below its long-term average of about 1.5 percent a year. As the U.S. labor force is growing by about 1 percent a year, job growth well in excess of this means that there are more jobs than people. Under this scenario, unemployment falls and wages rise as people can be more selective in the jobs and wages they accept. Job growth is easily tracked. On the first Friday of every month, at 8.30 a.m. Eastern Time, the Labor Department announces the previous month's employment numbers. Contained in this report is the number of nonfarm jobs created during the previous month (www.bls.gov/ces).

By the fall of 2010, there were approximately 800,000 more nonfarm jobs in the United States than in the same period a year earlier (Figure 3.4). While this marks a significant improvement, 800,000 jobs in a country of 300 million still represent a fairly anemic labor market. Until job growth really picks up, wage growth is likely to remain weak. This further pushes out the risk of inflation until at least 2012.

Figure 3.4 **U.S. Nonfarm Payrolls**

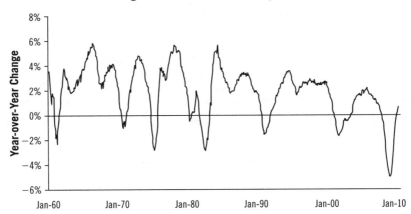

Source: Bloomberg and the Bureau of Labor Statistics, as of March 31, 2010.

INFLATION SIGNS: FACTORY BOTTLENECKS

In addition to the labor market, manufacturing levels also affect inflation. Specifically, the amount of spare, or unused, capacity in the manufacturing sector is a good leading indicator of future inflation. The Federal

Reserve tracks manufacturing capacity and how much is being used. It updates these statistics, known as *capacity utilization*, around the middle of every month (www.federalreserve.gov/releases/g17).

Just as the recession left the United States with too many people for too few jobs, it also left us with more manufacturing capacity than we need. With consumers buying fewer cars, appliances, and homes, manufacturers cut back on production. Typically, around 80 percent of factory capacity is utilized. When the economy is booming, as it was in early 2008, the country uses nearly 90 percent of its manufacturing capacity. With manufacturing plants running close to all out, bottlenecks start to ensue. When customers cannot get the goods they need, they start to bid up the price they are willing to pay, which in turn creates further price pressure and inflation.

During the recession of 2009 to 2010, capacity usage fell to as low as 68 percent. By the end of 2010, capacity utilization had rebounded to about 75 percent (Figure 3.5). In other words, roughly a quarter of the nation's factories and manufacturing capacity are not being used. With so much excess capacity, manufacturers are more willing to accept lower prices to offset the fixed costs of running their factories. Just as tight

Figure 3.5 **U.S. Capacity Utilization Rate**

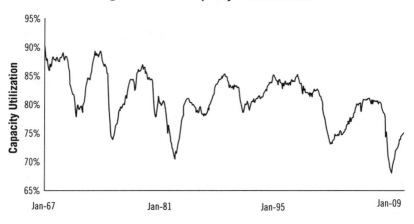

Source: Bloomberg and the Federal Reserve, as of March 31, 2010.

capacity utilization creates pricing pressure and inflation, low capacity utilization keeps a lid on prices and inflation. Historically, inflation does not start to pick up until capacity utilization rates are at least back at their long-term average. Even then, it generally takes about a year for prices to really start to accelerate. Until capacity utilization gets and stays back above the 80 percent level, there is less of a threat of inflation over the next year.

INFLATION SIGNS: WATCH THE MONEY

Next, we come to the growth in the money supply, which is arguably the most important factor to watch in assessing the inflation outlook. When the money supply grows too fast, this ignites inflation. While we have had inflation with a weak economy, we have never had inflation without a pickup in the money supply. This will be the most important indicator to watch when assessing the risks for future inflation. As with capacity utilization and other economic factors, this information is conveniently provided on a weekly basis, Thursday afternoons, by the Federal Reserve (www.federalreserve.gov/releases/h6/current/h6.htm).

The last time there was a significant resurgence in inflation was the late 1960s, followed in short order by a period of stagflation of the 1970s. In both cases, inflation was preceded by acceleration in the growth of the money supply. Instructively, in both cases long lags were evident. The year-over-year rate of growth in the money supply went from approximately 4 percent in late 1960 to over 8 percent by 1962 (Figure 3.6). Yet it was not until early 1966 that inflation really began to accelerate. Consumer prices went from rising at less than the year-over-year rate of 1 percent in late 1965 to over 4 percent by the summer of 1968. Inflation continued to climb over the next two years, reaching a peak of just over 6 percent in early 1970. From there, prices started to decline. By the middle of 1972, consumer price increases had slowed by less than 3 percent per year.

Figure 3.6 **U.S. Money Supply**

Source: Bloomberg and the Federal Reserve, as of March 31, 2010.

Then something strange happened. In contrast to most economic theory, which suggests that inflation should decelerate when economic growth slows, inflation started to accelerate. This acceleration occurred despite the fact that the U.S. economy began to contract in 1973. Over the next several years, the U.S. economy endured a particularly brutal recession. Unemployment, which was below 5 percent in the summer of 1973, rose to nearly 9 percent two years later. Despite the rise in the unemployment rate, inflation went from 3.6 percent in early 1973 to over 12 percent by the end of 1974.

The inflation of the early 1970s was a shock for everyone, but particularly for economists. A spike in inflation and a contracting economy were not supposed to happen together. While the inflation of the 1970s is difficult to explain by looking at economic growth or the labor market, it is remarkably easy to explain once you watch what the Federal Reserve was doing. Money supply growth was a relatively slow 2.5 percent at the start of the 1970s. By the end of 1971, the supply of money had skyrocketed. In December 1971 the nation's money supply was 13 percent higher than it was in the previous year, and its growth remained stubbornly high for the next two years.

So while overall economic growth, wage growth, and excess capacity are all significant determinants of inflation, the 1970s serve as a valuable reminder that in assessing inflation, you must pay particular attention to how much money is in the economy and how fast it is growing. As a general rule of thumb, the money supply should be growing in line with nominal GDP growth. Practically, that means that the most popular measure of money supply, known as M2, should not be growing by much more than 6 percent a year, which is also in line with the average growth rate over the past 25 years. If M2 were to grow much faster than that for a prolonged period of time, that would indicate future inflation. However, even then it will take a long time. As the example of the 1960s illustrates, inflation does not normally take off until at least two to three years after the money supply has started to spike. By looking at the money supply, we are unlikely to see much in the way of inflation before 2013.

Inflation Signs: How Big Is the Fed?

There is one final inflation indicator to watch. In Chapter 2 we introduced the concept of monetizing the debt. Should the Fed continue to expand its purchase of U.S. Treasuries, it runs the risk of eventually putting too much money into circulation. Should this occur, inflation will eventually follow.

Buying even more Treasuries and other financial assets will have the practical impact of expanding the Fed's balance sheet. While the Fed's balance sheet has steadily risen since the fall of 2008, the longer this goes on, the more dangerous it becomes. Assuming that the Fed buys the instruments from the banks, this creates new reserves for the banks. Under normal economic conditions, the banks will lend that money, and we will see a spike in the money supply. If the Fed purchases the debt directly from the government, the government will turn around and spend that money; this will also lead to a sharp rise in the money supply. Under either scenario, you raise the risk of inflation.

So far, the Fed's buying binge has not caused inflation; this is mostly because the banks have not been lending. In other words, bank lending is the typical mechanism that takes the Fed's policy actions—that is, buying securities—and translates that into more money in the economy. In late 2010, that mechanism was still not working as bank loan growth was pretty much nonexistent. Once demand for capital starts to increase and loan demand picks up, the Fed will need to shrink its balance sheet very quickly to prevent all that new money from entering the economy and increasing the money supply. If the Fed waits too long, there will be too much money chasing too few goods, and we run the risk of repeating the mistakes that led to such bad inflation in the 1970s.

Tracking what the Federal Reserve is buying and selling sounds esoteric, but it is actually quite easy. In late 2010, the Fed's balance sheet was approximately $2.3 trillion, which was roughly triple the size it was back in the summer of 2008. Going forward, you can monitor the size of the Federal Reserve holdings on a weekly basis on its Web site (www.federal reserve.gov/releases/h41/current/h41.htm). As a simple rule of thumb, from mid-2011 on, the Fed's balance sheet should be stable, and soon thereafter should start shrinking. If the Fed's balance sheet is still at or above current levels in 2012, that would be another warning sign.

INTEREST RATES AND INFLATION: WHEN TO ACT

For investors looking out over the next 10 to 20 years, there is plenty to worry about: slow growth, higher taxes, higher interest rates, and potentially higher inflation. The good news is that higher rates and inflation are likely to be delayed by the residual effects of the recent financial crisis. The bad news is that markets normally move in advance of the news. For this reason, you will need to keep a close eye on economic developments. Protecting your portfolio and positioning your finances will not require your becoming an amateur economist, but it will necessitate your being aware of a few basic developments.

First, watch the pace of economic growth, particularly the labor market and manufacturing sector. While inflation can happen in the absence of a robust economy, as the 1970s proved to everyone's discomfort, higher rates and higher inflation are less likely when demand is weak and supply is plentiful.

Second, look at consumer and corporate debt. As the economy starts to recover, consumers will eventually rediscover their love affair with debt. Corporations will do the same. When that happens, the Treasury will find itself in competition with other borrowers. At that point higher rates will be needed to attract buyers and fund the deficit. A more robust economy will raise the risks of both higher interest rates and higher inflation.

Third, look at the buyers of our debt. The United States has become dependent on others to finance our savings shortfall. If the Chinese and other foreign investors start to buy fewer Treasuries, rates will rise.

When it comes to inflation, you'll want to pay attention to job creation as measured by the annual change in nonfarm payrolls and capacity utilization. Inflation will start to rise when demand eclipses supply. There are lots of ways to measure this, but nonfarm payrolls and capacity utilization have proven useful in the past.

Finally, and most importantly, watch the supply of money and the size of the Fed's holdings. When the money supply starts to rise, inflation becomes a much bigger risk. And as the money supply is unlikely to rise before the banks start to lend, watch bank lending as well (which can also be tracked on the Federal Reserve's Web site). As long as banks refuse to lend, the mechanism by which the Fed influences the money supply is hampered. When banks start to lend again, that relationship will reassert itself, and the money supply will likely accelerate with inflation following.

Now that you know how to figure out when you need to start reallocating your portfolio, we will move on in the next chapter to discuss how you should reallocate.

CHAPTER 4

How to Manage Your Cash and Debts

F OR CLOSE TO 30 YEARS, U.S. interest rates mostly moved in one direction: down. From a peak of approximately 15 percent in 1982, long-term interest rates bottomed at a multidecade low of around 2 percent in late 2008. Since then, long-term rates have remained close to their lowest levels in decades. Short-term interest rates have followed a similar path. As of the end of 2010, they were effectively at 0 percent.

The low-rate regime may last a bit longer, but it will not last forever. By 2012 both short- and long-term rates should be on the rise. Just as the last three decades represented a more or less continuous decline in rates, the general direction over the next decade is likely to be up. What should you do to protect your assets in a rising interest rate environment? In this and each of the next five chapters, we'll explore how to respond to the economic and financial challenges of the coming decades. In this chapter we'll focus on two distinct but related aspects of your personal finances: cash and debt.

What you need to do in order to manage your debts in a rising inter- est rate environment will be the exact opposite of what you should do with your cash: look to borrow long and lend short. In other words, lock in your borrowing costs for the long term, but keep your cash in short- term instruments that will benefit from rising rates.

If you are looking to buy a house or refinance an existing mortgage, you should look for a long-term conventional mortgage to lock in your borrowing costs. For much of the past two decades, it has paid to have an adjustable-rate mortgage (ARM). However, in an environment of rising interest rates, an adjustable-rate mortgage will lead to higher payments over the life of the loan. Instead, take advantage of today's low rates to lock in a fixed-rate 15- or 30-year mortgage. This will be the best deal you are likely to see in your lifetime.

For most of the last decade, banks have paid virtually nothing on savings or money market accounts. As the economy stabilizes, the Fed will start to raise short-term interest rates. For those with extra cash lying around that is earning 0 percent interest, this is good news. Savers will finally start to be rewarded for their thrift. As rates start to rise, you will want to keep your extra cash in liquid vehicles such as savings accounts, money market funds, or short-term (less than two years) certificates of deposits. This way, you will benefit as interest rates reset higher.

MORTGAGES: FIXED RATE AND ADJUSTABLE RATE

Over the past few decades, bankers have invented ever more creative ways for consumers to take out mortgages. The last decade introduced us to an exotic zoo of loans, including ALT A, interest only, negative amortization, and "no doc" or "liar" loans. Suffice it to say, most of these innovations did not quite work as advertised. Too often, these products were poorly understood, came with underappreciated risks, or were simply mechanisms for borrowing more money than homeowners could safely handle. While your own personal finances and tax situation will determine the precise type of mortgage that will be best for you, there is one principle that you should follow in selecting a mortgage in an environment of rising rates: favor a fixed rate, not an adjustable one.

Fixed-rate mortgages, as their name implies, allow you to lock in an interest rate for a long period, normally either 15 or 30 years. The rate you pay is largely determined by the prevailing level of long-term rates at the time you take out the loan. Once you lock it in, the rate does not change for the life of the loan. If today you take out a 30-year fixed-rate mortgage at 5 percent, the interest rate on your outstanding balance will remain constant, regardless of what happens to short- or long-term interest rates.

In contrast, an adjustable-rate mortgage is a loan with an interest rate that changes over time. Unlike traditional mortgages where the rate is based on long-term rates, the cost of an ARM is typically determined by short-term interest rates. Adjustable-rate mortgages may start out with lower monthly payments than fixed-rate mortgages, but the rate will change as short-term interest rates fluctuate. The interest rate on an ARM changes periodically, usually in relation to an index, and the payments may go up or down accordingly. Generally the initial interest rates for ARMs are lower than the rates for fixed-rate mortgages that are being offered at the same time. At first, this makes the ARM cheaper than a fixed-rate mortgage for the same loan amount.[1] Home buyers are often tempted into taking out an ARM based on the low initial rate. But always keep in mind that the low initial rate comes with a cost. The cost is the risk that eventually your monthly payments may go much higher.

While all ARMs come with an adjustable interest rate, there are some important nuances on how that rate is calculated and when it adjusts. In general, it will adjust with some lag and after a set period of time. The interest rate on an ARM will remain in effect for a limited period, normally ranging from just one month to five years. For some ARMs, the initial rates and payments can vary greatly from the rates and payments later in the loan term.

Even if interest rates are stable, your rate and payment amounts can change quite a bit. If the annual percentage rate (APR) listed for your loan is significantly higher than the initial rate, then it is likely that your rate and payments will be a lot higher when the loan adjusts, even if general interest rates remain the same.[2] This is important when considering an ARM. If the terms of the ARM would require rates to not only remain constant but drop to maintain your current monthly payments, this is a bad bet. Short-term rates are unusually low, with many benchmark rates still close to 0 percent. They cannot drop any further. Should the global economy take another downturn, there are things the Fed could and would do—buying more long-term government debt and mortgage-backed bonds top the list—but it cannot lower short-term rates below zero.

With most ARMs, the interest rate and monthly payment change every month, quarter, year, three years, or five years. The period between rate changes is called the *adjustment period*. For example, a loan with an adjustment period of one year is called a *one-year ARM*, and the interest rate and payment change once every year. The actual interest rate that is applied is made up of two parts: the index and the margin. The ARM's index tracks a particular interest rate—normally a short-term rate— and the ARM's margin is an extra amount that the lender adds. If your loan comes with caps or limits, they will affect how high or low your rate can go.

For example, let's assume a $200,000 loan and a 30-year term, and a first-year monthly payment of 6 percent, made up of a 3 percent interest rate and a 3 percent margin. Under this scenario, the monthly payment is $1,199.10. Let's say that the following year the interest rate rises to 6 percent, so your interest rate once you add the margin rises to 9 percent. Now monthly payments would go up to $1,600.42, a one-third increase. In some cases, the increase would not be as great. If there is, for example, an 8 percent cap on your loan, then the interest rate the second year would be 8 percent and your monthly payment would be $1,461.72.[3]

In choosing whether to take out a fixed- or floating- (adjustable) rate mortgage, it is bad financial logic to look at just the low initial rate on the ARM. You want to consider the cost during the whole life of the loan, not just the first few years.

Over the past 15 years, ARMs proved cost effective because short-term rates for the most part trended lower. But that was then. Today, short-term interest rates are at a historic low of effectively 0 percent. As the economy recovers, they will climb much higher over the next 3 to 5 years. This will mean more expensive mortgage payments for anyone with an ARM.

A fixed-rate mortgage is likely to prove the better bet over the next decade, and it would be a good idea to act sooner rather than later. As Treasury yields rise, they will push fixed-rate mortgages higher. In addition, there are other reasons to lock in your mortgage today. One is that fixed-rate mortgages may climb even faster than Treasury yields. Conventional mortgage rates are artificially cheap today, even when compared to generally low yields on government bonds. This makes them a particularly good deal at these levels.

Lock in Today: Fixed-Rate Mortgages Are Going Higher

In the summer of 2010, a 30-year fixed mortgage was pegged at less than 5 percent, which was cheaper than at any time since the 1960s. Compare this rate to the long-term average. Since the early 1970s, the rate on a conventional mortgage has averaged approximately 9 percent, nearly twice today's levels (Figure 4.1). To put that difference in dollar terms, on a $200,000 mortgage at 5 percent, borrowing today costs $8,000 a year less than if interest rates had remained closer to their long-term average. Low interest rates are one of the key reasons that the economy in general, and the housing market in particular, did not suffer a worse decline during the recent recession. Lower rates helped make housing more affordable and allowed many individuals to keep houses that would have otherwise become unaffordable.

This bargain will not last too long. A large part of the reason of why mortgage rates are so low is that Treasury yields are so low. But there is

Figure 4.1 **Rates for 30-Year Conventional Mortgages**

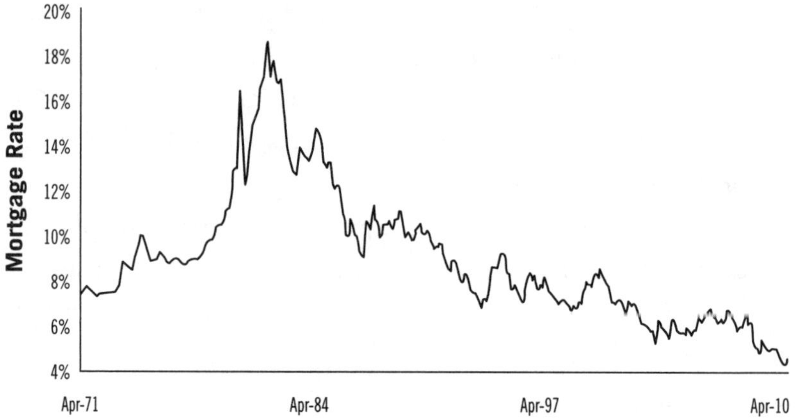

Source: Federal Reserve, as of March 31, 2010.

another reason why mortgage rates have remained so low: because the Fed wanted it that way.

Back in December 2008 the yield on the 10-year Treasury note hit an all-time low of 2 percent. By the spring of 2010 yields on the 10-year Treasury note had nearly doubled to around 3.5 to 4 percent. Despite the rebound in Treasury yields, mortgage rates barely budged. From a low of 4.81 percent in the spring of 2009, they were still below 5 percent more than a year later. This is highly unusual. Typically, the two rates—long-term Treasury rates and conventional mortgage rates—move more or less in lockstep. In fact, if you go back and compare the two rates, historically the correlation has been approximately 0.98 out of a possible 1. If long-term Treasury yields ultimately set rates for conventional mortgages, why did the yield on the 10-year Treasury note increase by nearly 2 percentage points while the rate on a 30-year mortgage rose by one-tenth of that amount?

The relationship between long-term Treasury yields and conventional mortgage rates began to break down in mid-2009. By November of that year the correlation between the two rates was the lowest it had been since 1976. The reason for the divergence, and the explanation for why mortgage rates have remained so low, is that the Federal Reserve took the unusual step of buying mortgage-backed securities—which are, effectively, bundled mortgages that the banks sell to investors—directly onto its balance sheet. In doing so, it created additional demand for mortgage-related products, which kept the price of mortgage-related products high and the yield low.

Beginning two days before Thanksgiving 2008 and continuing through March 2010, the Fed was directly purchasing mortgage-backed securities onto its balance sheet. Around the time of the Fed's announcement in 2008, the market for these securities had frozen in the midst of the financial crisis. The freeze in the mortgage market was a serious problem for the Fed and its efforts to stave off a more severe recession. The mortgage-backed market had become not only a crucial financial market but also a critical support to the housing market. Banks were able to offer cheaper mortgages because they could immediately sell off those mortgages to investors rather than keeping them on their books. In an effort to unfreeze the market for mortgage-backed securities and help push down mortgage rates, the Fed began buying these instruments directly.

The program was so effective that the Fed actually extended and expanded it on several occasions. When the Federal Reserve initially announced its intention to purchase mortgage-backed securities directly, the intent was to limit the purchases to $500 billion. The Fed began its program in January 2009, and in March of that year, it announced that it was raising its goal to $1.25 trillion. While the program was set to expire on December 31, 2009, in September of that year the Fed once again extended the program.[4]

While unconventional, the program worked brilliantly in bringing down mortgage rates, which in turn helped to cushion the housing downturn (yes, it could have actually been much worse). Back in late 2008, the spread, or difference, between a 30-year fixed-rate mortgage and the yield on a 10-year Treasury note exceeded 2.5 percentage points. This was nearly twice as wide as the historical spread. By early 2010, at the conclusion of the program, the difference between the yield on a 10-year Treasury and a 30-year mortgage had converged back toward its long-term average.[5]

Mortgage rates have remained near historical lows as a result of this deliberate Fed policy. In lieu of private demand, the Fed stepped in and created an artificial market for mortgages, and in doing so, it kept prices higher and rates lower than they otherwise would have been. This policy has now come to an end. As of the spring of 2010, the Fed is no longer purchasing mortgage backed securities. This removes a critical source of demand from the market. And at some point in the future, the Fed will need to sell some of its entire inventory of mortgage-backed securities in order drain money out of the financial system to tighten monetary policy if it wants to curb inflation. When the Fed starts to sell, it will put downward pressure on prices, and upward pressure on rates and the cost of mortgages. Even if the Fed does not sell—it could just let the mortgage bonds mature—there will be less artificial demand for mortgage-backed products. If nothing else, this will remove one of the factors that helped keep mortgage rates so low.

We are at or have already seen what is likely to be a generational low in mortgage rates. While a slow recovery may keep rates low for another year or two, for anyone looking out 10 or 20 years—a reasonable time frame for homeownership—today's rates will eventually seem incredibly cheap. The deficit will push rates higher, and the Fed will be unable or un-willing to stop this. One of the easiest ways to prepare for this is to lock in your largest borrowing cost, your mortgage, today.

ARMs and Short-Term Rates: Nowhere to Go but Up

The prescription for rising mortgage rates is to lock in today. This works only for conventional mortgages. For those with or thinking about an ARM, the very nature of the product prevents you from fully protecting yourself from higher rates. Short-term interest rates will rise. Today's zero rate policy is a residual effect of the financial crisis. The Fed may hold short-term rates low for the remainder of 2011, but absent another recession, they are likely to go up after that. Here's why.

The Fed generally sets the level of short-term interest rates based on both its expectations for inflation and economic activity. While not explicit, it is understood that the Fed is trying to keep inflation at around 2 percent over the long term. In addition to its mandate to keep prices stable, that is, to maintain low inflation, the central bank balances this goal with a second mandate. The Fed is also charged with promoting maximum employment.

In managing these dual mandates, short-term interest rates have traditionally been the Fed's primary tool. For example, the Fed may actually set short-term interest rates below the level of inflation, that is, at negative real rates, if the economy is threatened with a severe recession or deflation. This will encourage borrowers to take out loans and use the money in ways that will boost the economy. If the economy is too strong and in danger of overheating and boosting inflation, the Fed will raise short-term rates so that even after inflation, the price of borrowing will remain high. This will eventually slow the economy and reduce the risk of inflation. While rate policy will fluctuate based on the prevailing economic risks, over the past 50 years short-term interest rates have generally averaged approximately 2 percentage points above the CPI.

With inflation running at between 1 and 2 percent and short-term rates set at zero, current real short-term rates are decidedly negative. This policy of low real rates is justified as long as the economy remains weak and inflation is decelerating. As these trends start to reverse, the Fed will need to raise short-term interest rates. This suggests that even in the absence of much inflation, short-term rates will eventually revert back to at least the 4 percent range (2 percent inflation plus a real yield of 2 percent).

If inflation begins to accelerate above the Fed's comfort zone, there is a distinct threat that over the longer term, short-term rates will climb substantially higher. When they do, people with adjustable-rate mort-gages will see a big increase in their monthly mortgage payments. Unless you are convinced that the United States is in or about to enter a defla-tionary spiral, one in which prices generally fall, then you should not be considering an ARM.

THE LIBOR AND ADJUSTABLE-RATE MORTGAGES

There is one more reason to be cautious on ARMs, or more specifically one particular type of ARM. Adjustable-rate mortgage payments are based on one of several benchmark rates. Among the most common in-dexes are the rates on one-year constant-maturity Treasury (CMT) se-curities, the Cost of Funds Index (COFI), and the London Interbank Offered Rate (LIBOR).[6] What these all have in common is that they are all proxies for short-term interest rates.

The LIBOR is determined by the cost of *intra-bank borrowing*—that is, the cost for large banks when they borrow from one another. If your ARM is benchmarked to the LIBOR, investors' attitude toward risk could actually impact your monthly mortgage payment.

Normally, the LIBOR will move with other short-term rates, such as the rate on three-month Treasury bills, which in turn closely track the short-term interest rates the Fed sets, known as the *fed funds rate*. How-ever, during periods of financial stress, investors become more concerned with whom they are lending to. Under these conditions, banks would rather lend money to a sovereign entity, like the U.S. government, than to another bank, even a large, well-capitalized bank. When this happens, investors park more of their money in Treasury bills, which are consid-ered riskless. (They are riskless to the extent that the U.S. government has never defaulted.) As a result, the LIBOR tends to rise during periods of market turbulence, even when short-term rates, such as those on Trea-sury bills, are falling.

This is exactly what happened during the financial crisis of 2008. While the yield on Treasury bills was dropping, the LIBOR was rising. Banks were worried about loaning money to their peers even on an overnight basis. During this period, banks in need of funds had to pay a large premium to borrow. The LIBOR rose even while the Fed was pushing short-term rates lower. During this time, if you had the misfortune of having an ARM set to the LIBOR, your monthly payments would have increased even though most short-term rates were falling.

To the extent that your ARM interest rate is driven by a LIBOR benchmark, you should be aware of two things. First, the LIBOR will generally be approximately 50 basis points, or one-half of 1 percent, above the prevailing risk-free rate. Second, during periods of financial stress this spread will go up, potentially much higher as investor fear drives everyone into the safety of government-secured investments like Treasury bills. If your mortgage rate is tied to a LIBOR benchmark, you want to ensure that these risks are reflected in the mortgage spread over the index and other terms of the loan. In general, a loan pegged to a LIBOR benchmark will have a higher index rate so the margin should be lower to ensure that you're not paying more for the mortgage. Given that government deficits are likely to prove a semipermanent source of financial stress over the next decade, this is more than just an academic risk.

An Exception to the Rule

Despite all of the above, there are instances when home buyers or those looking to refinance should consider an ARM. If you think you can pay off your mortgage very quickly, then an ARM may make sense.

While ARM rates adjust with short-term rates, there is typically a grace period during which your initial rate is fixed and cannot change. Adjustable-rate mortgages with this feature are known as *hybrid ARMs*. These types of mortgages are often advertised as "3/1 or 5/1 ARMs." The loan is a mix of a fixed-rate period and an adjustable-rate period. The interest rate is fixed for the first few years of these loans. For example, for a 5/1 ARM, the interest payment is fixed for five years. After that, the rate may adjust annually (the "1" in the 5/1 example), until the loan is paid off. In general, the first number in a hybrid ARM tells you how long the fixed interest rate period will be, and the second number tells you how often the rate will adjust after the initial period. These loans are sometimes quoted as "2/28" or "3/27 ARMs"—in this case the first number tells you how many years the fixed interest rate period will be, and the second number tells you the number of years the rates on the loan are adjustable. Some of these ARMs adjust every six months rather than annually.[7] To the extent that the next several years will be characterized by a rising interest rate environment, you will want an ARM that resets less frequently. This will allow you to keep the lower rate for a little longer.

For those willing to take on more risk with their monthly payments, the hybrid ARM offers some opportunity if you think you can pay off your loan before the fixed period ends. As the initial rate on a 5/1 ARM is likely to be lower than the long-term rate for a conventional mortgage, it may still make sense to use an ARM if you are confident that you will be selling the house within the first five years or you will have the wherewithal to pay off the mortgage during that period. Assuming that you can terminate the mortgage through either method before the expiration of the lock-up period, your financing costs are likely to be lower with an ARM. Just be aware that you run a significant risk of higher monthly payments if you miscalculate and you have not paid off or sold the house when the rate starts to adjust.

How Much to Borrow?

Apart from how to borrow, the deficit also affects how much you should borrow. If you have the financial flexibility for a down payment in excess of what the bank requires, should you do it? There are many aspects to this decision including your tolerance for debt, individual tax circumstances, and your time horizon. But from the perspective of the deficit, the answer is simple. If deficit spending results in higher inflation—watch the signs discussed in the previous chapter—then you want to take out more debt. The higher inflation, the more you want to leverage yourself and take out a larger loan.

Inflation favors debtors. You borrow a dollar, and by the time you pay it back, it is worth much less. Effectively, like the Romans described in Chapter 2, you get to repay your debts in a currency that is less valuable. For this reason, individuals with high debt loads have normally preferred inflation over deflation. Deflation makes it harder to repay your loan, while inflation makes it easier as the loan is worth less over time.

A second reason to favor more debt when inflation is rising is that your income is likely to rise quicker. While incomes don't always keep up with inflation, wages do tend to rise faster when inflation is higher. Back in the day when inflation was more of an issue, employees regularly received cost-of-living adjustment (COLA) increases. If your wages rise faster than inflation, it makes your obligations easier to pay off, particularly if you have a fixed-rate mortgage.

Finally, when inflation is higher, you will earn more on the money you have in savings. When rates are low, the opportunity cost of putting down a big down payment is lower because you would not be earning much interest on your cash. In contrast, when inflation is higher, cash earns a much better rate of return. Under this scenario, you will want to make a smaller down payment and leave the extra cash in the bank or other investment vehicles that can generate income.

This does not suggest that you should leverage your finances beyond your comfort zone. Personal considerations and tax consequences certainly need to be taken into account. That said, you still should keep an eye on the inflation signs. To the extent that there is evidence of rising inflation, you should consider borrowing more to finance your home.

SAVINGS: THE GOOD NEWS

While the last decade has been a great time to borrow, it has been a miserable time to save. Stocks lost money over the course of the decade, something that had not happened previously in modern times. Nor has the situation been any better for more conservative individuals who avoided the stock market. Rates on savings accounts, money market funds, and short-term certificates of deposit (CDs) have been a fraction of where they were in the 1980s or 1990s. The Fed's policy of propping up the economy and bailing out the financial markets with low rates has effectively punished those dependent upon their savings for income.

So if there is a silver lining in our economic future of rising rates, it is that interest rates on savings vehicles will rise. The key to benefiting from this trend will be to follow the opposite advice given to borrowers. While borrowers want to borrow long and lock in low rates, savers want to keep their money in liquid instruments in which the interest rate will readjust with the market. Practically, this means favoring savings accounts, money market funds, and short-term CDs.

All of these are short-term savings vehicles in which the interest rate paid is periodically adjusted to reflect market rates. The interest rate you will receive will be primarily determined by the price the Fed sets for short-term interest rates. At the outset, savings accounts and other money market funds generally pay lower interest than bonds. Unlike bonds, however, once you invest your money in them, the rate paid resets when short-term interest rates rise. As a result, your income will rise as well.

For savings accounts and money markets, rate adjustments are typically made on a monthly basis. For certificates of deposit, the rate is set for the duration of the CD. In order to have the opportunity to benefit from rising rates, you'll want to favor CDs with short maturities so that, as they mature, you can reinvest the proceeds in other CDs, hopefully at a higher rate of interest. As a rule of thumb, look for CDs that will mature by 2012. After that, favor money markets and savings accounts that will reset monthly. Banks can provide all three of these vehicles. Money market funds, which are open-ended mutual funds, can also be purchased directly from asset managers or brokers.

In shopping around for the best rates, smaller banks are likely to pay slightly more than larger institutions, but the difference will not be huge. The major determinant of the interest rate you receive will be the maturity of the instrument. Savings accounts and money market funds are effectively cash. Like a checking account, you can access your money immediately. As such, they will pay a lower rate than a certificate of deposit, which has a specific maturity date. And if you do invest in a CD and decide you need your funds prior to the maturity date, there will normally be some type of a penalty. The only other difference in the savings vehicles is that the CDs will normally require a minimum $1,000 investment, with additional amounts in $1,000 increments.

In terms of safety, as long as you invest through an FDIC-insured bank, your deposits are insured to $250,000 per account for a single individual. Joint accounts are insured up to $250,000 per owner. You can even be insured for more than $250,000 per bank to the extent that the funds are in different accounts in different categories. Ownership categories include single accounts, joint accounts, and certain types of retirement accounts.[8]

Debt Long, Cash Short

As discussed in Chapter 3, interest rates are likely to remain close to their recent lows while the economy recovers and the Federal Reserve remains more concerned about another recession and deflation rather than inflation. As a result, we will not see a meaningful increase in short-term rates prior to 2011. Even then, to the extent that inflation is likely to remain well contained until at least 2012, the Fed is likely to adopt a slow and measured policy for future rate hikes.

After that, things are likely to get more interesting. As the excess slack in the economy gets worked off, the risk of inflation will rise. Adding to this, in two or three years' time we are at significant risk of an explosion in the money supply, another harbinger of inflation. The Fed massively expanded its balance sheet in 2008, 2009, and 2010. If the Fed does not reduce the size of its balance sheet and if it does not remove the excess reserves from the banks, all of that excess money will find its way into the real economy through bank lending. When that happens, inflation will become more of a threat. For that reason, from 2012 and beyond, expect higher short-term interest rates.

In order to protect yourself and take advantage of this dynamic, follow two simple rules: keep your debts long and your cash short. Before rates start to surge, use the current situation to your advantage and lock in your borrowing costs. Unless you believe that the United States is likely to enter a period of deflation, reminiscent of the Great Depression or modern-day Japan, we are unlikely to see long-term rates this low again. While many parts of the current market environment are, and will become more, challenging for investors, a 5 percent fixed-rate mortgage represents a rare opportunity. Take advantage of it.

On the cash side, simply follow the opposite advice. Expect short-term rates to start rising in 2011 and really pick up the following year. Accordingly, avoid savings instruments with a maturity much beyond 2012. Instead, keep your cash liquid in savings accounts, money market funds, or short-term certificates of deposit (one to two years) so as to take advantage of rising short-term rates. This way, as rates rise, the money you earn on your savings will rise with them.

CHAPTER 5

Bonds: How to Make Money in a Rising Interest Rate Environment

CHAPTER 2 HIGHLIGHTED THE MAIN impacts of higher deficits: slower growth, rising rates, and potentially inflation. And in Chapter 3 we highlighted the likely timing. The first of the three impacts, slower growth, is already evident, and it is actually good for bonds. One of the reasons bonds have done so well over the past couple of years is that the economic recovery has been anemic by the standards of other postrecession bounces. But as described in Chapter 3, as the economy slowly normalizes, rising rates start to become more of a problem, particularly given the federal government's need to finance its chronic deficit spending.

The first thing you should do to protect your portfolio in an environment of rising interest rates is to reduce your bond holdings, particularly U.S. Treasuries. Some stocks can withstand higher interest rates, particularly if the economy is strong. There are even some companies such as those in the energy sector that will actually benefit from higher inflation. When it comes to bonds, however, there are few silver linings.

The rule of thumb in the past has been for younger investors, for whom retirement was still many decades away, to keep around 30 percent of their portfolios in bonds and most of the rest in stocks. The logic behind a higher allocation to stocks when you're younger is that stocks do a better job of protecting purchasing power over the long term. In addition, younger investors can withstand more volatility in their portfolios as they are still decades away from retirement and have time to make back any losses. Then, as individuals age, the conventional wisdom has been to gradually raise their allocation to bonds. The rationale is that older investors will want to reduce the risk in their portfolio as they near retirement age, and bonds are inherently less risky than stocks. In addition, as individuals retire, a larger bond portfolio would generate more income.

Today, while individuals will still want more bonds and fewer stocks as they approach retirement, young and old alike should be reducing the part of their portfolio invested in bonds. If the main motivation for owning a bond is income, this is an awful time to be buying bonds, particularly Treasuries, as interest rates are close to historic lows. The current yield on the 10-year note is barely above 3 percent. After inflation and taxes, your real return is zero. Rising rates will create much better buying opportunities down the road. And as interest rates rise, bonds will become more volatile. Investors under the age of 50 should cut their bond allocation to around 20 percent of their portfolio. Even older investors, who are more income dependent, should try to lower their allocation to bonds and consider other income-producing investments like preferred stock or common stocks with high dividends.

Once you've lowered your overall allocation to bonds, what else should you do? You should focus your bond portfolio on shorter maturity bonds. You should also allocate a significant portion of your fixed-income portfolio to tax-exempt municipal bonds. This is particularly important for higher-income taxpayers. And in your remaining taxable bond portfolio, you should favor corporate and international bonds over U.S. Treasuries. Finally, while they carry some unique risks, you should look to allocate a portion of your portfolio to inflation-linked bonds. These are the only types of bonds that will provide some protection in the event of rising inflation.

As with stocks, bonds can have very different characteristics depending on the type and issuer. For this reason, in the part of your portfolio that remains in bonds, you will want to favor some types over others. This chapter will focus on how to structure your bond portfolio, what bonds to favor, and how to buy and sell those instruments.

What Is a Bond, and Why Own One?

There is nothing inherently wrong with bonds. They provide income, stability, and a sound night's sleep for many a retiree. But like any investment, there are times when they will perform well and times when they won't. Stocks are a great long-term savings vehicle, but the spring of 2000, when prices were nearing a peak, was a lousy time to buy them.

The problem with bonds today, or more specifically U.S. government bonds, is that they are expensive, particularly when you consider the risks explained in the first several chapters. "Expensive" for a bond means that the real or after-inflation yield is very low. Today, the real yield on longer-dated U.S. government debt is barely 1 percent. And that is before taxes (while the interest on certain obligations of states and municipalities is tax exempt, interest on federal obligations is taxable for federal income tax purposes). The second problem with government bonds today is that a slew of supply will eventually push prices down. As the pressure increases, bonds will become less stable and more volatile.

A little primer here on bonds will help you understand what characteristics you want to look for in the part of your portfolio that remains in bonds.

Bonds are also known as *fixed-income instruments*, in part because their interest payments are generally fixed. In effect, a bond is a loan to the bond issuer for a period of time. The bond issuer normally pays interest to the bondholder at some regular interval, often semiannually. When the bond matures, the buyer gets his or her money back. You don't invest in bonds to get rich; you invest in them so you know where your money is. So when considering bonds, first and foremost you want to look for an issuer who will pay you back.

Second, you want a bond that produces income, obviously the more the better. The tricky part is to balance your need for income with your tolerance for risk. As with stocks, a bond's return is also a function of its risk. There are no free lunches. If one bond is paying 4 percent a year and another is paying 8 percent, there is a reason. It may be that the higher rate is to compensate you for accepting a much longer maturity because that will subject you to a higher risk that interest rates will rise in the interim. It might also be the case that there is a greater risk that the issuer of the higher coupon bond will default, in which case you would lose all or a portion of your principal. This is the reason that the Treasury can borrow so cheaply, despite its massive debt; investors still believe that the U.S. government is less likely to default than almost any other borrower.

Another thing you want from a bond is tranquility. This is different from getting your money back. Some bonds may not be at any real risk of defaulting, but they may be very volatile before they mature. In other words, you may have to live with violent daily price swings. Bonds in general are a lot less volatile than stocks—historically, bond prices have recorded only about one-quarter the volatility of stock prices—but some bonds are more volatile than others. And unlike stocks where volatility has an upside, with bonds you're still going to get the same amount back when it matures, regardless of how many sleepless nights you have in the interim. As we'll discuss, you'll want to invest in bonds whose creditworthiness is likely to improve, not deteriorate—practically, that means bonds of companies, countries, or states whose debt level is manageable relative to their income or tax revenue. These bonds will have less volatility.

Finally, bonds can serve one other function: diversification. Depending on the economic conditions, they behave differently than stocks. During the recent financial crisis, Treasury bonds went up while both stocks and commodity prices were crashing. While both bonds and stocks tend to decline when interest rates and inflation are increasing, bonds generally help you to achieve greater diversification in your portfolio. Bonds generally do better when the economy is weak, while stocks suffer as earnings growth slows. During these periods, bonds will offer diversification from stocks. This is important because diversifying your investments—having different assets that respond differently to various economic conditions—will further lower the overall volatility of your portfolio. As we'll discuss later in the chapter, the diversification argument favors buying more international and fewer U.S. bonds.

So you don't want to banish all bonds from your portfolio, but you need to invest in the right types of bonds. You want to focus on bonds that will pay you your money back—preferably in a currency that is worth something, produce a reasonable real after-tax income, and help lower the volatility of your portfolio.

BOND RISKS: TIME AND CREDIT

Since investing in any asset class is always a matter of trading off risk for return, investors should understand how to evaluate the risks on their bond portfolio. There are many variables to consider when investing in bonds, but the two most important are interest rate and credit risk. When interest rates are rising, bonds are generally not a great asset to hold. This is why the deficit will be so bad for bonds.

The interest rate on a bond is generally fixed for the life of the bond. Unlike a savings account or money market account where the rate will rise and fall with short-term rates, whatever rate you get when you buy the bond is the rate you live with. The other difference between a savings account and a bond is that with a savings account you can always get 100 percent of your money back at any time. In order to get all of your principal back out of a bond, you have to wait until it matures, at which time the issuer pays it off. The holder of a bond may choose to sell the bond to other investors before it matures, but when she does, she may not get back her full investment. If interest rates have risen since the bond was purchased, the bondholder can only sell the bond at a discount.

This is easy to understand. A 30-year bond with a face value of $100 and a stated interest rate of 6 percent will pay the owner $6 a year for 30 years. If interest rates remain at around 6 percent, the price to buy or sell that bond will be about $100. But if interest rates were to suddenly rise to 9 percent, a bond with 30 years left to maturity and a 6 percent *coupon*—the interest rate the bond pays—would be worth around only $70. The purchaser of the bond will still get $6 a year, but the $6 is less attractive in an environment where a new 30-year bond is paying 9 percent a year. As a result, investors would be willing to pay the holder of that bond only around $0.70 on the dollar. When interest rates rise, investors can get a higher yield on new bonds so the value of the old bonds declines.

However, if your bond will mature next year rather than maturing in the distant future, the drop in price will not be nearly as steep. If your 6 percent bond is going to mature next year, even if interest rates have risen to 9 percent, you can still get $100 for it if you just wait a few months for the issuer to pay it off. Other investors are going to recognize this, so even if you decide to sell now, you will still get close to *par*, that is, $100. But if the bond isn't going to pay off for 20 years, that's a different story. Investors are going to be looking for a price that gives them the 9 percent annual return.

The longer a bond takes to mature, the more its price will decline when rates rise. This relationship between rates and price is known by the technical term of *duration*. There are different ways to measure duration, but the general principle is the same: how sensitive is the price of the bond to a change in interest rates? One measure of duration is the ratio of the percentage reduction in the bond's price to the percentage increase in the yield.[1] Bonds with higher duration will experience greater appreciation when rates drop, but they will depreciate more when rates rise. For example, a 2.5-year duration bond would lose approximately 1.25 percent on a 0.5 percent increase in rates. A bond with a 5-year duration would lose twice as much value.

Another way to think about duration and bond risk is based on when you get your money back. The longer it takes to get back all the money that the bond issuer promised you, both interest and principal, the longer the duration and the higher the risk.[2] This means that bonds with high interest payments will have a shorter duration, and they will be less sensitive to changes in interest rates. If a bond yields 10 percent, you will get back a larger portion of your total cash flow as interest, versus a bond with a yield of 5 percent. For this reason, higher coupon bonds typically have a lower duration than lower coupon bonds. This is important given today's bond market. Because interest rates are so low, you get most of your total cash flow when the bond matures. For that reason, bonds today will have a higher duration than when interest rates were higher. As duration equals risk, this means that bonds today are more risky than they were in the past.

But *duration*, which measures the risk of losing your principal as interest rates rise, isn't the only factor you have to consider. The second major risk factor for bonds is *credit risk*, or the likelihood that the issuer of the bond will not pay back all the interest and principal owed. Bonds with better creditworthiness are less of a risk, and therefore they pay less interest than securities issued by riskier borrowers. For example, despite the government's current budget deficit, the federal government has a long and consistent record of paying its debt on time and in full. In contrast, some countries, for example, Argentina, have frequently defaulted on their sovereign debt. For that reason, U.S. bonds pay a much lower interest rate than the bonds of most other countries as investors are more comfortable loaning money to the United States.

The same general principle regarding creditworthiness applies to other issuers as well. When IBM issues a bond, it is able to pay a lower interest rate than a small, less well-known company. IBM has been in business for decades, and investors are comfortable that it will be able to pay the interest and principal when the bond matures. Investors are likely to have less confidence that a small company they are less familiar with will be around in a decade's time. As a result, they will demand a higher interest rate from that company.

WHEN BUILDING A BOND PORTFOLIO, USE A LADDER

The big problem for bond investors is that interest rates are going to rise, but it is not clear when. In addition to owning fewer bonds, you can protect your portfolio by owning bonds with a shorter duration. This serves two purposes. As described above, when rates rise, shorter duration bonds will be less impacted, and they will experience less price volatility. Second, by owning shorter duration bonds, your bonds will mature more frequently, and you'll be able to reinvest the money at a higher rate.

The drawback to shorter duration bonds is that they pay less. When building a portfolio of bonds, one of the key challenges is to balance the extra return generated by buying longer maturity bonds with the extra risk. We first mentioned the concept of the yield curve in Chapter 2. As you will recall, typically the yield curve will be upward sloping or positive—that is, the longer the maturity, the higher the interest rate.

Why is it that longer-dated bonds should pay more than shorter-dated bonds? The longer it takes for a bond to mature, the more things that can go wrong. Interest rates can rise, which means you can be stuck with less income for a longer period of time. Inflation can rise, which would not only be likely to drive up interest rates but also likely to lower the purchasing power of your principal. Finally, the longer you hold the bond, the greater the chance that the issuer may default or attempt to change the terms of the bond. If you buy a 30-year corporate bond as opposed to a 3-year corporate bond, you will need a much higher level of conviction in the long-term viability of the company. For these reasons, investors who are willing to purchase longer-dated bonds are typically rewarded with higher interest payments.

So is there a way to minimize the trade-offs between the lower income of the short duration bonds and the higher risk of the long duration bonds in a rising rate environment? Yes. Rather than buying bonds with the same short maturity, let's say five years, you can purchase bonds of different maturities including longer bonds but with an average maturity of around five years. This is known as *laddering*, and it can be a very effective way to structure your bond portfolio, particularly when the yield curve is positive and steep, as it is today.

The basic concept in laddering is to invest in bonds with staggered maturities so that a portion of the portfolio will mature each year. To maintain the ladder, the money that comes in from maturing bonds is typically invested in bonds with longer maturities within the range of the bond ladder. Laddering does well against other bond strategies for a couple of reasons. First, laddering captures price appreciation as the bonds age and their remaining life shortens. Second, laddering reinvests principal from maturing limited-term bonds (low yielding) into new longer-term bonds (higher yielding). The goal of a laddered portfolio is to achieve a total return that compares favorably to the total return of a longer-term bond, with less risk. The way to do this is to invest approximately equal amounts in your bond portfolio in each year of the selected maturity range.[3]

Here is why laddering helps to lower your risk in a rising rate environment. While bond values initially drop as rates rise, they do recover value as they move toward their maturity (remember, assuming the bond issuer has not defaulted, you get back par when the bond matures). Unlike owning an individual bond, owning a ladder of bonds of which some mature each year gives the portfolio a stream of cash flow to reinvest in new, higher-yielding bonds. Without maturing bonds, you can only sell bonds at depressed prices in order to generate cash for reinvestment. As proceeds from maturing bonds are reinvested in higher-yielding bonds at the far end of the ladder, the portfolio's yield gradually increases. This built-in reinvestment feature offsets some of the price depreciation that occurs throughout the ladder when interest rates rise. It also results in a rising income stream. As maturing proceeds are reinvested at the end of the ladder, the yield of the portfolio is greater than what would be expected by the average maturity of the bonds, because of the positive slope of the yield curve.[4] Today, with interest rates likely to rise over the longer term and the yield curve very positive, laddering offers an effective mechanism for lowering the risk of your bond portfolio while still helping you maintain a reasonable income on your holdings.

BUYING TREASURY BONDS

Even though you should look to lower the allocation and duration of the U.S. Treasuries in your portfolio, many investors, particularly risk-averse ones, will still want to hold some portion of their assets in short-term Treasury bills and notes. For the portion of your portfolio that remains in Treasuries, what is the best way to buy and hold these instruments? There are several ways to buy Treasuries. The easiest, and cheapest, may be to buy them directly from the government. For decades the Treasury has enabled individual investors to buy and hold their instruments without going through a broker or a bank. The service is known as Treasury Direct, and it can be accessed at www.treasurydirect.gov.

There are several advantages to using this service. First and foremost, there are no fees to open or maintain your account with the Treasury. Another advantage is that the account is directly with the Treasury. While it is rare, a broker or bank can go out of business—think of Lehman Brothers in 2008. This is unlikely to happen to the U.S. Treasury. Whatever the challenges facing the government, for the foreseeable future it is likely to be a safe custodian of your funds. A third advantage is that the service allows you to purchase, reinvest, and sell securities directly online.

For investors with larger portfolios who want to build a laddered Treasury portfolio, purchasing bonds directly makes sense. For smaller investors who want to avoid the time and hassle of yet another account, it may be easier to let someone else do the work. To the extent that you are looking to diversify across different maturities, let's say holding a portfolio with maturities ranging from three months to five years, the burden of buying, selling, and maintaining an account may not be worth it. For these investors, it may make more sense to pay a small fee to invest through a traditional open-ended mutual fund or exchange-traded fund (ETF). The advantage of both is a much more diversified portfolio. The disadvantage is the fee. Fortunately, if you stick with an index fund, or ETF, the fees are relatively low, on average around 0.15 percent per year.

Throughout this and the next few chapters, I'll be recommending various mutual funds and exchange-traded funds. These are meant purely as examples, in order to provide some practical basis for implementing the ideas discussed. Investors should do their own homework to identify the funds or products that are right for them. While investigating which fund or ETF to invest in, always consider whether that product is engaged in active or passive management.

Active funds employ fund managers who try to outperform a given benchmark, like the Dow Jones Industrial Average. Their goal is for the fund to add value through security selection. For example, an active manager running an S&P 500 fund would be trying to outperform or beat the returns on the S&P 500 by a few percentage points each year. An active manager attempts to beat the benchmark by owning securities in different proportions to those in an index. So if IBM makes up 1 percent of an index and the portfolio manager likes the stock, he may choose to have IBM make up 3 percent of his portfolio. If the portfolio manager does not like a particular stock, he may not own any despite the fact that the stock is represented in the index. The success or failure of an active manager will be measured by the margin by which the fund beats the benchmark, in this case the S&P 500.

In contrast, an *index*, or *passive*, *fund* will seek to simply replicate, rather than surpass, the performance of a given benchmark. In the case of an index fund manager who is running an S&P 500 fund, he will simply own all the securities, and in the same proportion, as those listed in the S&P 500.

Active funds will add value to the extent that the manager has skill in "beating the market." If the manager does not have skill, or if his or her particular methods are ineffective in a given year, the fund may underperform the benchmark. So when you invest in an active fund, in addition to the market risk, you are also taking on additional risk, that of the manager. Finally, always remember that active funds charge higher fees. This means that not only does the manager have to beat the market, but she has to beat the market by enough to justify her fees. Most of the recommendations I make in this book, including the ETFs, will involve an index fund.

While most investors are familiar with mutual funds, they may be less familiar with ETFs. *Exchange-traded funds* are effectively open-ended mutual funds (almost all of which are passive) that trade on an exchange like a stock. In a traditional mutual fund, when you buy into the fund, you buy directly from the fund company. The price you pay for the fund will be the closing price from that day. With an ETF, unless you are a very large institution, you buy the fund from other investors, and the fund price fluctuates throughout the day—though the price will generally remain very close to the value of the underlying securities in the fund (the *net asset value*, or NAV). You can purchase either an ETF or a traditional open-ended fund through a broker. In the case of a mutual fund, you can also invest directly from the investment manager.

Exchange-traded funds offer several advantages over traditional index funds. For starters, they are typically cheaper. The average expense ratio for all ETFs in the United States is 0.54 percent, compared with an average of 0.99 percent for conventional index funds. Exchange-traded funds may also be more economical to the extent that many brokers are now offering commission-free trading for ETFs. The trend began back in the fall of 2009 when Charles Schwab entered the ETF market with four funds that featured no commissions for Schwab investors who trade online. Since then, other brokers, including Vanguard and Fidelity, have offered similar arrangements.[5]

Another advantage for ETFs over traditional mutual funds is that exchange-traded funds tend to be more tax efficient. When investors sell an ETF, they sell shares to other investors rather than redeeming them with the fund. As a result, you control the timing of the taxable disposition of your investment. In contrast, when a traditional fund needs to sell securities to meet redemptions requests, it must distribute the resulting net taxable gains to all the fund's investors. With a traditional fund, you have less control over the timing of your capital gains.[6]

Exchange-traded funds are an effective way to gain access to not only the Treasury market but also most asset classes. As they can also be used for stocks, commodities, and even more esoteric asset classes, such as volatility, here are a few words on what to look for. Obviously, as with any investment product, keep the fees to a minimum. Remember, most ETFs are index funds. In other words, they are trying to replicate, not beat, an index or benchmark. Therefore, their fees should be low. This is particularly important for Treasury or bond ETFs because the expected returns are lower and high fees will eat up a greater portion of the returns.

After fees, be aware of the size and liquidity of the ETF. As a rule of thumb, larger ETFs, as measured by their asset size, will be more liquid and easier to trade. This is critical because part of the cost of an ETF is the bid/ask spread you will pay when you buy and sell the fund.

Larger funds are more likely to have smaller spreads and are therefore cheaper and easier to trade. Finally, pay attention to the index that the ETF uses. This is less of an issue with a product like Treasuries, where there are fewer indexes and less of a difference between them. However, it can make a huge difference for a commodity fund. Here, depending on the index the ETF is supposed to be tracking, returns can differ substantially.

MUNICIPAL BONDS

High deficits don't just mean slower growth and higher interest rates. The deficits are also likely to mean higher taxes, particularly on the more affluent. Fortunately, there is a solution to the tax side of the problem: municipal bonds, or *munis*. The best, and arguably only, way to shield yourself from a high deficit-inspired tax bite will be to raise your allocation to municipal bonds. For wealthy individuals in the top tax brackets, munis should form the core of their bond portfolios. The good news is that today, on an after-tax basis, municipal bond yields look reasonably priced.

Municipal bonds are issued by states or other local municipalities. The interest on a municipal bond is not subject to federal taxation, and if the municipal bond is issued by the state in which you live, it is not subject to state or city taxes. For investors in the higher tax brackets, this is a huge savings. And even if marginal rates rise further, the after-tax income on your municipal bonds remains constant.

When comparing a municipal bond to a taxable bond, you will want to calculate what is known as the *tax equivalent yield*. To do this, take the yield on a municipal bond and divide it by 1 − your tax rate. If your marginal tax rate is 35 percent and a municipal bond yields 5 percent, you will need to find a taxable bond yielding at least 7.6 percent [5 percent/(1 − 35 percent)] to make you whole.

As your tax rate goes up, either because overall marginal rates are rising or you are in a higher tax bracket, muni bonds become more and more valuable. Consider two taxpayers and one muni bond paying a 4 percent coupon. Assume both taxpayers live in the state of issuance, so in both cases the bond will be exempt from federal, state, and city taxes. As illustrated above, if the first taxpayer's combined state and federal tax rate is 50 percent, she will need to find a taxable bond yielding 8 percent in order to produce the same after-tax income. If the other individual is in the 40 percent bracket, he will need to find a taxable bond with only a 6.7 percent yield to produce the same income. In other words, the higher your combined state and federal marginal tax rate, the more valuable a municipal bond will be.

While munis may yield more on an after-tax basis, are they safe? Obviously, this is going to depend in large part on the issuer, but generally speaking, muni defaults are exceedingly rare. For munis issued by a state, as opposed to a town or municipality, there has not been a default in decades. The last state to default on a state-issued bond was Arkansas in 1933!

Tax-free muni bonds generally come in two flavors: general obligation (GO) and revenue bonds. *General obligation bonds* are backed by the full taxing authority of the state or municipality, while *revenue bonds* are tied to a particular source of revenue, such as a toll road or a hospital. Generally, GO bonds are considered safer as there are more potential sources of revenue to back the bonds. For that reason, a GO bond will generally yield less than a revenue bond because yield, or return, is again a function of risk.

Beyond whether a bond is a GO or revenue, the relative safety of the bond will be determined by the entity issuing the bond. Today, because of its perpetual budget problems California is considered a greater credit risk than Iowa. Accordingly, the yield on a California GO bond will be higher than the yield on an Iowa bond of the same maturity. The perceived safety of the municipal bond will be driven by a number of factors, including the potential gap between revenue and expenditures for a state, the size of its tax base, its unfunded pension liabilities, and its demographics.

In general, though, municipal bonds are about as safe as any fixed-income instrument, outside of a U.S. Treasury. And in a number of respects, they may even be safer. Munis have one significant advantage over Treasuries or corporate bonds: unlike the federal government, most states are legally prohibited from running a budget deficit. Of the 50 states, 16 are required by their constitution to balance their budgets. Also, unlike a corporation, states cannot file for bankruptcy protection under Chapter 9 of the bankruptcy code.

Not all munis are issued by states, so what about those munis that are issued by cities or other municipalities? Here again, there are several safeguards that help to ensure a very low default rate. First, in only 26 states can municipalities file for bankruptcy, and in those states they may do so only with state oversight or approval. Even for those localities with the legal authority to file, bankruptcy is not an attractive option. There are several notable detriments. A municipality that files for bankruptcy protection will lose market access for future borrowings.[7]

There is potentially one other reason to favor munis over Treasuries in your portfolio. As explained in earlier chapters, the supply of Treasuries will only increase over time. Eventually, demand will struggle to keep up with that supply, and prices are likely to drop. State governments are also struggling to get their own finances under control. However, depending on the future of one key piece of legislation, they may have another option besides selling tax-free bonds. A little-known portion of the 2008 financial stimulus package has been helping to ensure that the supply of tax-free municipal bonds in 2008 and 2009 was less than it otherwise would have been.

In an effort to provide funding for what were euphemistically known as "shovel-ready projects," the U.S. government allowed traditional tax-exempt municipal issuers to finance certain qualified projects in the taxable bond market. These bonds are known as Build America Bonds, or BABs. In order to offset the additional interest expense of taxable bonds—recall that the reason municipalities can issue debt bonds so cheaply is that their bonds are exempt from federal taxes—the Treasury provides each issuer with a 35 percent direct subsidy. In 2009, BAB issuance totaled $64 billion. Supply doubled in 2010 and represented over 30 percent of municipal issuance. These bonds have proven very popular with institutional investors and foreign investors who are looking for a high-quality alternative to the Treasuries market. They have grown so popular that they are likely to be included in bond indexes, a move that would engender even more demand as bond fund managers will then need to purchase them in order to track that particular bond index.[8]

For our discussion, the significance of BABs is that they allow states and other municipalities to fund more of their projects in the taxable rather than nontaxable bond market. This decreases the supply of tax-exempt municipal bonds. Previously, these projects were likely to get funded anyway, but with tax-free bonds rather than BABs. To the extent that the federal government maintains the program (it was scheduled to expire at the end of 2010, but there were numerous efforts underway to extend it) and BABs continue to grow in popularity, this will remove future supply from the tax-free municipal market.[9] With less supply, prices of tax-exempt munis (the kind individuals buy) are likely to remain more stable than prices in the bond markets (that is, Treasuries) that will be flooded with an ever-growing supply over the coming years. An extension of the BABs program will raise the relative attractiveness of tax-free municipal bonds relative to Treasury bonds.

So there are a number of good reasons to favor municipals within your bond portfolio. And from a price perspective, municipal bonds look cheap relative to Treasury instruments. In 2010, long-term, 10-year general obligation municipals were yielding more than Treasuries. Historically, long-term GO municipal bonds have typically traded 100 basis points below the yield on the 10-year Treasury. As a rule of thumb, with a top marginal tax rate of approximately 35 percent, if GO 10-year muni yields are within around half a percentage point of the yield on the 10-year Treasury, municipals represent a good deal. If yields are actually *above* the comparable Treasuries, they are arguably an even better bargain. And while it is true that some states, particularly California and Illinois, look like economic basket cases, they are still unlikely to default. Even in California, for all its economic woes, municipal bondholders are near the top of the line when it comes to being paid.

BUYING MUNIS

For investors looking to add to their muni portfolio, what is the best way to do so? First, realize that rising yields will hurt the prices of municipals as well as of Treasuries. And while you may want to gain more of your bond exposure through munis rather than Treasuries, you will still be better off favoring shorter maturity issues.

Second, when it comes to revenue versus general obligation bonds, this decision is largely a matter of risk tolerance. Because revenue bonds, as their name implies, are normally tied to a single revenue source, they are perceived as more risky, and therefore they generally provide higher yields than general obligation bonds. Over the past 30 years, long-term (approximately 20 years) revenue bonds have yielded about one-half of 1 percent—that is, 50 basis points—over GO bonds of the same maturity. As of this writing, the spread between revenue and general obligation bonds is close to its long-term average, implying that revenue bonds do not look particularly cheap or expensive compared to GO bonds.

An even more important issue is whether most investors should be buying individual muni bonds in the first place. Unless you are willing to do your homework researching the particular characteristics, duration, and ratings of various muni bonds, the answer is probably no. For most individual investors, it will be easier to assemble a broad, diversified portfolio of municipal bonds through a mutual fund or ETF.

There is a second reason to consider using a mutual fund rather than buying municipals directly. The muni market is notoriously opaque and expensive to trade. While you can buy Treasury bonds or stocks cheaply—that is, there is a small difference between the price to buy and the price to sell—municipal bonds have much wider spreads for small investors. Practically, this means that you will pay more when you buy the bond and receive less when you sell. The more you pay, the lower the effective yield. The advantage of using a professional money manager is that he can transact at institutional rates, and he can buy or sell bonds more cheaply than even a large, individual investor.

When investing in a municipal bond fund or ETF, in addition to watching the expense ratio, pay attention to the geographical reach of the fund and duration of the fund. As with Treasury funds, most mutual fund providers offer funds targeted at different maturities. For example, Vanguard offers tax-free bond funds with short-, intermediate-, and long-term durations. The short duration fund will own municipal bonds with an average duration of a little over a year, while the average duration for the long-term fund is approximately 6.9 years. Favor short and intermediate duration (five years or less) tax-free bond funds.

Also pay attention to the geographical reach of the fund. While municipal bonds are always exempt from federal taxes, they qualify for the state tax exemption only if you happen to live in that particular state. For a broad, national fund, you will have to pay state taxes on the income generated from out-of-state bonds. If you live in a high tax state like California or New York, this can reduce the income by 10 percent or more. Fortunately, most large fund complexes do offer specific funds for large, high tax states. Again, going back to Vanguard, it offers specific funds for California, Florida, Massachusetts, New Jersey, New York, Ohio, and Pennsylvania. As with other types of bond funds, the expense ratio on all of these options should be low. Look for funds with an expense ratio of approximately 0.20 percent.

In addition to traditional mutual funds, there are also a number of municipal bond ETFs that you can invest in as well. BlackRock is the largest provider in this category, and it offers both short and longer duration municipal bond funds, as well as funds targeted specifically for California and New York. Expense ratios are similar to those for bond funds.

To summarize, for most investors but particularly those in high tax brackets, munis should form a significant part of their bond portfolios. While there is some risk associated with specific states, this can be significantly reduced, along with transaction costs, by using a mutual fund or ETF, which will provide better diversification between different bonds and issuers. Investors should favor short or intermediate duration funds that will hold up better when rates start to rise.

Corporate Bonds

The U.S. deficit and national debt could be compared to the income statement and balance sheet of a corporation. The country can't fund its operations from its current revenues, so it has been running a deficit and it needs to borrow money (issue debt) to pay its bills. It has been doing this for a long time, so there is a large accumulation of debt that needs to be paid off. And since it is unlikely that it will be able to fund its operations any time soon out of available revenue, in this case taxes, it will need to continue to issue more and more debt. If the U.S. government were a corporation, you would not want to invest in it.

Fortunately, real U.S. companies are actually in much better shape than the government. Unlike consumers, corporate America entered the recession with relatively manageable debt levels. Even after the recession, U.S. corporations look healthy and have been paying off debt. As a result, while the government appears to be a bad credit risk, corporate America does not. Individual investors should look to corporate bonds as a good substitute for government debt.

In addition to generally having good credit quality, corporate bonds usually pay more interest than Treasuries. In fact, well-known, established companies typically pay a higher interest rate than the government. In the past, long-term corporate bonds from companies with the highest credit rating, AAA, have paid approximately 1 percentage point over the prevailing Treasury rate. For slightly smaller, less established but still creditworthy companies, those with a Baa rating, the spread over Treasuries has been nearly 2 percentage points. Currently, the increase in income on corporate bonds is particularly attractive. Despite the fact that large companies' finances are improving while the government's are falling, corporate bonds offer an even wider interest rate spread today than the long-term average. Part of the reason is that investors are still sufficiently scared of another financial meltdown and prefer the safety of Treasury bonds and notes. While this may have made sense in the past, it makes much less sense at a time when large corporations are in better financial health than the government.

While investors want to modestly lower their overall bond allocation, for the percentage of their portfolio that remains allocated to taxable bonds, they should favor corporate over government bonds. Because of the rich yield of good-quality corporate bonds, the corporations' relative financial strength, and the government's ever-growing debt problems, investors should prefer corporate bonds, particularly investment grade, to Treasuries.

BUYING CORPORATE BONDS

While corporate bonds look to be a good bet in general, investors face the same dilemma as with municipal bonds. What bond to buy? Most individuals don't have the resources to evaluate the creditworthiness of individual companies, so investors should gain their exposure to the corporate market through a broader portfolio, either using a mutual fund or an ETF. That way, even if a few of the bonds default, they will lose only a small portion of their investment.

When buying corporate bonds through a mutual fund or an ETF, you'll need to make two broad decisions: how long and how much risk. *How long* refers to whether you want to invest in short-term, intermediate-term, or long-term bond funds. Given that all bonds, including corporate bonds, will be negatively impacted by rising interest rates, you should select intermediate-term funds over long-term funds. While intermediate-term funds will pay a bit less interest than longer-term funds, you will be less exposed to rising interest rates.

The second decision is *how much credit risk* you'll want to take. Most bond funds are divided into two categories: investment grade and high yield. *Investment-grade bonds* are issued by established companies whose bonds are considered less risky. *High-yield bonds*, as their name implies, provide a much higher interest rate but also much higher risk. Companies that issue high-yield bonds tend to default more. As a result, funds that invest in high-yield bonds will be much more volatile than those that invest primarily in investment-grade issues. Also, high-yield bonds behave a bit more like stocks, with their price declining more when the economy is weak as investors worry that a weak economy will lead to more corporate defaults. Your choice of investment-grade versus high-risk bonds is primarily one of risk tolerance. If you can take a bit more risk and volatility, high-yield bonds will provide more income, but at the risk of a few sleepless nights.

Both types of bonds are available through mutual fund providers like Vanguard or Fidelity. You can purchase the fund directly from the firms or through your brokerage account. When researching a fund, pay attention to the expense ratio the fund charges. The higher the fees, the more they will eat into your returns. As a rule of thumb, high-yield funds will generally charge more than investment-grade funds.

Investors can also access the corporate bond market through ETFs. BlackRock runs a number of different corporate bond products, based on both maturity and credit risk. For investors looking for investment-grade bonds, there is the LQD. This fund has a relatively cheap annual expense ratio of 0.15 percent with nearly 99 percent of its funds invested in investment-grade corporate bonds. The fund obtains diversification partly by investing in a variety of industries. The average maturity of the bonds in the fund is 12 years. For those looking to move a bit further out on the risk curve, there is the HYG, which invests primarily in high-yield bonds. The expense ratio on this fund is higher, at 0.50 percent a year. The bonds in this fund tend to be a bit shorter in duration, with an average maturity of approximately 5 years. Other companies offer similar funds. State Street also offers a high-yield bond fund, the SPDR Barclays Capital High Yield Bond ETF (JNK). This fund is also highly liquid and charges a 0.40 percent expense ratio.

INTERNATIONAL BOND MARKETS: REASONS TO INVEST

In addition to lowering your bond exposure, the other key principle of this plan is to look for places to loan money other than the U.S. government. States are a good option, primarily due to the tax advantages. Corporations make sense because their balance sheets look better than the government's and they pay more interest. A third alternative is to look for the securities of governments outside of the United States. Just as the United States has a bond market in its debt, other countries have similar markets. In the United Kingdom government bonds are offered on the Gilt market. Japan's bonds are known as Japanese Government Bonds (JGBs).

Before going through the reasons to consider international bond markets, it is worth addressing one potential objection. While the United

States clearly has its share of fiscal problems, aren't other countries in even worse shape? Why avoid U.S. debt only to invest in Europe, which based on the events of 2010, seems to be an even bigger risk for a fiscal catastrophe?

While there are other countries with severe fiscal problems, notably Japan, that should be avoided, by a number of measures the United States looks worse than most other developed countries. In 2009 and 2010, U.S. deficits as a percentage of GDP were among the highest in the developed world. And on another metric, the United States looks even worse than the Mediterranean countries investors were fleeing during the summer of 2010.

The problem with using deficits to GDP as a measure of debt is that the GDP represents a country's entire production. While a government can theoretically tax anything and everything to pay its obligations, in practice there are limits to what governments can extract from their citizens. Those limits vary from country to country. In Europe, governments are generally able to tax citizens at a higher rate. As a result, government revenues have historically been larger relative to the GDP in Europe than in the United States. For example, in 2009 German government revenues were 44 percent of its GDP, while in the United States they were less than 15 percent. U.S. citizens simply don't like paying taxes, and unless you believe that is going to change, then the U.S. government's revenue will be limited.[10]

When you compare the U.S. national debt (what we owe) to the U.S. government revenues, which will ultimately be used to repay those obligations, the United States looks far worse than just about any other developed country. Government debt is 165 percent of the revenue in Germany. It is 248 percent of the revenue in Ireland, one of the countries investors view as a significant risk. In Greece, the epicenter of the debt crisis, the debt is more than 300 percent of the revenue. In the United States, it is over 350 percent, more than double the ratio in Germany and even worse than Greece.[11] This does not mean that investors should be piling into Greek or Irish debt. These countries do indeed have real fiscal problems that may eventually lead to a default. But it is also worth remembering that the United States is not necessarily the best sovereign borrower. Compared to the United States, countries like Germany look to be a reasonable credit risk.

Beyond better finances, there are other reasons to consider international debt markets. Bonds are influenced by cyclical factors such as the economic cycle as well as longer-term factors such as fiscal deficits. In some instances countries' interest rates and inflation may be falling, which is when you want to buy bonds (remember the United States in the early 1980s, a great time to be a bond buyer). As bond prices fall when inflation and/or interest rates are rising, investing outside of the United States will help prevent a situation in which all of your bonds are falling at the same time due to rising rates. For this reason, a portfolio composed of both international and domestic bonds should have less volatility than a purely domestic portfolio.[12]

Finally, an international bond denominated in a foreign currency helps you to diversify your currency holdings. As we will discuss more in the next few chapters, one way to hedge against the negative implications of deficit spending is to own more assets that are denominated in a currency other than the U.S. dollar. That way, if the dollar depreciates because of inflation, you will be partially hedged as your non-dollar-denominated assets will appreciate. By holding foreign bonds, if the dollar declines, you will profit not only from the interest payments on the bond but also from the appreciation in the foreign currency.

THE ATTRACTION OF THE EMERGING MARKETS

The United States is not the only country in the world that has promised its citizens more benefits than it can pay for. What is surprising is that many countries that previously were described euphemistically as "emerging markets" are actually in a much better position. Given the fiscal prolificacy of many industrialized countries, investors will want to go a step further and increase their allocation to emerging markets, most of which are not facing the same fiscal challenges.

One of the great ironies of the financial crisis, and one that probably foreshadows the shifting balance of global power, is that many of the less developed countries, the ones known as the *emerging markets*, actually came out of the financial crisis in a much better fiscal position than many of the developed ones. In 2010 both the United States and the United Kingdom had budget deficits close to or exceeding 10 percent of their gross domestic product. In contrast, three of the largest emerging markets—China, Brazil, and India—all had deficits of 5 percent or less.

After having come through the crisis relatively unscathed and with their fiscal balance sheets cleaner than many older, wealthier countries, emerging markets enjoy two other advantages that suggest favoring their bonds: better demographics and the prospects for a *secular* downturn in inflation. The central banks of emerging markets are starting to be afforded the inflation fighting credentials that central banks of the developed markets won back in the 1980s. This will help their bond markets going forward (note: an exception to this rule is India, which is still grappling with high inflation).

It has now been well documented that much of the so-called developed world, that is, the United States, Japan, and Europe, is aging while many emerging markets still have relatively young populations. The statistics back this up. Japan is in the worst position. Nearly 25 percent of its population is over the age of 65, while less than 13 percent is under 15. In Europe, the proportions of the population over 65 and those under 15 are roughly equal. In the developed world, the United States actually looks somewhat spry, thanks to a higher birthrate and a more liberal immigration policy. In the United States the proportion of the population over 65 is 13 percent, while nearly 20 percent is under 15. While that looks promising compared to a rapidly aging Europe and an even grayer Japan, we can't match the youth explosion in the emerging markets. In India, Brazil, and Indonesia, the proportion of 15- to 65-year-olds is approximately four to one! While China will actually age quicker than other emerging markets, thanks to decades of a one-child policy, its ratio of under-15-year-olds to over-65-year-olds still looks better than most developed countries at more than two to one.

The demographics of the population matter because they ultimately drive the number of working-age citizens. A population with more young people and fewer retirees is a huge benefit for governments; it means more people paying taxes, and fewer receiving retirement benefits. As discussed in Chapter 1, one of the biggest drivers of the current U.S. fiscal mess is demographics. We have a pension and medical system in place that is groaning under the weight of too few workers supporting too many retirees, and it only gets worse as more of the baby boomers retire. If you're thinking about the long-term risks a government faces, and by extension where to invest, demographics are destiny, and it is better to favor bonds of governments with better demographics (or at least more rational policies).

This demographic advantage is already evident in today's numbers, with recent history confirming what is likely to be a long-term trend. Emerging market countries are now providing credit on a regular basis to older, more developed countries. Beginning late last decade, for the first time almost every major emerging market country is a *net creditor* (provider of capital) to the global economy.[13] Remember, it is now the Chinese whose savings the U.S. government has come to rely on to fund its deficit.

The second argument for investing in emerging market bonds is that, as a group, they are winning the same fight against inflation that the United States won 30 years ago, but just as with the United States back in the early 1980s, there is still a lot of residual skepticism on the part of bond investors. Take Brazil. Brazil was one of the few countries in which real interest rates remained significantly positive throughout the crisis.

After decades of double-digit inflation and more recently a strenuous effort to contain inflation, the Brazilian Central Bank left real interest rates high throughout the crisis. Investors in Brazilian bonds are now benefiting from the same paranoia, albeit a healthy paranoia, that infected the bond market in the early 1980s. While many emerging markets were witnessing a cyclical increase in inflation—one brought about by too strong an economy—in late 2010, their collective response suggests that these countries are taking any inflation threat seriously. Remember, the best time to buy an asset is when it is cheap, and other investors are unconvinced.

Finally, because emerging markets are all different and they undergo different economic cycles, their bonds will help to diversify your portfolio. In the past, emerging market debt has enjoyed a low correlation with most other fixed-income asset classes. This means that their bond markets tended to do different things and at different times than other types of assets. The correlation between traditional emerging market debt and U.S. Treasuries is approximately 0.15.[14] Recall that the advantage of including uncorrelated assets in your portfolio is that it lowers the overall risk—that is, some assets will appreciate while others are depreciating. Your goal is to find different asset classes and individual assets that do not do the same thing at the same time; emerging market bonds meet this criterion.

BUYING INTERNATIONAL BONDS

While it is cheap and easy for a U.S. investor to buy Treasuries, it is likely to be considerably more expensive to purchase foreign bonds. You will need to find a broker who can transact in these markets. And the broker will almost certainly charge you a higher fee than would be the case if you were purchasing a Treasury security. In addition, you may need to convert the interest payments from the home currency into dollars. Depending on the conversion rate that the broker is willing to offer, this may wind up being an expensive proposition—so expensive, in fact, that it can eat up most of the gains from the foreign bonds. In addition, varying trading rules and tax treatments also suggest that the best way to get exposure to this asset class is again through a mutual fund or exchange-traded fund. While this will be slightly more expensive than investing in a domestic bond fund, it is still likely to be far cheaper than doing it yourself.

While investing in international bonds has become easier, there are still a number of unique issues to face even if you are investing through a mutual fund or an ETF. One of the first questions to ask is, does the fund hedge its currency exposure? *Hedging* refers to the practice of selling futures or other derivative contracts on foreign currencies as part of the investment process. The reason a manager would do this is to eliminate the foreign currency risk of the bond. In doing so, with varying degrees of success the manager would be eliminating the foreign currency component of the return.

The foreign currency, or *f/x*, component will add to the volatility of your returns. In addition to your fund moving up or down based on the prices of the bonds in the fund, returns will also be driven by the price of the currency that the bond is denominated in. Take a simple example. Imagine a fund that owned only one bond, denominated in euros. If the bond appreciates 1 percent but the euro falls by 2 percent against the dollar, your overall return is −1 percent. Of course, the euro can also appreciate against the dollar, in which case the currency would add rather than detract from your returns. But either way, the return on your bond funds will be more volatile than it would be in a similar domestic fund.

Despite the additional volatility, I would recommend focusing on unhedged funds. As discussed above, lowering your exposure to dollar-denominated assets is one of the advantages of investing internationally. To the extent that a fund hedges its foreign currency exposure, you lose that benefit. As most of the vast majority of your assets and income are already denominated in dollars, look for opportunities to use other parts of your portfolio to diversify into different currencies. If you can live with the volatility, look for unhedged bond portfolios and ETFs.

For example, you can purchase an international bond ETF, which focuses on international government debt. Funds in this category will charge a management fee of approximately 0.30 to 0.40 percent, compared to a fee of approximately 0.15 to 0.20 percent for a fund focused on U.S. Treasuries. Given the transaction costs you're likely to face if you try to buy these bonds on your own, a fund or an ETF will still be cheaper. If you are willing to dip your toes into emerging markets, there are also funds that allow you to invest directly in emerging market bonds. As a general rule, and this will apply to stocks as well, you will always pay a higher fee for emerging markets.

TREASURY INFLATION-PROTECTED SECURITIES (TIPS)

For most bonds, but particularly Treasury bonds, inflation is deadly. For a 1 percentage point increase in the rate of inflation over a one-year period, the nominal return on a long-term government bond declines by 1.3 percentage points. In addition, long-term Treasury bonds are the worst-performing asset class in the immediate aftermath of an *inflation shock*—that is, an unexpected spike in inflation.[15]

When there is inflation, the companies that issue stock can raise prices and make more money. Funds that hold commodities will see the value of those physical assets rise with inflation. But for bonds, there is no reprieve. As bond payments are normally fixed, they are worth less as inflation erodes the value of that fixed sum of dollars. Bonds are further hurt because principal also loses its value.

In a world where rising inflation is a significant long-term risk, investors should always be thinking about purchasing power. What investments are best situated to protect the value of my money? When it comes to bonds, the best way to hedge inflation risk is with *inflation-linked bonds* (ILBs). In the United States, these government bonds are known by the acronym TIPS, which stands for Treasury Inflation-Protected Securities. While you generally want to reduce, if not eliminate, your exposure to U.S. debt, this is the one exception. As inflation is a long-term threat, investors should be thinking about purchasing power in every segment of their portfolio. As such, investors should be allocating a small portion of their bond portfolio to TIPS.

Unlike a typical bond in which $100 is invested (principal) and is then returned at the maturity of the bond, ILB principal adjusts in accordance with some measure of inflation. An ILB protects an investor from the risk of higher-than-expected inflation. Like a nominal bond, an ILB pays an investor a semiannual coupon on a principal investment. Unlike a nominal bond, however, the principal on an ILB grows over time by the amount of the rise of inflation. Inflation in this context is typically measured by the domestic consumer price index (CPI), and the level of the index provides the mechanism for adjusting an ILB's principal for inflation. When an ILB is issued, it is assigned a base CPI value, which is simply equal to the level of the CPI on the date of issuance. If, for example, the CPI is 100 on the day a particular bond is issued, and it stands at 103 one year later, the inflation-adjusted principal of the bond is equal to the principal multiplied by 103/100.[16]

While these types of bonds have been around for a long time, the market for inflation-adjusted bonds has grown exponentially over the past decade. The first inflation-linked bonds (ILBs) were launched by the United Kingdom back in 1981. Today the United States, France, Germany, Italy, and Japan are all major ILB issuers. The size of the market has grown from under US$100 million in 1997 to over US$1.4 trillion in the fall of 2009.[17]

In the beginning of the chapter, I advocated a small position to ILBs. Given the significant risk of inflation, why not a larger position? While inflation-linked bonds can do a reasonably good job of providing an inflation hedge, there are some cautions. It is important to understand what TIPS can protect you from and what they can't. An ILB will protect the holder from an increase in inflation, assuming the bond is held to maturity. The TIPS will not insulate the holder from a rise in real interest rates. Also, the extent to which the TIPS insulate you from inflation will be determined by the inflation expectations that are embedded in the bond and the breakeven level, as well as the holding period. The *breakeven level* refers to the amount of inflation that the TIPS bondholders are expecting. If the expectations are too high, and you don't hold the bond to maturity, you may still be better off with a plain vanilla bond.

To better understand this, recall the different components of the nominal bond yield. The yield is equal to a real, or after–inflation, yield and an expected level of inflation. This expected level of inflation is the difference in yield between an ILB and a normal bond. If TIPS and Treasuries of the same maturity, respectively, yield 2 and 5 percent, the difference between them, 3 percentage points, means that the expected level of inflation over the life of the bond is around 3 percent. This is also known as the *breakeven inflation*. It can be thought of as the amount of annualized inflation required for an investor to "break even" when purchasing an ILB instead of a nominal bond.[18]

As inflation is almost always positive, ILB yields will generally be below the yields of normal bonds. An exception to this occured in late 2008, when TIPS and Treasuries of the same maturity were trading at near-identical yields. This signaled that the market was so worried about deflation that investors were assuming that the inflation rate over the next decade would be effectively zero. In retrospect, this was a great time to buy TIPS as you would receive the same yield as a normal Treasury with the added benefit of having your principal reset upward as inflation actually rose.

Even if you expect inflation to rise, as an investor in TIPS, you need to compare the expected inflation rate embedded in the price of the TIPS with your own expectations. If the current breakeven rate for 10-year TIPS is 4 percent and you expect average inflation of 3 percent, you will be better off buying an ordinary Treasury. This illustrates an important point when considering TIPS: check the price. For TIPS, the price is the breakeven rate. If it is too high, then inflation will need to accelerate significantly for the TIPS to be worth the price. Even if inflation accelerates from current levels but never gets as high as what is assumed in the breakeven rate, you would be better off investing in a traditional Treasury.

One way to think about the breakeven rate is that it is similar to the price-to-earnings (P/E) ratio for a stock. A stock may be a great company, with better-than-average growth prospects, but if the stock is priced too aggressively, it may still be a bad investment. For this reason, TIPS represent the best bargain when their breakeven inflation rate is low.

In addition to the breakeven level, investors must also consider whether they plan to hold the TIPS to maturity. TIPS will perfectly hedge inflation as measured by the CPI, but only under certain circumstances. If TIPS are held to maturity, they will provide a guaranteed real yield equal to the TIPS yield, or interest rate, at purchase. This means that the investor will have earned a realized return equal to the TIPS yield plus CPI over the life of the bond.[19]

But, as discussed above, a bad time to purchase TIPS is when real yields are low and breakeven inflation is high. When TIPS are not held to maturity, their returns will depend upon their relative price, that is, the breakeven rate at purchase and sale. If you buy when TIPS breakevens are high and sell when they are low, you will not necessarily match or exceed inflation. The longer TIPS are held, the more likely their returns will hedge the inflation realized over the holding period. With TIPS, if you don't plan to hold until maturity, investors will do best if inflation rises above expectations after purchase and real rates fall. Conversely, TIPS perform worst on a relative basis when inflation falls below expectations after purchase and real rates rise.[20]

This nuance to TIPS is critical when considered in the context of the U.S. deficit. Recall from Chapter 2 that while real and nominal interest rates are almost certain to rise due to deficit spending, inflation may not.

In the event that bond yields rise not because of inflation fears but because of supply pressures, TIPS will get hurt along with plain vanilla government bonds. As a simple rule, if the government looks to be cutting the deficit through austerity and reforms to entitlement spending, an unlikely but possible scenario, inflation is less likely and TIPS become less necessary. In the absence of any meaningful effort to rein in the deficit, inflation becomes more of a risk, and investors should consider TIPS as an alternative to traditional Treasury bonds and notes.

There is one other risk that needs to be applied to the TIPS warning label. First, as described above, the mechanism by which TIPS are adjusted for inflation is the consumer price index (CPI). The CPI is a monthly statistic that is meant to capture the overall price changes, at the consumer level, in the United States. The CPI is based on samplings from hundreds of different products and services, everything from the price of grade-A eggs to the cost of a haircut. While it is meant to be a broad measure of inflation, remember that it will not necessarily match your definition of inflation. If the stuff you buy and the services you use are very different from the national average, your personal inflation rate may be very different from the CPI.

The government's housing component is a good example of where the official CPI can deviate significantly from real-world inflation. Housing is a big part of the CPI. There are two separate housing-related components in the CPI. The simpler and smaller of the two is based on rent. The larger and more controversial one is the so-called owner's equivalent rent (OER). Here the government tries to get at the cost of housing by asking the following question: "If someone were to rent your home today, how much do you think it would rent for monthly, unfurnished and without utilities?" Based on changes to the answer, the Bureau of Labor Statistics calculates changes in housing costs, which in turn drive about one-third of the overall consumer price index.[21]

The obvious problem with this measure is that it has little to do with how most people think of their housing costs. If you live in a house that you own, the theoretical rent you could charge has no impact on your expenses. If rents rise, you are not any better or worse off, as long as you continue to live in your home. In early 2010, one of the key factors driving down headline inflation was the drop in OER. For those whose expenses were driven more by health-care spending, education, or gasoline—that is, most people—their experience of inflation was very different from the one the government recorded each month.

None of the above caveats imply that you should avoid TIPS. Rather, they need to be there for the right reasons and under the right conditions. If those are met, TIPS are arguably the one exception to the general rule of avoiding U.S. government debt. First, while TIPS are bonds, if they are held to maturity, they offer a reasonable hedge against rising inflation. The proportion of TIPS in your portfolio should be in proportion to your inflation concerns. If you believe that the Fed will maintain its role as the guarantor of price stability, then you do not need to be considering TIPS unless breakeven levels are very low. However, if you believe that the government plans to go on spending as it currently is, you should own some protection against inflation, even in your bond portfolio. For investors with no opinion on the outlook for inflation, over the next five years look to allocate a modest portion of your bond portfolio to TIPS whenever the breakeven level on the 10-year notes is below 2 percent; if it falls below 1 percent, buy more.

Buying TIPS

So far we've discussed TIPS in the abstract. To actually purchase TIPS, you have several options. You can buy them directly at government auctions through the Treasury Direct Web site, or you can purchase them on the secondary market. That is, you can buy bonds that have already been issued, through a broker. In either case, you will be purchasing a particular bond with a particular maturity date. As diversification is always a good thing and you would rather assemble a portfolio of TIPS with several maturity dates, you can also gain exposure to TIPS through traditional open-ended mutual funds or ETFs.

There are even funds that allow you to invest in ILBs outside of the United States. State Street Global Advisors (SSgA), the world's second-largest ETF provider, manages an ETF based on ILBs from other countries. The SPDR DB International Government Inflation-Protected Bond ETF is an exchange-traded fund that invests in ILBs outside of the United States, including those in the United Kingdom, France, Canada, and Germany. Most of the bonds in the portfolio are longer term, and the fund has an average duration of approximately nine years. The annual management fee is 0.50 percent.

THE BALANCED BOND PORTFOLIO

When thinking about your bond portfolio, remember why you own bonds in the first place. Bonds produce income, but they also provide safety and stability. Most people would not sleep well if all of their wealth were invested in stocks. Bonds are much less volatile, and assuming they are held to maturity, they provide a much better chance of your getting your money back. Today, you need to pay special attention to the latter point. Remember that getting your money back does not only mean return of principal but, more importantly, return of purchasing power.

Because of that, the U.S. fiscal deficit represents two threats to the bond portion of your portfolio. All else being equal, a larger supply of Treasuries will push real yields up and prices down, and the longer the duration of your bonds, the bigger will be the hit to their price. The second threat is less certain but potentially more deadly. High government deficit spending often leads to inflation. Inflation will push interest rates up further, and it will also erode the purchasing power of your principal.

To address these twin risks, start by lowering your allocation to bonds. If you need income, look at preferred and dividend-paying stocks as bond substitutes. If nothing else, the stocks will provide a better inflation hedge. If you are a younger investor, keep your bond allocation to a fifth or less of your financial assets. For the bonds that remain in your portfolio, keep the maturities short. You can accomplish this by owning shorter duration bonds, say, five years or less, or using a ladder approach. A ladder approach allows for some longer duration bonds in your portfolio, but you balance those out with shorter duration bonds with different maturity dates. This way you always have a portion of your bond portfolio maturing so you can take advantage of higher rates by reinvesting whatever is maturing at a higher yield.

The third key is to maximize your after-tax income with a high allocation to municipals. For the remaining, taxable portion of your bond portfolio, I would advocate roughly 40 percent to corporate bonds, 40 percent to international, and 20 percent to TIPS, assuming that breakeven levels are 2 percent or less or you plan to hold the bonds to maturity. As discussed in Chapter 2, inflation is not a certainty, but it is a significant risk. TIPS are not the perfect hedge against inflation, but assuming you hold them to maturity, they will at least match the official rate of inflation. To the extent that the market gives you an opportunity to buy TIPS at a breakeven inflation rate of 2 percent, take advantage of that. Even if the Fed keeps a lid on inflation, given recent government spending, inflation is likely to be more than 2 percent for the next decade. And if the Fed continues buying government securities directly, inflation may go much higher than 2 percent. Under that scenario, TIPS will help preserve real purchasing power. In other words, you will not only get your money back, but it might actually be worth something.

CHAPTER 6

STOCKS: HOW TO MAKE MONEY WHEN GROWTH IS SLOWER AND RATES ARE HIGHER

I T WAS HARD NOT TO make money in the stock market between 1982 and 2000, particularly toward the end of that period. From 1995 to 2000, U.S. stocks advanced by approximately 20 percent a year. The returns were so good for so long that investors eventually just started to assume that such gains were normal. Given this extraordinary run, it is not surprising that investors began to convince themselves that stocks, like housing this decade, were a one-way ticket to riches. "Buy and hold" was the mantra.

That was before the bubble burst in 2000. The last decade has been a lot less fun. Investors who bought into the market in the late 1990s have at best broken even and are probably still underwater in their portfolios. The decade from 2000 to 2010 represented the worst 10-year stretch for U.S. stocks since the Great Depression.

The problem for equity investors going forward is that despite two brutal bear markets, U.S. stocks never really got that cheap, at least when compared with other market bottoms. So while stocks are reasonably priced today, they are nowhere near the bargain basement prices that typically mark the start of a new, long-term bull market.

The situation is made less promising by the huge and continuing U.S. budget deficits. As I have already described, the three main economic risks of big deficits are slow growth, high real interest rates, and potentially higher inflation. All three are bad for stocks. Slow growth will be a drag on corporate earnings. Higher interest rates increase the cost of capital for corporations, depressing stock prices. Finally, inflation hurts most companies by raising their input costs, putting downward pressure on profits and stock prices.

Despite all these headwinds, there will be places to make money in stocks over the next decade. While a slower economy and higher interest rates do suggest that you should trim your allocation to equities, or at least U.S. stocks, don't sell everything just yet. For starters, even during a secular bear market (I'll come back to this), which is the kind we are likely to get, there will be periods, often prolonged ones, when stocks do rise. You'll want to buy stocks when valuations are cheap. Second, many countries, particularly in emerging markets, are not facing the same problems the United States is. The easiest and best way to improve your equity returns will be to increase your investments outside of the United States. Third, while higher rates and inflation are generally negative for stocks, some businesses will be more resilient than others, and a few stocks will even benefit from higher inflation. Finally, there are ways to make money even when the market is moving sideways. More aggressive investors, who are willing to take more risks, should consider alternative investment approaches that don't depend on a bull market for profits.

U.S. Stocks: 12 Lost Years

Before trying to understand where the stock market is going, it will be useful to review where it's been. In short, U.S. stocks have gone nowhere for a very long time. In the summer of 2010, the stocks of large U.S. companies—known as *large-capitalization companies*, or *large cap*s for short—were trading at roughly the same levels as the summer of 1998. In the past 12 years, stocks have managed to generate a lot of volatility, but few returns.

The fact that U.S. stocks have gone nowhere for more than a decade is evidence of what is called a *secular bear market*. Most investors are familiar with the more common variety of bear market, which is when the stock market goes down by 20 percent or more and then rebounds after a year or two. These are relatively common, and for most of the past 60 years, they have presented good buying opportunities.

A secular bear market is different. We have had three in the last century: 1906 to 1921, 1929 to 1952, and 1968 to 1982. Again, for those who have been under the impression that stocks generally rise, it is worth pointing out that cumulatively these secular bear markets accounted for approximately half of the past century. Secular bear markets tend to last a very long time. During these periods, equities will have some big rallies, and some bigger pullbacks, but basically the market goes nowhere for a decade or two.

There are no shortages of reasons why stocks have struggled over the last decade, including the collapse of the Internet bubble, the collapse of the housing market, and the near collapse of the banking system. But the main culprit for this secular bear market, as with the previous ones, was a grossly overvalued stock market. The U.S. stock market was severely overvalued in 2000, and we've been working off those excesses ever since.

STOCKS NEED *UNEXPECTED* GOOD NEWS

Markets don't always need good news to rise. Sometimes it's enough that the news is just less bad than investors were expecting. Conversely, even when everything is going well, the economy is humming, and corporations are making lots of money, stocks can drop if investors have already bid up stock prices too high. Secular bear markets happen when too much good news is discounted and is already reflected in prices. This was exactly what happened in 1929, 1968, and 2000.

When assessing what is already reflected in stock prices, start with the market's valuation. One of the simplest but still most useful ways to value stocks is to look at what they earn versus what they cost, known as the *price-to-earnings*, or *P/E*, *ratio*. If we look at the S&P 500 back at its peak in 2000, the index was trading for approximately 33 times the earnings of its component companies over the previous 12 months (Figure 6.1). This ratio was roughly double its long-term average. Put differently, the market was charging twice as much to buy a dollar of earnings as it typically did. For the most overhyped stocks on the Nasdaq exchange, it was not uncommon to see P/E ratios in the triple digits. The market has gone nowhere for 12 years because back in 2000 investors expected too much and have been disappointed ever since.

Just as secular bear markets begin when investors are too optimistic, they end when they're too pessimistic. Back in the early 1980s, investors had abandoned stocks after having been beaten down by nearly 15 years

Figure 6.1 **S&P 500 Cyclically Adjusted P/E Ratios for 1900 to 2010**

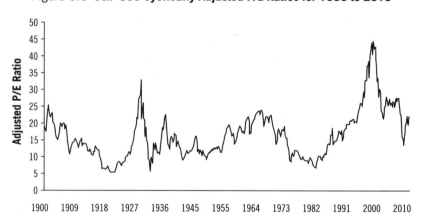

Source: Robert Shiller, Online Data, www.econ.yale.edu/~shiller/data.htm.

of losses. When everyone has decided stocks will never go up again, that is usually when they do begin to go up because the market has become very cheap. Typically, at the bottom of secular bear markets, stocks are so cheap that investors are paying just seven or eight times earnings, half of what they normally do.

Since the market's peak in 2000, market valuations have fluctuated dramatically. The market was cheapest at the bottom in 2009, but even then the price of U.S. companies was still much higher than what was reached in previous bear market bottoms, such as 1982. This is important for your equity strategy going forward. It suggests that U.S. equities may not have bottomed, or at the very least, they may experience several more years of sideways action.

The deficit is likely to make the situation worse. Stocks tend to rise when economic conditions are improving. A great year in which to buy stocks was 1982 because the economy was starting to recover, inflation had already peaked, and interest rates were falling. Today, we are likely to face the opposite set of conditions. Interest rates are already so low they are unlikely to drop further, and they will eventually start to rise. The same holds true for inflation. The stock market is likely to get some boost as the economy recovers, but even then the average rate of growth for the U.S. economy will be slower than it was in the 1980s and 1990s. All of which suggest that the U.S. stock market is unlikely to stage a prolonged bull market any time soon.

A Slower Economy Means Slower Earnings Growth

Higher deficits result in lower economic growth and higher interest rates. Both these developments suggest you should trim your holdings in U.S. companies. When thinking about the impact of the fiscal deficit on your stock portfolio, remember that stocks are primarily impacted by two factors: earnings and interest rates.

Let's start with earnings. Earnings are what you are ultimately paying for: the higher the earnings, the more a company can pay out to shareholders in the form of dividends and the more the company will increase its book value through retained earnings. While earnings growth is impacted by many factors, not surprisingly the rate of overall economic growth has an enormous impact on earnings.

When the economy is strong, most CEOs look like geniuses, and when it is weak, they can't seem to get anything right. This is not a coincidence nor is it a reflection on executive talent. When the economy is growing, it is much easier for companies to grow. When economic growth is slower, companies find themselves competing for a dwindling number of dollars. Even those that win that competition find that it is harder to raise prices, and profit margins tend to be weaker. In addition, most companies have fixed costs that can't be pared back, even during a recession or slowdown. As a result, companies in many industries have what is known as *operating leverage*, meaning that a small increase or decrease in revenue can have a huge impact on their profits. For all these reasons, economic growth is critical for corporate earnings.

We are already at a point where the deficit and national debt are going to be long-term drags on economic growth. Higher government debt will lower real economic growth even further. Recent studies suggest that for each 10-point increase in the ratio of government debt to GDP, economic growth eventually falls by approximately 0.2 percent. This implies that the expected increase in the ratio of U.S. federal government debt to GDP, from 62 percent in 2007 to 98 percent in 2011, could shave three-fourths of a percentage point off GDP growth.[1] There is also reason to believe that very high debt levels will be particularly toxic for growth. In other countries where debt levels exceeded 90 percent of debt to GDP—a level we are likely to hit over the next decade—growth rates fell by more than 1 percent on average.[2]

Slower growth will be a big headwind for corporate America. Some companies that rely on sales outside of the United States may be able to mitigate this effect to the extent that they can sell their wares abroad. But few companies sell most of their goods or services overseas. Most still rely on U.S. customers, which means overall corporate earnings grow more slowly.

How much slower will earnings grow? In the past, corporate earnings have generally grown at about four times the rate at which the U.S. economy has grown. Figure 6.2 compares economic growth, represented on the horizontal axis, with earnings growth, represented on the vertical axis. It is easy to see that when the economy accelerates, earnings grow faster, and when it slows, so do earnings.

Figure 6.2 **Economic Growth versus Corporate Profits**

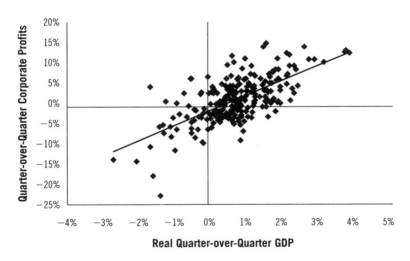

Source: Bloomberg, July 2010.

The fact that earnings grow quicker than the economy reflects the fact that most companies have operating leverage, which means that small increases in revenue drive larger changes in earnings. This means that if the U.S. economy grows at an average rate of 1 percent slower over the next decade than it otherwise might have, corporate earnings growth will be approximately 4 percent slower.

While earnings growth that is 3 to 4 percent slower may not sound like much, it will make an enormous difference over time. If a company is currently earning $1 a share and it can grow earnings at 10 percent a year in a healthy economy, the company will be earning roughly $2 a share in seven years. In the case where the company is growing its earnings at 7 percent a year, rather than 10 percent, its earnings in seven years will be $1.60 per share. Assuming that the market values those earnings with a P/E multiple of 15, under the first scenario the company would be worth approximately $30 a share, while under the second scenario the value would drop to $24, a difference of 20 percent.

Interest Rates, Inflation, and Market Multiples

Rising interest rates will further lower equity returns. Higher rates raise the cost of capital, which cuts into earnings. And higher rates also slow economic growth. Historically, each 0.10 percentage point increase in long-term yields typically leads to an average 0.30 percentage point decline in the S&P 500. Even when market conditions are favorable and corporate profits are rising, the direction of interest rates usually makes a difference (see Table 6.1). In years when profits were up but interest rates higher, equity returns were nearly 40 percent below those years when profits were up but rates were down.

Table 6.1 Corporate Profits, Rates, and Equity Returns, S&P 500 Average Annual Gains, 1962 to Present		
	Long-Term Rates Up	Long-Term Rates Down
Corporate Profits Up	8.08%	13.14%
Corporate Profits Down	−1.58%	3.15%

Source: Bloomberg, as of July 2009.

Not surprisingly, the same negative relationship between interest rates and stock returns holds for inflation and stocks, at least over the short to intermediate terms. While stocks do a decent job of keeping up with inflation, historically this has worked only over very long periods of five years or more.[3] Stocks also perform very poorly when inflation rises unexpectedly. This is known as an *inflation shock*. Equity returns decline in the months following an inflation shock and do not experience a meaningful recovery for a long time thereafter.[4] This is important today because investors are generally not expecting much inflation over the next decade. Recall that today's real interest rates assume that inflation is likely to stay low for much of the next 10 years. If at any point prior to then inflation starts to rise quickly, equities will get hurt.

How much inflation will it take to hurt stocks? Table 6.2 looks at average P/E ratios on a monthly basis based on different inflation regimes. As a general rule, investors place the highest multiple or valuation on stocks when inflation is low, but not too low. As inflation rises, the market has generally been less willing to pay up for earnings, and market multiples have been lower. Interestingly, when inflation is too low, less than 1 percent, P/E ratios also tend to drop as investors begin to worry about deflation, which can hurt company earnings.

The difference in valuations based on inflation can be significant. When inflation is low, defined as between 1 and 3 percent, investors generally will pay a little less than 20 times earnings for U.S. stocks. However, if inflation rises to 5 percent, the average multiple drops to about 13 times earnings. So if you bought a company that was earning $1 a share in an environment of low inflation, you would expect that company to trade for around $19. Buy that same company when inflation is around 5 percent, and the market is more likely to value it at $13, a 30 percent discount. While this is a very simple example and it leaves out a lot of other important factors, like how quickly the company is growing, it illustrates an important point. Inflation will create a headwind for stocks when it begins to rise.

Table 6.2 **U.S. Equity Market Valuations and Inflation, S&P 500 Multiples and Inflation Levels**	
	Avg. P/E Ratio
Year-over-year CPI Less than 1%	15.62
Year-over-year CPI 1–3%	19.24
Year-over-year CPI 3–5%	16.95
Year-over-year CPI 5–7%	13.18
Year-over-year CPI 7–9%	10.34
Year-over-year CPI above 9%	8.77

Source: Bloomberg

When inflation does start to rise, it does not take much to hurt stock prices. As illustrated in Table 6.2, even a small acceleration in inflation has typically hurt market multiples. Should the CPI go from the 2 to 3 percent range up to the 3 percent to 4 percent range, history suggests that market multiples would fall by around 10 percent. While the stock market probably would not fall by that much given the fact that earnings are likely to be higher, it illustrates an important point. When inflation is rising, companies need to grow their earnings faster just to compensate for the negative impact of inflation on valuations. As a result, markets rarely do as well when inflation is rising as when it is falling. If inflation starts to press up against the 3 percent level, lower your allocation to U.S. stocks.

BE TACTICAL

When deciding where to put their money, investors need to start by thinking about how much return they expect a particular asset or investment to generate. All else being equal, the higher the expected return, the more of your money you should put into it. The expected return on an asset is a function of many factors, including the economic environment, inflation, interest rates, and investors' preference for risky assets. Expected returns are also highly dependent on value. Put simply, if you buy an asset cheaply, it is more likely to go up than when you are paying a premium.

Despite recent declines, stocks are still not particularly cheap by most valuation standards. Going forward, add to that the U.S. debt's triple threat of slower earnings growth, higher rates, and potentially higher inflation, and you get a poor environment for U.S. stocks. Stock returns are likely to be lower and more volatile than in the past. Accordingly, as you think about your allocation to equities, it should, on average, be modestly lower.

As I mentioned in the previous chapter, the rule of thumb has generally been for younger investors to keep approximately 60 percent of their financial assets in stocks. The rationale for such a high level is that stocks typically do much better than cash or bonds over the long run. This is particularly true once you adjust for inflation. Even though most stocks are hurt by inflation, they do a much better job of keeping pace with inflation than do bonds.

In an environment where growth is slow and rates and inflation are rising, younger investors should probably be looking to modestly lower their allocation to equities to perhaps 45 to 55 percent of their portfolio. In the event that we have higher inflation but also higher growth, equities are likely to do somewhat better, and you should raise your allocation toward the upper end of the range. As will be discussed in the next chapter, some of the money you take out of stocks and bonds should be invested in physical assets, such as commodities.

Now even with the deficit, there are circumstances in which investors may want to have higher allocations to stocks. If equities take another turn down and P/E ratios get back toward the high single digits, this would be a good opportunity to increase your holdings of stocks back closer to the 60 percent range. The reason is, while there is a lot of potential bad news to come, much of it related to the deficit, if the news is already reflected in stock prices—evidenced by low valuations—you can still make money. Even during secular bear markets, stocks can and do rally for prolonged periods of time. This typically happens after stocks have gotten too cheap. The flip side of this is to further lower your allocation to stocks when they are more expensive. This means further reducing your allocation to stocks when P/E ratios are above 20. If stocks do become that expensive, lower your allocation even further, to around one-third of your portfolio.

A one-third allocation to stocks is still a lot of money. If the environment for equities is likely to be so bad, why have anything in stocks? The key will be what you do with your equity allocation. Some stocks will do better than others, either because the companies are based in different countries or because their business model will work even under adverse conditions. The next few sections will focus on what markets and stocks to invest in over the next decade.

INTERNATIONAL INVESTING

Most individuals and even many institutional investors suffer from what is known as a *home country bias.* In effect, they invest too much of their money in their own country. The United States currently accounts for roughly 25 percent of the world's GDP and a slightly higher percentage of the world's stock market value. Yet most Americans have the majority of their investments in U.S. assets. While there is a certain comfort in owning what you know, like it or not, the United States makes up a shrinking portion of the world's economic activity. You want your portfolio to reflect the growing importance of other countries and regions as this is where future economic growth is likely to be fastest.

There is another benefit to diversifying out of the United States. Just as was the case with bonds, foreign stock markets will be impacted by different factors than are domestic markets. Some foreign countries' economies may be going up while ours is going down. Owning different markets provides diversification, and diversification lowers the overall risk of your portfolio without lowering your return.

So far we've confined the discussion of equity investing to the U.S. markets. Arguably, the best defense you have in your equity portfolio is to dramatically increase your exposure to stocks outside of the United States. The triple threat of slower growth, higher interest rates, and potentially higher inflation is not confined to the United States. Large parts of Europe, including the United Kingdom, and Japan face similar dilemmas. Some of these governments, most notably the United Kingdom, seem to be addressing their structural deficits, mostly through spending cuts. Others are simply postponing the day of reckoning.

But there are still plenty of places in the world to invest, even within Europe—Germany looks structurally sound. And once you leave Europe, you'll find that much of the rest of the world came through the recent financial crisis in much better shape. Among developed, industrialized countries, Australia, Canada, and many of the smaller Asian markets like Singapore and Hong Kong look set for better growth and certainly lower deficits. And as discussed in the previous chapter, most emerging market countries are now in a significantly better fiscal position than their more developed peers. Further, in addition to better fiscal positions, emerging markets offer better long-term demographics and growth prospects. As a result, the best and easiest way to insulate your stock portfolio is to diversify outside of the United States.

So how much should you invest in foreign markets? I would argue that the majority of your stocks should be based in markets outside the United States. If the United States represents only about one-fourth to one-third of the global equity markets, why would you have most of your money invested in U.S. stocks? Unless you believe that despite everything discussed so far, the U.S. market is likely to benefit from some combination of faster economic growth, perpetually low interest rates, and stable inflation, you should be looking for better opportunities, and you will find them overseas.

One example of a country in a much better fiscal condition than our own is Australia. For a variety of reasons, including a more solid banking system and the good fortune to have significant natural resources, Australia came through the recent financial crisis in much better condition than most other developed countries. One way to measure this is to quantify how much debt the Australian government needs to sell to finance its deficit spending and roll over its existing debt. In Japan the amount of debt is equivalent to roughly 64 percent of its GDP (Japan has the highest debt-to-GDP ratio of any of the developed markets). In the United States it is 32 percent. By contrast, in Australia the number is barely 7 percent.[5]

Another advantage of investing in Australia is that the market is levered to natural resources, and as such is likely to hold up much better under rising inflation than the United States, Europe, or Japan—all of which have relatively small mining sectors. Countries that do best under rising inflation are those dominated by natural resource companies. When inflation rises, natural resource prices—such as for copper or oil—also tend to rise. As a result, you can make money by owning positions in countries that produce commodities, particularly energy. Australia and Canada are two examples of developed countries with a heavy exposure to natural resource companies.

Emerging Markets: Follow the Growth

In the previous chapter I talked about the potential advantages of investing in emerging market bonds. The arguments for doing so were higher potential growth, declining inflation, better demographics, and better fiscal positions. These same arguments hold even more for equities. Countries that are categorized as emerging markets are making up an ever larger share of the world's economy. They should also comprise a larger share of your portfolio.

In addition to the advantages described in Chapter 5, it is worth reiterating how much better many of these countries look from a fiscal perspective. In the past, many of these countries were better known for International Monetary Fund (IMF) bailouts, occasional defaults, and the odd political insurrection. Today it is a very different story. While the United States, the United Kingdom, Japan, and much of what is considered developed Europe are laboring under budget deficits of 5 to 10 percent or more, most emerging markets are close to balanced budgets, even in the wake of the financial crisis. In late 2010 deficits for emerging markets were estimated at 1 percent in Peru, 2 percent in China, 3.5 percent in India, and 1 percent in Indonesia. South Korea was actually running a surplus.

In addition to running lower deficits, they also have less debt. The differences can be huge. Japan currently has a debt-to-GDP ratio of approximately 200 percent. While the U.S. gross debt-to-GDP ratio is much lower, it is still daunting at around 90 percent, even before you add in the additional debt of states and municipalities. In contrast, South Korea, South Africa, Taiwan, and Chile—all emerging markets—all have debt-to-GDP levels below 50 percent.[6] Recall that high debt levels tend to hamper growth. Lower debt levels represent an additional advantage when compared to more developed countries. Less debt translates into faster economic growth, which in turn means higher earnings growth and a more robust stock market.

For those investors who want to benefit from the faster growth in emerging markets but are uneasy about investing outside of the United States, there is another way to take advantage of these trends: invest in U.S. companies that get the majority of their revenue from international sales through exports. As their sales are more dependent on foreign economic growth than domestic, these firms will benefit disproportionately from strong overseas growth. And if the dollar weakens due to deficit spending, it will further help exporters. A less expensive dollar makes U.S. products cheaper for foreign buyers, and therefore it typically helps the sales of U.S. exporters. As a rule of thumb, industrial companies that make machinery and technology firms generate a high percentage of their profit in overseas markets, so this is another segment of the market to favor in trying to increase your international exposure. For example, in 2009 Intel—the largest manufacturer of computer chips—generated roughly 80 percent of its sales outside the United States.[7]

In short, the world has changed. Today, U.S. stocks comprise less than one-third of the world's stock market value, and the United States accounts for only about one-fourth of the global GDP. Your portfolio should reflect these realities. This means that more than half of your stock market allocations should be invested in companies outside of the United States. I would advocate that your allocation reflect the above percentages and that you direct approximately two-thirds of your equity investments to countries other than the United States. And as an additional step, for the portion of your equity portfolio that remains in the United States, you'll want to favor companies and sectors that are focused on selling abroad rather than to U.S. consumers.

Outside of the United States, favor countries with better growth prospects and less debt. Practically, this means places like Canada, Australia, Germany, and some of the smaller developed countries in Asia (Hong Kong and Singapore). Also give more weight to emerging markets. These are the countries that will grow fastest over the long term. Within emerging markets, Brazil looks particularly attractive based on its growth prospects, abundant natural resources, and established property rights.

Buying Abroad

When it comes to investing abroad, you will face many of the same issues that you would face in buying bonds that were discussed in the previous chapter. First, do you want to invest directly in companies, or do you want to buy a broader basket of stocks through a mutual fund or exchange-traded fund? Second, if you invest in a fund, should it be an active one where the manager is attempting to beat an index or a passive one, which simply aims to replicate the index? Third, as was the case with bonds, if you go the fund route, do you want a fund that attempts to neutralize the currency exposure? Finally, should you invest in single country or in regional or global funds?

In terms of whether to buy individual companies or a mutual fund, consider a few things. First, do you have any specific reason for investing in a particular company? When investing outside of the United States, you're faced with a universe of literally thousands of different stocks. Why are you favoring one or two names in particular? In the absence of a very strong rationale, you'll want to favor a fund. The reason is that when you invest in an individual name, you're assuming a lot of risk on things that are idiosyncratic to a particular company. For example, let's say you believe that continued growth in emerging markets and improving living standards will increase the world's need for oil, and as a result energy companies will do particularly well over the next decade. What is the best way to implement this strategy?

You could go out and buy a couple of energy companies directly. The problem with that strategy is that in addition to gaining exposure to increasing oil prices, you'll also be exposed to all sorts of other risks you did not intend. (Think about owning BP in the summer of 2010.) The handful of stocks you bought will be influenced not only by oil prices but also by management issues, the success or failure of that company's drilling, and a host of other issues related to that particular company. If that is not what you intended to bet on, you would be better off owning a broad basket of energy stocks that will help to minimize the risks associated with any one company. In short, you want to take the bet you intended to take—in this case a bet on energy stocks—and to the extent possible, neutralize the other risks. In the absence of specific knowledge of a company, this favors investing in a fund, which will help you diversify away from the specific risks of any one stock.

Assuming you're going to invest in a fund, the second big decision you'll have is whether to invest with an active manager or an index fund. Here the trade-off is the same as described in Chapter 5. An active fund may produce higher returns if the manager has skill. But, at the very least, you will be charged a higher fee for the fund. Again, you should be aware that the manager can underperform an index as well as beat it. The choice really comes down to whether or not you have any reason to believe that a particular manager has enough skill to consistently beat the market by enough to justify the management fee.

When considering this, there is one thing you should keep in mind. Historically, the managers that did the best in the past are not necessarily the ones that will beat the market in the future. Favoring funds purely on the basis of past performance has been an ineffective strategy. Investors have lost a lot of money over the years buying funds at the wrong time.[8]

Managers often outperform not based on any inherent skill but simply because their style of investing happens to be working. For managers who looked for inexpensive companies, value investors, the period from 2000 to 2007 was a great time. But that same group was out of favor for much of the late 1990s as the market ignored cheap stocks and favored those with the fastest earnings growth. What works during one period rarely works in the next.

As is the case with bonds, when you invest in a foreign stock or fund that invests in foreign stocks, you'll be exposed to the fluctuations in currency as well as the stock prices. Most traditional funds and exchange-traded funds do not neutralize their currency exposure. The performance of the fund will be driven in part by the performance of the foreign currency against the dollar as well as the performance of the individual stocks. That is okay. The U.S. deficit represents a long-term threat to the dollar. In addition, the U.S. currency looks overvalued against the currencies of many of the emerging market countries, most notably China. Having exposure to other currencies through your international portfolio is likely to be a profitable trade over the next decade, particularly for Asian countries.

Finally, you'll need to address the issue of how broad or narrow a region in which to invest. If you're particularly bullish on one country, there are exchange-traded funds that can provide focused exposure to a single country. This may be useful to the extent that you want to focus on one country rather than a region. An example to consider is Germany.

While there are many reasons to avoid a significant position in Europe, not the least of which is that much of the continent is plagued by larger budget imbalances than the United States, Germany may be an exception. German stocks are reasonably valued, German exporters will benefit from the weaker euro, and Germany has already managed to address most of its fiscal problems.

Germany aside, as a basic rule, favor broad portfolios. As with buying individual names, buying a single country fund entails additional risk associated with that one country. If you have a particularly strong opinion that the country will produce high returns, it may be worth taking on that additional risk. But to the extent that you're looking to gain broad exposure to markets outside of the United States, a more geographically diversified fund is likely to prove a better bet.

SECTOR SELECTION AND INTEREST RATES

In addition to investing the majority of your stock portfolio outside of the United States, what other segments of the market should you focus on? As one of the big risks of higher deficits is higher interest rates, one key will be to emphasize stocks and sectors that are more resilient to rising rates. Practically this means overweighting stocks in the energy, health-care, and technology industries and owning less of financial, utility, and consumer discretionary companies. (*Consumer discretionary* companies sell nonessential goods and services to consumers. Restaurants and department stores are examples of companies in this sector.)

Historically, health-care, energy, and technology companies have been less sensitive to higher rates. Another way of putting that: companies in these sectors typically experience fewer multiple contractions—that is, lower valuations—than companies in other parts of the market. Why is that? One of the key reasons is that these companies typically carry a lower debt burden than the average U.S. firm, and they have much lower debt levels than those sectors that are most sensitive to rising rates, namely, financials, utilities, and consumer discretionary.

One of the key reasons that companies are hurt by rising rates is that higher interest rates increase a company's cost structure. As rates rise, a firm needs to pay more interest on bank loans and on new bond issues. Higher interest raises their costs and lowers their profits. Conversely, companies that are less reliant on debt tend to be less impacted by rising interest costs. Just to be clear, it is not as if these lower-debt companies benefit from rising rates. Many of the companies in this sector will still have some debt, although there are some technology firms that are virtually debt free. For the debt they do have, their costs will go up as well. In addition, rising interest rates are generally a drag on overall economic growth, so there is some negative impact. The key is that historically the negative impact has been less. So think of these companies as places to hide rather than as huge moneymaking opportunities.

In contrast, the three sectors most negatively impacted by rising rates do tend to have very high debt levels, particularly financials and utility companies. As a result, their interest costs go up faster than the average company's and their earnings drop more. There are, however, other reasons why a company's or sector's sensitivity to interest rates will vary. Utilities, for example, pay high dividends. In addition, utility companies are highly regulated in what they can charge customers. As a result, investors normally buy utility companies more for their high, regular, and predictable dividends than for their quick appreciation. In this sense—stable prices and high income—utility stocks resemble bonds. As with a bond, they get hurt when rates rise.

There is another reason why the deficit is likely to hurt utility stocks in particular. Higher deficits are likely to mean higher taxes, and not just on income. If the government resorts to raising the tax rate on dividends, utility stocks will be less attractive to investors, and their prices will be particularly hurt.

Back in 2003, the tax rate on dividends was reduced. The Jobs and Growth Tax Relief Reconciliation Act of 2003 (JGTRRA) reduced the maximum individual tax rate on dividend income. Prior to passage, dividends were taxed at rates identical to other types of ordinary income such as wages and interest. A taxpayer in the top bracket in 2003 would have faced a 38.6 percent tax rate on both wage and dividend income. The JGTRRA lowered the top individual rate on dividends from 38.6 percent to 15 percent.[9] This represented an enormous tax cut on dividends, and it made those stocks that paid high dividends more valuable to own.

Since the 2003 tax cut, utility stocks have been much more expensive relative to the market than they were prior to the tax cut. Traditionally, utility stocks have traded at a lower valuation than the overall market. This is because most utility companies are regulated. In other words, they can charge only what the local regulator allows them to charge, and as such they tend to grow slower than companies in less regulated industries.

From 1995 through the end of 2002, the utility sector traded at less than half of the market's valuation. However, after the 2003 tax cut, investors were willing to put a higher valuation on utility stocks, in part because the dividends were now worth much more after taxes. Now rather than having utility stocks trade at less than half the market's valuation, they traded at over 70 percent. While this is still a discount to the broader market's valuation, it is a much smaller discount. Utility stocks are still regulated; the only difference between today and 10 years ago is that their dividends are now worth more after taxes. If in 2013 (when the Bush tax cuts are currently expected to expire) the dividend tax rate goes back up, some of that increase in relative valuation will reverse, and these stocks will get hit particularly hard.

Consumer discretionary companies are another example of how the deficit can hurt companies in different ways. Consumers tend to be very rate sensitive. In the 1990s, one of the drivers of the consumption binge was falling interest rates. As rates fell, people refinanced their home mortgages, and in doing so, freed up excess cash. They then spent the cash, which is one reason why personal consumption was so strong in the late 1990s. When rates rise, fewer people can refinance their homes, removing an incremental source of demand. In addition, when rates rise, homeowners with adjustable-rate mortgages have to devote more of their income to mortgage payments, and therefore they have less left over to spend. Along with energy prices, interest rates are one of the key economic factors that quickly impact individual spending patterns. If rates rise, not only do the expenses of retailers go up but their revenue is also likely to drop. For these reasons, you'll want to avoid the stocks of specialty retailers, department stores, apparel manufacturers, and restaurants in a rising rate environment.

Finally, financial industry stocks get hit on multiple angles. Financials carry large fixed-income portfolios. Even the loan portfolio of a bank can be thought of as a collection of fixed-income obligations. When interest rates go up, the value of this portfolio drops, lowering the book value of financial companies. In addition, rising short-term rates increase a bank's financing cost. This is particularly damaging to a bank's profitability if short-term rates are rising faster than long-term rates, a situation in which the yield spread is narrowing. Under these conditions, banks have to pay more to depositors but can't recoup all of the additional costs when they lend money out to borrowers. So for banks, in addition to watching long-term rates, also pay attention to the spread between the short- and long-term rates. All else being equal, a narrowing yield spread—short-term rates are rising faster than long-term rates—is very negative for bank stocks.

INFLATION AND SECTOR PERFORMANCE

Over the short term, inflation is even a tougher headwind for stocks than rising interest rates. Stock valuations in general contract once inflation starts to edge above the 3 percent level, and few sectors are immune. An analysis of inflation and sector performance is very instructive. When you control for other factors, the only sector that exhibits a positive correlation with inflation—that is, it tends to have positive returns when inflation is higher—is energy. Both oil producers and oil service companies tend to exhibit positive performance with inflation. This is not a mystery. Normally, when inflation is rising, so are oil prices. In fact, oil prices are often one of the main components that are driving inflation higher. As a result, energy companies have historically done well even with higher inflation.

What sectors do you want to be most cautious of under rising inflation? Here the list is very similar to the losers under rising rates. Traditionally, financial companies, like banks and brokers, and consumer discretionary businesses, such as restaurants and department stores, have done the worst when inflation is rising. Again, this is not difficult to explain. Banks and brokers have large inventories of paper assets like loans and bonds that lose value when inflation is rising. Rising inflation also encourages the Federal Reserve to hike interest rates, which raises their cost of capital and in turn hurts their margins.

For retailers and restaurants, the problem with inflation is twofold. First, recall that wages rarely keep pace when inflation is accelerating. As a result, even if people's nominal wages are rising, their purchasing power is declining. When purchasing power drops, individuals normally cut back on discretionary purchases, and in particular, they cut back on new clothing (apparel) and eating out (restaurants). To some extent, you don't even need overall inflation. In the past, rising gasoline prices have been enough to cut into the revenue of retailers and restaurants as higher gasoline prices are one of the first things to hurt most consumers.

CHANGING YOUR SECTOR EXPOSURE

When it comes to adjusting the sector exposure of your portfolio, exchange-traded funds are likely to be your best tool. ETFs have traditionally offered more choices on investing by sector, and because they are almost all index funds, fees are low. While index mutual funds are sometimes a cheaper alternative to ETFs, there are fewer traditional mutual funds that offer exposure to specific sectors. In contrast, sector ETFs have been popular for over a decade, and as a result, there are a number of different managers offering cheap and liquid products. All of the large ETF providers have a number of popular products for all three sectors you may want to overweight: energy, health care, and technology. For example, State Street's sector products are known as SPDRs, and there is a particular sector SPDR for technology (XLK), energy (XLE), and health care (XLH).

You can choose to boost your energy and health-care holdings by buying these ETFs directly. Alternatively, if you are more adventurous, you can also profit by *shorting* those ETFs of sectors you expect to go lower. If you want to profit by a drop in the price of consumer discretionary companies, you can short the XLY, which is State Street's Consumer Discretionary ETF. When you *short a stock or ETF*, you borrow the stock or ETF from your broker and sell it, with the expectation that you will buy it back and return it to your broker when its price drops. The difference between its price when you sold, or borrowed, the stock and its price when you bought it back and repaid the loan represents the profit or loss.

When shorting, there are a couple of things to keep in mind. First, be careful. Shorting theoretically carries infinite risk. In other words, when you buy a stock, you can lose only 100 percent of your investment. When you short a stock, since the stock can continue to rise without any limits, you can lose much more. For that reason, when you short any stock or ETF, you should have a limit in mind on how much you're prepared to lose, and you should close out the position if you reach it.

The other consideration when you do a short sale is the cost of borrowing the stock or ETF you are shorting. The broker from whom you borrow the stock or ETF charges you a fee to borrow the security. The amount can vary, and it will reduce your returns. If a stock or ETF is particularly expensive to borrow, then the cost of borrowing might exceed the expected profit on the trade. Generally, the smaller the company or ETF, the more expensive it will be to borrow. Securities that trade more frequently will be cheaper. When deciding whether or not to short, keep in mind the trading costs.

For those who want to bet against certain industries but don't feel comfortable shorting, there is another mechanism for doing this: *inverse ETFs*. These are ETFs that are based on the opposite of an index or benchmark. When the index goes down, the ETF rises. However, these products come with a number of warning labels that should keep most individual investors on the sidelines. First, they tend to be smaller, less liquid, and more expensive than traditional ETFs. Second, they are really meant for short-term trading as opposed to long-term investing. Due to the way they are constructed, the funds don't track the inverse of an index over the long term, and they are really suitable only for short-term traders.[10] For example, if you buy an inverse ETF on the consumer discretionary sector and it declines by 20 percent over a year, you will not see a 20 percent return on your investment.

Betting on a price drop, whether done through shorting or an inverse ETF, is something most investors should leave alone. Unless you have significant experience managing your money, these techniques are more likely to cause trouble then be the source of additional profits. But even if you are not directly profiting from those parts of the market that are likely to be hit the worst by the U.S. deficit, knowing what to avoid can be equally valuable. Look at your portfolio, and see what types of companies you are exposed to. To the extent that you own, either through mutual funds or direct stocks, a significant percentage of U.S. banks, retailers, or utility companies, you'll want to lighten up on those holdings. Instead, favor positions in energy, technology, and health care for the longer term.

Making Money When the Market Goes Nowhere

With the exception of the preceding discussion on shorting, all of the investment ideas contained above assume that you're going to buy some type of stocks or funds, whether they are Brazilian index funds or energy ETFs. This is how the vast majority of individual investors invest.

However, many institutional investors and a few wealthy individuals have engaged in a different type of investing based on an investment vehicle that can invest more aggressively than your average mutual fund. These are known as *hedge funds*. Hedge funds are like mutual funds, although the legal structure is very different and they are actually partnerships. But what really differentiates hedge funds from traditional mutual funds is their increased flexibility. Hedge funds invest in a much broader array of instruments, including derivatives, than traditional mutual funds. In addition, they also short stocks and other instruments so their returns are not as dependent on the market rising.

While hedge funds offer more flexibility, they come with a long, long list of warnings. Hedge funds are not nearly as transparent as traditional mutual funds, which are legally required to report their holdings. How hedge funds operate and what they invest in will be very opaque. In the extreme, this can be a cover for outright fraud—think of Bernie Madoff. Even in less severe instances, it is often difficult to understand the investment strategy and approach of the manager.

Then there are the fees. Hedge funds are the most aggressive form of active management, meaning that the fees will be much higher than those for an index fund or even an actively managed fund. That means that the manager has to be particularly skilled in order to generate a large enough return to cover the expenses. Finding managers with this level of skill is difficult. This is particularly true given that most of the most successful hedge funds are actually closed to new investors.

Beyond fees, hedge funds come with much more onerous terms than mutual funds. You will need to satisfy certain minimum requirements as to your net worth and earnings. And once you find a successful hedge fund that will actually let you invest, you need to be aware that you may not be able to get your money back immediately, or when you necessarily want it. Investing in a hedge fund also often means locking up your money for a period of time. Unlike stocks or even mutual funds, which you can sell on a daily basis, hedge funds are generally organized as limited partnerships and have their own terms. One of those terms is referred to as a *lock–up,* which means that the fund is restricted as to when, how, and in what amount you can get your money back.

Perhaps most importantly, hedge fund investors need to make sure that the returns they are getting are derived from the manager's skill, rather than from simply hoping that the market rises. With all the obligations and limitations of investing in hedge funds, the expected trade-off is that these types of investment vehicles can make money, or at the very least avoid losing much, in good times and bad. Here the evidence is mixed. Using data from the Barclays Hedge Fund Database, hedge fund returns over the last few years were heavily influenced by how financial markets did. In 2008 when stocks and corporate bonds were experiencing a brutal bear market, hedge funds lost over 20 percent. In the following year, when markets rebounded, so did hedge funds, producing a 23 percent return on average.[11] This suggests that many hedge funds were just taking bets on the direction of the market. While this was a good thing in 2009, you do not need to pay managers a high fee for this. If you are convinced the markets are about to skyrocket, you can simply invest in an index fund at a fraction of the cost and get your money back whenever you want.

One class of hedge funds that did show some promise in avoiding the markets' gyrations consisted of the market neutral funds. *Market neutral funds* are hedge funds that try to profit by buying undervalued stocks and selling overvalued ones. In executing this strategy, they balance their long and short positions so that they are, at least in theory, completely hedged against the market. If good, cheap, high-quality companies are outperforming overpriced ones, these strategies should produce a modest return, 5 to 10 percent a year, regardless of the market's direction. During the financial crisis, these strategies had some success in dampening the market's volatility. Market neutral strategies in the Barclay Database were down nominally, about 1 percent, in 2008 when the market crashed.[12] While these strategies have struggled of late, market neutral funds are likely to do better in an environment where investors focus on value and investing in safe, reliable companies. In an investment environment characterized by more financial and economic headwinds, that probably is a sensible approach for those who have the wherewithal, risk tolerance, and experience for hedge fund investing.

Volatility: How to Invest in Turmoil

There are a number of different factors that drive the performance of a stock. One factor is the country in which the company is located. When the U.S. stock market is doing well, as it did in the late 1990s, almost all stocks do well. A rising tide lifts all boats, as they say. Another factor is the company's sector or industry. When investors fled banking stocks in 2008, it didn't matter much if a bank had a good or bad business model; investors simply sold all bank stocks. In that case, the bank's sector was the biggest factor influencing its stock's performance.

Country and sector are relatively straightforward, but there are more abstract stock characteristics that also impact performance. One of those is volatility. *Volatility* refers to how much the stock price varies in a given year. Some stocks, such as those for technology companies, tend to be more volatile than the overall market, while stocks for more stable businesses like those in health care tend to be less volatile. Small companies also tend to be more volatile than larger, established firms. When investors want to take on more risk, more volatile companies do better because they tend to appreciate faster when the market is rising.

In addition to measuring the volatility of an individual stock, you can also measure the volatility of the overall market. The typical amount by which the S&P 500 changes in a given year can be used as a proxy for the market's volatility. For example, over the last several decades, the average volatility of the S&P 500 has been around 20 percent a year. In practice, this means that if the market's average annual return is around 8 percent and if the market's typical volatility is around 20 percent, there is roughly a two-thirds chance that the market's return in a given year will be between −12 percent and 28 percent. The 20 percent volatility defines the band within which the market is likely to trade. In some periods the band is narrower, indicating a less volatile market, and at other times it is wider, indicating more volatility. The index that tracks the volatility of the overall U.S. stock market is known as the *VIX Index*. It is often referred to as the *fear index* because it tends to spike during times of market turmoil when investors are panicking.

Today, many institutional investors buy and sell volatility as they would a stock. When the market is very quiet, investors will buy volatility on the expectation that the market will become less stable in the future. When the market is going through extreme gyrations, the way it was in 2008 and 2009, investors can also sell volatility on the expectation that the market will calm down in the coming months.

Generally, several factors influence how much volatility the stock market exhibits. These include monetary conditions, short-term economic indicators, and credit conditions—that is, how easily companies can borrow money. If we think about how the deficit is likely to impact most of these factors, it suggests a stock market that is likely to be more volatile in the future than in the past.

For example, lower GDP growth has in the past lead to higher equity market volatility. Slower growth and the accompanying threat of a recession scare investors, and that nervousness manifests itself as higher volatility. This does not necessarily mean that the market will go down. Volatile markets can also rise. But it does mean that if the U.S. deficit leads to slower growth, it will also lead to more equity market volatility. You can take advantage of this by allocating a small, say, 4 or 5 percent, portion of your equity portfolio to buying volatility. Buying volatility is the financial equivalent of buying an insurance policy. It will be a waste of money when things are going well, but it will help protect your portfolio during a crisis.

There are several ways that investors can buy volatility. One is to buy options on stocks or the market. *Options* are instruments that give you the right to buy or sell a stock or an index at a fixed price for a certain period of time. There are also *futures contracts* that allow you to buy and sell volatility directly. Futures contracts are similar to options in that they are what are known as *derivatives*—that is, they are financial instruments that are based on another index or product. Basically, a futures contract obliges you to buy or sell something, in this case volatility, at a specified price on a specific date. The buyer of a futures contract expects the price to rise, while the seller expects the price to fall.

Today, there are futures contracts on the VIX Index allowing you to buy or sell volatility. It should be noted, however, that buying and selling any futures contract is much more complicated, and time-consuming, than buying and selling stocks or bonds. To trade volatility directly using futures, you'll need to open a futures account. Also, unlike stocks, which have no expiration date, futures expire and have to be *rolled over*. Most futures trade with *quarterly expirations*. This means that if you have a position when the futures contract is set to expire, you'll need to sell the old contract and buy a new one with an expiration date further out in the future. In short, futures are probably a reasonable solution only for very sophisticated investors who have the time and energy to devote to actively managing their accounts.

For those uncomfortable with options or futures but who are still interested in owning volatility as an insurance hedge, there are other instruments that allow you to buy volatility. There are products known as *exchange-traded notes*, or ETNs.

Where an ETF represents an ownership interest in the underlying assets, ETNs are generally senior, unsecured debt of the issuing company. The securities obligate the issuer, usually a large bank, to pay a return based on a designated index. Like exchange-traded funds, they trade daily on an exchange.[13]

There are a few products currently trading based on the VIX Index; two examples are the iPath S&P 500 VIX Short-Term Futures ETN (VXX) and the iPath S&P VIX Mid-Term Futures (VXZ). Both of these products are issued by Barclays Capital and are based on the VIX futures (the difference between the two has to do with which futures contracts are used). In effect, they give you the chance to buy and sell volatility without having to go to the trouble of opening a futures account. Each trades with a 0.89 percent management fee.

The VIX Index changes every day, and it is tracked in most financial newspapers. For those willing to take on additional risk, using a futures or ETN to buy volatility is a direct way to profit on market turmoil. If the VIX Index is trading in the mid-teens (its long-term average is 20), this may represent a good buying opportunity. While buying "fear" seems like a strange financial strategy, given all the headwinds the United States is facing, allocating a small percentage of your portfolio to an instrument that will do well during times of panic means that, in effect, you are buying insurance against the market's next big stumble.

AVOIDING THE HEADWINDS: MAKING MONEY IN STOCKS

As is true of bonds, the U.S. deficit will impact the stock market, and not for the better. Slower growth, higher interest rates, and higher inflation will not help a secular bear market already into its second decade. Investors will want to modestly lower their allocation to equities and dramatically reduce their exposure to U.S. stocks, which will bear the brunt of the deficit's side effects. We should also try to forget the buy-and-hold mantra that was endlessly repeated at the peak of the bull market. Stocks can go down, and depending on what you pay for them, by quite a lot. Even good companies can make for bad stocks if you overpay.

To avoid another lost decade, start by paying attention to where the market is valued. When companies in developed markets are trading at a price-to-earnings ratio of significantly more than 15 times the previous 12 months' earnings, around the historical average, lower your allocation. When stocks are comfortably below this level, add to your positions. One of the biggest mistakes individual investors tend to make is buying near market peaks and selling at the bottoms. Watching the market's valuation level will help you to avoid this mistake.

In terms of what to buy, remember that other parts of the world will grow faster than the United States over the next decade. The bull market that lasted between 1982 and 2000 went for so long because the United States entered a period of steady growth and falling interest rates and inflation. The bull markets of the next decade will occur in countries entering a similar phase. Countries in this position include emerging markets, much of Asia, and developed countries likely to benefit from higher inflation—including Canada and Australia. So, as with bonds, increase your allocation to emerging markets. You should have at least half of your stock portfolio invested outside of the United States.

For your U.S. positions, favor companies that will be resilient in, or even profit from, a higher interest rate and/or inflationary environment. This means investing in energy, health-care, and technology companies. At the same time, minimize your investments in banks, utilities, and anybody who sells anything to consumers that they don't absolutely need. This means avoiding the stocks of restaurants, department stores, and apparel companies.

Finally, and with all the warning labels attached above, the most experienced investors with adequate resources may consider allocating a small portion of their portfolio to investments that are not dependent on the market's direction. These could include hedge funds, ETFs, or mutual funds that replicate hedge funds, or other investment vehicles that are theoretically uncorrelated with equity markets. While hedge funds and other alternative investments can prove diversifying, you need to be very careful in terms of both fees, which tend to be high, and disclosures, which tend to be small. Investors need to consider whether the after-fee returns will be sufficient to justify the complexity of these products. Most importantly, you need to make sure that what you're buying is really differentiated from a typical portfolio of stocks. Otherwise, you'll be paying a big fee for something you could get much more cheaply by just buying an index fund.

CHAPTER 7

COMMODITIES: THE BENEFITS OF OWNING REAL ASSETS

M UCH OF THE LAST two chapters was spent highlighting what not to own or what to own less of. I have just advised you that in the coming environment of slower growth, rising interest rates, and possibly inflation you should seriously rethink your investing strategy. I have said that you should reduce your bond holdings, specifically Treasuries, and modestly lower your allocation to stocks, particularly U.S. stocks. Now, you might notice that taking those actions leaves a large hole in your portfolio. In this chapter I will talk about what should fill the hole.

Part of the answer is commodities. Unlike stocks and bonds, commodities do not represent an ownership claim or a liability attached to a company. Instead, commodities are real physical assets, including everything from oil to agricultural products. As physical assets, commodities produce no income. Nonetheless, they are good to own in an inflationary environment because as money becomes less valuable, prices will rise and commodities will become relatively more valuable. The result is that commodities not only hold their value when inflation is rising, but they will also help you to make money even after accounting for inflation.

Remember, large federal deficits do not mean that inflation is inevitable, but they do mean that it is more likely over the long term. If the Fed continues to expand its balance sheet and purchase U.S. government bonds, this will raise the long-term risk and we will eventually see a sharp spike in inflation Even without an explicit decision to monetize the debt, higher government spending in the absence of a permanent pullback in private consumption will eventually translate into inflation. In this chapter, I am going to show you why commodities are the best-performing asset class when inflation is rising.

In a sense, commodities represent an insurance policy on a potential economic outcome. In the event of inflation, commodities will help you to maintain your purchasing power. Apart from the deficit and the likelihood of inflation in the United States, there are also other reasons to increase your allocation to commodities. Rising living standards in many emerging market economies will lead to increased demand for various commodities, from copper to grains. This additional demand will tend to keep commodities prices higher than they have been in the past. On the opposite side of the equation, supply for some commodities is likely to be constrained in the future, which will also put upward pressure on prices.

A final argument for allocating a greater percentage of your portfolio to commodities is diversification. As commodities do well during times of inflation, they behave very differently from paper assets.

How much of your portfolio should you allocate to commodities? I would say to start with at least 10 percent. Then, if the leading indicators of inflation—job creation, capacity utilization, and most importantly the supply of money—start to rise, raise that allocation to closer to 20 to 25 percent of your portfolio.

INFLATION AND PHYSICAL ASSETS

As we've discussed, it has been a long time since investors have had to worry about real inflation (Figure 7.1). Long-term interest rates have been trending lower since the early 1980s. The same holds true for inflation. Consumer inflation peaked at nearly 15 percent in the spring of 1980, and it has been heading lower for most of the past three decades. In the wake of the 2008 to 2009 recession, inflation actually turned briefly negative. This meant that overall, consumer prices were lower than they were a year earlier, something that had not happened since 1955. While consumer prices have since stabilized, they still remain close to their multidecades low. This is particularly true when you look at *core inflation*, which excludes changes in food and energy prices because they tend to be the most volatile.

Figure 7.1 **U.S. Consumer Price Index (CPI) 1951 to Present**

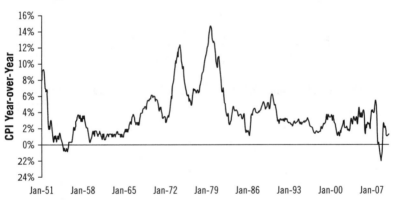

Source: Robert Shiller, Online Data, www.econ.yale.edu/~shiller/data.htm.

Based on spare capacity in the labor market and manufacturing sectors, coupled with the anemic growth rate in the money supply, inflation is not a near-term threat. The yearly change in inflation is likely to remain low for at least the next one to two years. However, large deficits, what appears to be a permanent increase in government spending, and the Fed's unusual and aggressive response to the financial crisis all raise the risk of higher inflation beyond 2013.

When inflation starts to rise, investors get nervous. Higher inflation leads to higher interest rates, which hurt both stocks and bonds. So
after an *inflation shock*—an unexpected and sudden rise in inflation—
investors' kneejerk reactions are to sell stocks and bonds and buy commodities. For this reason history suggests that commodities are the best
place to be positioned when inflation starts to rise, especially in the early
years of a new inflationary cycle.

Of all the asset classes, commodities tend to be the most closely tied
to inflation, falling when inflation falls and rising when inflation rises
(Figure 7.2). The reason is that inflation literally means that paper money,
dollars in whatever form, is less valuable because it buys fewer goods. Investors flee assets denominated in dollars—stocks and bonds—and look
for physical assets instead.

Figure 7.2 **Asset Class Performance Relative to
Economic Growth and Inflation**

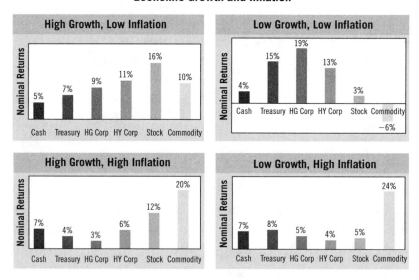

Source: BlackRock, Ibbotson Associates, and Bloomberg.

Changes in inflation have historically been the single most important determinant of commodity prices.[1] The same relationship between

inflation and commodities holds even if you simply own gold. Another way to think about the link between commodity prices and inflation is how much commodities will rise when inflation starts to pick up. Historically, every 1 percentage point increase in the annual U.S. inflation rate has led to an increase of between 3.8 and almost 10 percentage points among the different commodities.[2]

While it is a good idea to invest in commodities as a hedge against likely inflation, you should also be aware that commodities are not going to help you if interest rates rise but inflation does not. If the deficit pushes interest rates higher, not through inflation but because there is an over-supply of debt and investors get worried about risk, this will not benefit commodities. Higher real interest rates will act as a drag on the economy, and they will ultimately slow demand for many commodities, particularly for energy and industrial metals. Figure 7.2 illustrates the returns to commodities under different economic environments. As you can see, the return to commodities when growth is slow and inflation is low is only half the return when growth is slow and inflation is high. Commodities hedge against rising inflation, not rising real rates.

OTHER REASONS TO OWN COMMODITIES

Government deficit–induced inflation is probably a sufficient reason to raise your long-term allocation to commodities, but there are other reasons as well. Rising demand from emerging markets and a restricted supply for several key products, notably crude oil, are other good reasons to increase your portfolio's allocation to commodities.

Analyzing commodity prices is largely a matter of looking at the likely demand for a given commodity and the future supply. If supply is held flat, rising demand will lead to higher prices. If demand is held constant and supply is reduced—or supply becomes more expensive to produce—prices will also rise.

Starting with demand, why should you expect to see rising demand? The answer lies with emerging markets. As emerging markets grow, they are experiencing a significant rise in their middle-class population. Over the past several decades, several hundred million people have been lifted out of poverty, particularly in China and India. As incomes have risen, so have living standards. More and more people in China, India, and other emerging markets are now able to afford or aspire to middle-class Western lifestyles. As people move up the income ladder, their consumption of a host of commodities rises. Western diets make use of more meat (which in turn requires more grain to feed cattle) and sugar. More and bigger homes in turn demand more timber, steel, and copper. And finally, the middle-class aspiration of owning one's own car will put additional pressure on oil prices. All in all, a rising middle class is not only an encouraging sign of social development, but it is also a signal of rising demand for just about every commodity imaginable.

For example, Chinese energy demand has surged over the past decade (Figure 7.3). In 2010 China passed the United States as the world's largest energy consumer, although the United States still consumes much more energy per person than does China. Since 2000, China has gone

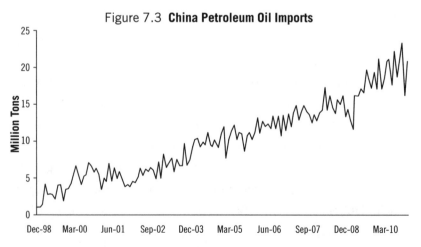

Figure 7.3 **China Petroleum Oil Imports**

Source: Bloomberg and the China Administrator of Customs, as of June 2010.

from importing roughly 5 million tons of crude petroleum each month to over 20 million today. China's appetite for raw materials is not limited to energy—imports of copper ore are up more than 200 percent since early 2004.

Nor is this trend likely to reverse any time soon. Future demand for commodities, particularly energy, will continue along the same trajectory. Over the next quarter century, world energy demand is expected to rise by 50 percent, from around 500 quadrillion British thermal units (BTUs) annually to approximately 740 quadrillion BTUs in 2035. (A *quadrillion* is actually a real number. It is equal to a million billion.) Of this 50 percent jump in world demand, the overwhelming portion will be driven by emerging markets, with countries outside of the developed world accounting for roughly five-sixths of the increase.[3]

For some commodities, upward price pressure will come not only from increasing demand but also from supply constraints as well. In certain cases, overall supply has been dropping. In many instances, particularly those commodities that need to be mined, the easy, low-cost mines have already been exhausted, and production is now moving to smaller, marginal mines.

There is already some evidence of this in the copper markets. Ore grades have fallen by roughly 25 percent over the past two decades. In addition, miners need to go deeper and deeper to find even the lower-grade copper. Over the past decade, a greater proportion of discoveries have required deeper mining methods when compared to the previous two decades.[4] When it comes to mining or drilling for oil, deeper means more expensive. Copper prices will need to remain high to justify digging such deep and expensive mines.

The cost of extracting oil is also on the rise. During the past decade, there has been a lot of controversy over the topic of "peak oil." Those who advocate this theory argue that global oil production has already peaked, or it will do so in the very near future. Geologists and industry experts have come down hard on both sides of this debate. In fairness to the experts, deciding how much oil is ultimately recoverable involves a lot of guesswork. For starters, the definition of what is recoverable changes every year as new technologies make previously inaccessible oil fair game. Second, much of the world's oil is in the Middle East, particularly Saudi Arabia. Getting accurate estimates on the age, production, and state of Saudi wells is notoriously difficult, leaving geologists missing a big part of the global puzzle.

While we probably won't know for years, or perhaps decades, if we're truly running out of oil in any meaningful way, what is clear is that we're running out of cheap oil. Increasingly, new oil production is being driven by reserves that are either technically difficult to produce, think deepwater Gulf of Mexico, or in politically unstable parts of the world. Both entail high risks and costs.

Even in the absence of a dropoff in supply, as it becomes more expensive to produce that next barrel of oil, companies will only ramp up supply as prices rise. If prices fall below a certain point, it no longer becomes economically viable to produce oil from 35,000 feet below the surface of the ocean or to extract it from Canadian oil sands. As a result, supply will fall if prices start to fall too low, which will cushion prices and provide a floor for oil.

By 2025, what is euphemistically known as *unconventional hydrocarbon*—read expensive—*oil production* is forecast to grow to over 20 percent of the global supply.[5] And as the oil industry becomes dependent on unconventional oil, the floor on oil prices will rise. As a result, energy in particular is likely to see higher prices as the cost of finding and producing oil keeps rising.

Apart from the likelihood of government deficit–induced inflation and the likelihood of price increases due to higher demand and higher costs, there is a final reason why most individuals should increase their allocation to commodities: diversification.

Commodities behave very differently than paper assets. For starters, they respond well to inflation, whereas stocks and bonds generally do not.

Second, unlike bonds, they also do well when economic growth is very strong, as a humming economy normally means more demand for most commodities.

To quantify how different assets move together, economists look at what is known as *correlation*. Correlation measures the relationship between two sets of numbers, like annual returns. If the two sets move in perfect lockstep, the correlation is 1. If the two are mirror images of each other, one always going up when the other falls, the correlation is −1. And if there is no relationship between the two sets of numbers, the correlation is close to 0. Ideally, in order to create a truly diversified portfolio, investors want to assemble assets that have either no correlation or a negative correlation with each other.

Looking at annual returns, the correlation between stocks and commodities has been 0.05 over the long term. This is effectively no correlation, indicating that stocks and commodities march to their own tune, which is what you want in a well-diversified portfolio. Looking at gold and stocks, the correlation is actually modestly negative, meaning gold has a slight tendency to rise when stocks are falling and vice versa. In general, owning commodities helps to diversify your portfolio.

There will be periods when this does not work as advertised. While commodities have in the past, and are likely in the future, proven the value of diversifying, it is important to note that this does not always hold over the short term, defined here as a year or less. During the bear market of 2008 and early 2009, commodities sank just as quickly as stocks. Large U.S. equities lost approximately 38 percent in 2008, while the broad commodities index dropped 36 percent. Faced with a potential meltdown of the global economy, investors sold all assets that carried any level of risk, including commodities. In this case, the normal benefit of diversification was temporarily lost. However, one asset that did behave differently in 2008 was gold. While stocks and other commodities sank, gold actually rose by approximately 5 percent as investors sought a safe haven in which to hide their money.

In 2009 when stocks, corporate bonds, and other risk assets rallied, commodities also ran right along with them, calling into question just how diversifying they really are. But it is important to remember that this is the exception rather than the rule. During an acute financial crisis, most investors want nothing to do with risk. Under these circumstances they tend to put all investments in one of two categories: ultrasafe assets like U.S. Treasuries and everything else. When investors finally decide that it is safe to crawl out from under the bed, they still behave in a herdlike fashion, just in the opposite direction, piling into assets regardless of risk, such as stocks, high-yield bonds, and commodities. During these periods, there is no such thing as diversification.

Most of the time, however, there are different factors affecting markets, including the strength of the economy, the pace of inflation, geopolitical events, and corporate profitability. It is rare for everything to be either good or bad at the same time. In these instances, which describe markets the vast majority of the time, diversification is critical. Some of your portfolio will respond well to prevailing conditions, while other parts will not, but overall you'll help dampen your portfolio's volatility by owning different types of assets. The advantage of commodities is that they do respond differently to inflation than stocks and bonds. This can mean that at times when your stocks and bonds are being hurt by inflation, commodities will help you make up for the losses.

ARE ALL COMMODITIES THE SAME?

Arguing for a higher allocation to commodities leaves open the question of which ones? Like stocks and bonds, all commodities are not equal. To the extent that investors are buying commodities specifically as a hedge against inflation, some work better than others. Also, the supply and demand for different commodities will vary over the next decade, which will affect their prices. In short, commodities come in lots of different flavors.

While there are dozens of different commodities, they can be broadly grouped into a few categories. Precious metals include gold, silver, and platinum. There are energy-related commodities, such as crude oil, natural gas, gasoline, and heating oil. Agricultural commodities are generally edible and include wheat, cattle, orange juice, and sugar. Industrial metals are those primarily used for building and manufacturing. This class includes copper, zinc, aluminum, iron, and steel.

While all of the above fall into the broad asset class of commodities, like different types of bonds, they all have their own nuances, and each will respond differently to various economic circumstances. Precious metals, particularly gold, are often thought of as a store of value or an alternative currency. As a result, gold and to a lesser extent silver and platinum tend to rise when the dollar is weak and tend to fall when it is strong. Gold also does well during a crisis. After several millennia of being used as a medium of exchange, investors have grown to trust gold during times of turbulence. Gold is for investors what a security blanket is for a toddler, something to hold onto when things get scary. The disadvantage of holding gold is that it produces no income. If you're not worried about inflation, a weaker dollar, or the collapse of Western civilization, then there is little reason to own gold.

Oil prices are in part driven by economic conditions. All else being equal, a stronger economy needs more energy than a weaker one, and oil prices rise on evidence of growing demand. But other factors influence energy as well. OPEC and Middle East production make up approximately one-third of global oil production, so instability in the region normally leads to higher oil prices. Finally, even weather can impact energy prices, at least over the short term. Every time a hurricane comes barreling through the Gulf of Mexico and shuts down oil rigs, there is a small bounce in the price of oil. While the price will slip as soon as the storm passes and oil production resumes, at least in the short term a misplaced hurricane or a particularly cold winter in the northeastern part of the United States can drive energy prices higher.

Like oil, industrial metals, particularly copper, are strongly influenced by economic growth. Due to its use in building and construction, copper is so sensitive to economic conditions that economists often use changes in its price as a leading indicator of economic activity. When copper prices are rising, this is generally interpreted to mean that the economy is likely to grow, at least over the near term.

Finally, agricultural commodities are largely driven by weather conditions in the near term, but they are likely to also be impacted for the longer term by global growth and the emergence of a large middle class in places like China and India. As hundreds of millions of people adopt a middle-class lifestyle and increase their consumption of meat and sugar, this will put upward pressure on many of the agricultural commodities, a trend that is likely to continue for years to come.

Precious Metals and Inflation

Since the theme of this chapter is how to use commodities to protect your portfolio from inflation, it is worth exploring the relationship between precious metals and inflation in more detail. As illustrated above, all commodities respond well to inflation. When inflation is high, they do well in an absolute sense—that is, their returns beat inflation. During periods of inflation commodities do well also in a relative sense in that they outperform stocks, bonds, and cash. But the commodity category most closely tied to inflation is precious metals.

Precious metals have historically performed best during periods of rising inflation, such as the late 1970s. From 1973 to August 1984, a period generally characterized by high inflation, precious metals were the top-performing asset class, easily beating stocks, bonds, and cash. During that period, the annual inflation rate was approximately 8.5 percent, while a portfolio including gold, silver, and platinum appreciated by over 20 percent annually.[6]

Precious metals offer another advantage. Because precious metals have an actual negative correlation with other asset classes, they are even more diversifying in a portfolio when compared to a broad basket of commodities. As a result, the unique characteristics of precious metals make them particularly useful as a diversification tool.[7]

Of the precious metals, should you favor any one in particular? When it comes to hedging inflation, at least historically gold has provided the best protection (Figure 7.4). Gold shows a much stronger correlation with annual changes in U.S. consumer prices in comparison to a broad, well-diversified basket of commodities. It has also demonstrated the ability to protect purchasing power over the long term. Between 1959 and the middle of 2010, U.S. consumer prices rose nearly 7-fold. During the same period, gold prices rose over 35-fold, despite the fact that gold prices were fixed until the early 1970s.

Figure 7.4 **Inflation, Gold, and Commodities, 1972 to Present**

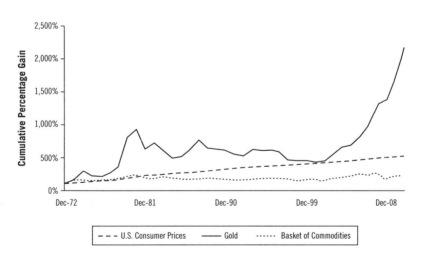

Source: Bloomberg and the Bureau of Labor Statistics, as of July 2010.

Now some may argue that the above is not a fair comparison. The period includes the 1970s, when the United States fell off the gold exchange standard and witnessed its worst bout of inflation in decades. Yet even during the last 25 years, a period in which gold prices were flat for long periods of time, gold has managed to beat inflation. Since 1984, U.S. consumer prices have risen by a bit over 100 percent, indicating that prices have generally doubled. Even during this 25-year period, which as been characterized by relatively low and falling inflation, gold prices are up over 200 percent, more than tripling since 1984.

Why has gold, at least historically, proven such a useful inflation hedge? Unlike other commodities such as copper or energy, it is not really good for anything. I would argue that it is precisely because gold serves no useful purpose that it has been such a good inflation hedge. The demand dynamics of other commodities like copper are heavily influenced by the global economy. The demand for agricultural commodities can be impacted by changing lifestyle patterns.

It is because gold serves no purpose other than as a store of value that its price is so impacted by inflation. When individuals are confident that paper money will hold its value, they have no reason to hold gold. This is one reason gold did so poorly during the boom years of the 1990s. Why hold a lump of metal when you feel confident that the Internet company you just bought will become the next IBM? It is primarily during periods when people are concerned about the stability of the financial system and the purchasing power of the dollar that gold becomes an attractive alternative.

Before moving onto the other precious metals, it is worth inserting a couple of notes of caution for those gold bugs who may now feel justified in putting all their money in gold bullion. No matter how attractive the investment case for any asset, investors should always pay as much, if not more, attention to risk as they do to return. Putting all or even most of your eggs in one basket is a bad idea, and it goes against the basic principle of portfolio diversification. Gold is a good inflation hedge, but remember that we may not get inflation for many years, and there is still a real possibility that we won't get it at all. Because economic events are notoriously uncertain, never overallocate to a single financial asset, no matter how convinced you are that the events in any one scenario or thesis will actually occur. Gold definitely has a place in most portfolios, but its attractiveness as an inflation hedge needs to be balanced by the fact that in the absence of inflation or a declining dollar, returns are likely to be muted.

What about other precious metals such as silver and platinum? Silver does do a modestly better job than other commodities in tracking inflation, but the relationship between silver and inflation is still only about half as strong as the one between gold and inflation. Part of the reason probably lies in the fact that while it is a precious metal, it is an industrial one as well. Industrial uses count for around 43 percent of silver end-user demand, including its use in batteries, photography, and thermophotovoltaic cells.[8] Similar to other commodities, there are lots of factors influencing the demand for silver besides the prevailing view on inflation. This does not suggest that silver may not be a good investment. As new technologies expand its uses, it may in fact turn out to outperform gold. But if you're goal in investing in precious metals is to hedge your inflation risk, gold has historically done a better job.

Similar to silver, platinum has a number of other uses besides sitting in a safety deposit box and adorning engagement rings. As with silver, roughly 50 percent of platinum use is for industrial purposes, particularly in the automotive sector, with the remaining demand being driven by jewelry and investment. As such, the price of platinum is strongly influenced by overall economic conditions. The impact of broader economic factors other than inflation is clear when you look at the historical relationship between platinum and changes in consumer prices. While platinum prices have more than kept up with inflation, the correlation between inflation and changes in platinum prices is much lower than it is for gold or even silver. Platinum has been a sound investment, but not necessarily a good inflation hedge.

COMMODITY ALLOCATION

Many factors will impact global commodity markets over the next decade. Most of them appear to be bullish for commodity prices. In addition, commodities will provide you with both an inflation hedge as well as better overall portfolio diversification. As a result, put at least 10 percent of your investable assets in commodities.

Given the many factors influencing commodity prices, it is beyond the scope of this book to make a strong, long-term recommendation on the relative merits of wheat versus copper. Too many supply and demand factors will influence the price over the next decade to bet strongly on one versus the other. For that reason, I would recommend that investors restrict their commodity investments to just two allocations: a broad commodity fund and gold.

In addition to acting as an inflation hedge, most commodities will benefit from rising emerging market consumption. In addition, crude oil and certain metals are also likely to benefit from supply constraints. To fully benefit from these trends, you'll want to own a broad cross section of different commodities.

The second commodity allocation should be directly to gold. The argument for an extra position in gold is that gold has proven the best inflation hedge historically, even when compared to other precious metals. Its utter lack of practical uses, other than being pretty to wear, has made it uniquely sensitive to inflation. If inflation returns, gold will arguably be the beneficiary.

The reasons for not allocating your full commodity position to gold are twofold. First, commodities like copper, crude oil, and even agricultural commodities are a more direct play on emerging market growth. Second, while gold offers great inflation protection, you never want to have too large of an allocation to a single asset. For that reason, allocate half your commodity position to the broad commodity basket and the other half to gold, or about 5 percent of your total portfolio to each. If and when the leading indicators of inflation start to flash yellow, increase your positions to 10 percent of your total portfolio to a commodity basket and 10 percent to gold.

How to Implement a Commodity Position

Up until around five years ago, futures were the only practical way for individual investors to own a direct position in most commodities—precious metals being the exception. And the truth is that for the vast ma jority of individuals, futures really aren't all that practical. Futures have expiration dates, so you have to sell out your position before it expires. Otherwise, you face the prospect of having a hundred barrels of oil or a thousand bushels of wheat dropped off on your doorstep. If you want to maintain positions in commodities by using futures, you need to continually buy and sell your contracts. Maintaining a futures portfolio requires more time and energy than the average investor can devote to it.

Even if you are willing to devote the time to maintaining a futures portfolio, you should be aware that constantly *trading out,* or *rolling out,* of expiring futures contracts and buying new ones can impact your portfolio in unpredictable ways. The returns generated on a futures position can diverge significantly from the performance of the underlying commodity. Depending on the relative price difference between an expiring futures contract and a new one, your returns may be hurt or flattered when you roll positions. This is a source of risk that has nothing to do with the performance of gold, crude oil, or wheat but is instead driven by the technical nature of the futures market.

For more sophisticated investors or for those with the resources to hire a financial manager, futures may still be a viable way to gain exposure to commodities. But if you don't have the resources to devote to managing your futures position, there are a number of mutual funds and exchange-traded funds and notes that can also provide exposure to both a broad basket of commodities as well as more specific indexes.

When looking to use an exchange-traded product (ETP) or mutual fund to gain commodity exposure, there are four issues to consider. First, if you are considering an exchange-traded product, is the product an exchange-traded fund (ETF) or an exchange-traded note (ETN)? Recall from Chapter 6 that while ETFs and ETNs look the same, exchange-traded notes come with an important difference: you don't have any actual ownership interest in the underlying assets. Instead, you basically hold a promissory note from the bank. The note promises to pay you a return that matches a particular index. The assumption is that the bank will be around to pay. Make sure you're comfortable that that assumption is valid. Exchange-traded notes entail some credit risk, in the sense that the issuing bank or brokerage may not pay the return it promised. That particular risk does not exist with exchange-traded funds; however, there are certain commodity products that are available only in the form of an exchange-traded note.

The second issue to consider is: What does the fund or note actually own? Does the instrument hold the physical commodity, or does it gain exposure to the commodity from futures contracts or other derivative instruments? This was not an important issue relative to the discussion of stocks and bonds. Most mutual funds or exchange-traded funds simply own the underlying stocks and bonds. Commodity funds are different. Many do not actually own the commodities but instead own futures contracts tied to the underlying commodities. As discussed above, owning futures, whether directly or through a fund, entails risks that have nothing to do with the underlying prices of the commodities.

Third, as always, what are the costs? When looking at funds, keep in mind the liquidity as well as the management fee. Smaller funds may wind up costing more if they are expensive to trade. Here the calculus is the same as with stocks and bonds. Start with the management fee of the fund, but also consider the other costs. If you are buying an exchange-traded fund or note, look at the size of the fund. In general, smaller funds—which I'll define as under $100 million—will be more expensive to trade, and those additional costs will detract from your return just as with a fee. As a rule of thumb, the larger the fund, the smaller the trading spread, which means you can buy and sell the fund at a low cost. If you're investing in a traditional mutual fund, is there a sales charge, or *load*. This will be a fee you'll have to pay when buying, selling, or potentially both. Add up all the fees, not just the annual management fee, when comparing your different options.

Finally, and perhaps most importantly, make sure you understand what commodities the fund owns. Is it a broad fund owning a well-diversified basket of commodities, or is it more concentrated in that most of the fund is made up of one type of commodity, such as energy? There is nothing wrong with investing in a fund that owns mostly energy commodities, if that's what you set out to invest in. But if your intent is to own a well-diversified basket of commodities, make sure that the fund delivers.

The advantage of owning a broad basket of commodities is that, to the extent that you don't have a strong opinion on the merits of one commodity versus another, it will help insulate you from the specific ups and downs of each separate commodity. With that in mind, make sure you look under the hood of the fund to confirm just how diversified the fund is. There are a few major commodity indexes that are generally used as the benchmarks for commodity funds, including the two most popular: the Goldman Sachs Commodities Index (GSCI) and the Dow Jones-UBS.

While each of these baskets will own a mix of different types of commodities, the relative weighting of these commodities in each index can vary dramatically. In the case of the GSCI, as of late 2010 the index was heavily weighted toward energy. Approximately two-thirds of the index was made up of energy-related commodities, with roughly one-sixth of the index invested in agricultural commodities. Only about one-sixth of the fund was invested in industrial or precious metals. Practically, this means that the fund will be driven predominately by oil prices and it will not be particularly influenced by changes in either copper or gold.

The Dow Jones-UBS Commodity Index looks very different. Again, in late 2010 energy made up less than one-third of this benchmark, while precious metals accounted for roughly one-sixth of the index, versus roughly 3 percent for the GSCI. The Dow Jones had a high percentage, approximately 30 percent, of agricultural commodities and about 20 percent of precious metals.

There is no ideal commodity index, just as there are no perfect stock or bond indexes. But comparing the two commodity indexes does illustrate an important point. Both the GSCI and the Dow Jones UBS Commodity Index can reasonably represent themselves as broad commodity indexes, but the commodities you are most exposed to are very different. If crude oil falls, returns on the GSCI will be modest, even if other commodities are performing strongly.

When thinking about the right commodity fund to invest in, ask yourself whether your intent is to gain exposure to a broad and diversified list of commodities, or if you would rather emphasize certain themes, such as precious metals or energy. If you agree with the call that energy is particularly attractive, even when compared to other commodities, then the GSCI is probably a good index to follow. It will provide that overweight to energy while still giving you exposure to a mix of other commodities. If, on the other hand, you are simply looking to gain exposure to a broad, well-diversified mix of different commodities, then funds based on the Dow Jones-UBS Commodity Index will be the better choice.

Buying Gold and Other Precious Metals: Stocks, ETFs, or Bars in the Backyard?

Earlier in the chapter I advocated a separate position in gold. Unlike other commodities, investors can actually buy and store physical gold, as well as platinum and silver. While some have argued that owning the physical commodity will come in handy in the event of a total breakdown in the financial system, I would be somewhat skeptical that owning a block of gold will be of that much use if civilization comes crashing down around you. Under that scenario, you probably want to go with the guns-and-livestock portfolio and abandon everything else.

That said, there are advantages to the physical metal. Unlike futures, or products that gain their exposure to gold through futures, owning the metal outright does not expose you to additional risks associated with maintaining a futures position. By owning physical gold, your return will exactly match the performance of the metal rather than being distorted by fluctuations in the price of one futures contract versus another. A second advantage is that owning the metal directly will not generate any management or brokerage fees, which will be the case with futures or a gold fund. When you buy physical gold, there will be costs associated with the delivery of the metal, and to the extent that you want to store it in a bank safety deposit box, there will be some incremental costs to maintain that box, but these are relatively minor expenses.

There are also some disadvantages to owning the physical gold. First, what do you do with it? If you are uncomfortable storing the gold in a safety deposit box, is there another safe place to store it that does not leave you vulnerable to fire or theft? Another consideration is the size of your purchase. If you're buying relatively small amounts, a few hundred dollars' worth, the cost of shipping the gold may represent a relatively high transaction cost compared to your investment.

Beyond physical gold, there are other options to gain exposure to the yellow metal. Investors can invest in gold futures, funds or ETFs that invest in gold, or even the stocks of companies that mine gold. Beginning with the stocks for gold mining companies, while there may be a place in your portfolio for gold stocks in general, they have proven much less useful as an inflation hedge than physical gold. Some commentators have offered up gold stocks as an alternative to physical gold on the notion that stocks can pay a dividend and produce income. Also, gold mining companies can offer greater earnings or operational leverage to the extent that gold prices are skyrocketing. (*Operating leverage* refers to the process by which a small increase in revenue, that is, the price of gold, leads to a big increase in earnings and therefore the stock price.)

While all of the above sounds reasonable, and gold mining stocks may make a good investment for other reasons, they have not been an effective inflation hedge in the past. The earnings of these companies can surge on a rise in the price of gold, but unfortunately their valuations can and do contract due to rising inflation. Even though these companies earn more due to rising gold prices, investors place a lower value on those earnings when inflation looks like it will rise. As a result, over the past 20 years, an index of large gold companies has had only a very weak relationship with U.S. consumer inflation.

Futures offer the advantage of not having to store the physical commodity. Gold futures are popular and liquid, and they are not expensive to trade, but they suffer from the same drawbacks as other types of futures contracts. Specifically, how the prices of different contracts relate to each other can have a large impact on your investment performance, and it can distort your returns away from the price of gold itself. Sometimes this can even work in your favor, but investors need to understand the idiosyncrasies of the futures market in order to be able to effectively use futures contracts.

This leaves exchange-traded funds. For those who are uncomfortable storing gold or trading futures, ETFs can provide exposure to the physical commodity. There are two large providers of gold exchange-traded funds: State Street and BlackRock. The larger fund is the SPDR Gold Share (GLD), which is managed by State Street. The fund holds the actual physical gold, and it charges a 0.40 percent expense ratio. BlackRock also offers a large, liquid gold ETF, the iShares COMEX Gold Trust (IAU). The ETF also owns the physical gold, and it charges a 0.25 percent management fee. As both funds trade like stocks, you can buy them and hold them within your existing brokerage account.

CONCLUSION: SELL SOME PAPER AND BUY STUFF

Owning a portfolio devoid of commodities was never a good idea, as having at least a small allocation to physical assets helps you to diversify your risk. Moving forward, however, avoiding commodities is going to be an even worse idea. In fact, in the current environment, you should consider allocating a nontrivial part of your portfolio to commodities.

Growing demand from emerging markets and constricting supply for many commodities suggest strong supply and demand fundamentals. On top of that, governments around the world are engaging in unprecedented monetary experiments. Today, these experiments pose little risk of inflation; down the road, the risk is likely to be greater. And finally, there is the government's deficit spending. Permanently higher government spending will be inflationary once private demand returns. The presence of large deficits also raises the risk that the government will increasingly monetize the debt, a step that can set up the United States for massive inflation.

To take advantage of these opportunities and insulate yourself from the risks, start with a 10 percent allocation in your portfolio to commodities. Divide that allocation equally between a fund replicating a broad commodity index and gold. The broad commodity basket will provide diversification from the ups and downs of any one commodity. It will also provide good exposure to rising demand for commodities from emerging markets. The position in gold is effectively an insurance policy against inflation. Like any insurance policy, it will sit there the vast majority of the time doing nothing. But like a real insurance policy, if and when inflation rises, you'll be glad you have it.

Be prepared to expand the commodity portion of your portfolio in the coming years. As the global economy recovers, the risk of higher inflation will also rise. Watch the excess slack in the economy—measured by both the rate of job creation as well as the percentage of manufacturing capacity that is being used. Also watch the banks and the money supply. When the money supply starts to accelerate, inflation will eventually follow. When these indicators start to rise, that will be the time to raise your overall commodity allocation to around 20 percent. Under this scenario, again divide your commodity allocation between a broad commodity basket and gold.

Owning commodities will be a new experience for most investors. But as I've tried to point out, the environment we're likely to live through over the next decade will look and feel very different from the past 30 years. And in a world in which economic growth comes from India and Indonesia and debt comes from Washington, commodities offer a reasonable investment solution.

CHAPTER 8

REAL ESTATE AND DEFICITS

W E'VE COVERED CASH, bonds, stocks, and commodities. But what we've neglected thus far is the one asset class most investors already own: real estate. For many if not most investors, real estate is their single largest investment. Given the primary role that real estate plays in most people's net worth, how should you think about owning property in an economic landscape dominated by large government deficits?

In the previous chapters, the prescriptions were fairly straightforward. Higher deficits will lead to higher interest rates and potentially inflation. Both are bad for bonds and domestic stocks, while at least inflation is good for commodities. How does real estate compare? Real estate is obviously not a paper asset like bonds or stocks. However, it will be hurt by many of the same side effects of the deficit that will negatively impact paper assets. Like stocks, real estate returns are correlated with economic growth. A slower economy will hurt real estate prices. Like both stocks and bonds, real estate performs best when interest rates are falling. Falling rates make real estate more affordable, and they support prices for both residential and commercial real estate.

However, when it comes to inflation, actual real estate has more in common with commodities (I'll explain why I added the qualifier of "actual" in a moment). Even over the short term, real estate has a positive correlation with inflation, although not as high as gold. And over the long term, real estate does a decent job of holding its value in inflation-adjusted terms. When the value of paper money is falling, the physical characteristics of real estate make it a good inflation hedge, if you hold it long enough.

In thinking about real estate in your portfolio, always consider what you already own. Most people start with a large real estate position in the form of their house. When times are good, the cyclical nature of real estate adds to their net worth, as most people enjoyed last decade. When economic conditions weaken, even a small drop in the value of people's homes can put a serious dent in their net worth, given how central home equity is in most portfolios. Therefore, the real question you should consider is not whether you should own real estate, but given the implications of the deficit, should you own more?

The answer, as we'll see, will largely depend on whether we get inflation. In the absence of a pickup in inflation, there are few arguments for increasing your exposure to U.S. real estate (international real estate offers some diversification benefits, and it is a different story). Slower economic growth will reduce the demand for both residential and commercial real estate, and higher interest rates will harm affordability. If you already own a house and that house represents a nontrivial portion of your net worth, you probably have all the real estate exposure you are going to want.

If we start to see signs of inflation, however, the story changes. You should then consider adding to your real estate exposure, through a bigger home or a second house. But before adding to your real estate holdings, consider two things. First, consider whether you plan to hold onto the real estate for a long period of time, which I'll define as at least a decade. Second, consider whether you will be borrowing to finance the purchase: adding to your real estate holdings on the expectation of rising inflation makes even more sense if you can borrow to finance the new real estate. Recall from Chapter 4 that it makes sense to take out more debt early in an inflation cycle as inflation erodes the value of your debt and makes it easier to pay off.

One important caveat to keep in mind if you want to use real estate as an inflation hedge is that it needs to be the real thing. In other words, you need to own an actual physical asset, not a share of a *real estate investment trust* (REIT). REITs are a type of publicly traded company that owns real estate. Investors often mistakenly believe that owning a REIT is a substitute for owning real estate. Investors need to be aware that there is a big difference in how physical real estate performs under inflation versus how REITs do.

In the case of whether or not to own real estate, the answer depends largely on what you actually own.

Thinking about Real Estate as an Asset Class

A house, undeveloped land, or an office building—all qualify as physical assets. Unlike a bond, which is effectively an IOU that you can trade, or a stock, which represents a fractional ownership interest in a company, real estate is obviously a tangible asset. In this sense, real estate resembles a commodity. It is for this reason that physical real estate has proved a good inflation hedge. During periods of inflation, you want to own hard assets rather than paper assets.

In other ways, however, real estate is more akin to stocks or bonds. First, unlike commodities, real estate produces income. Both residential and commercial real estate produce rent. You can rent out a vacation or second home. And to some extent, your primary home has an imputed rent (*imputed rent* is the rent you save by owning rather than renting your house). And because real estate produces rent, its value is largely a function of how you value those rent payments. This means that like stocks or bonds, real estate is hurt by rising interest rates. This is because the future value of those rental payments goes down when interest rates rise.

Second, like stocks and bonds, no two real estate investments behave exactly alike. A bar of gold has the same value as every other bar of gold, but two properties even if they produce the same income are still likely to have different values as other factors—such as location, condition, and local economic environment—impact price. Unlike commodities, the investment properties of a piece of real estate are idiosyncratic to that particular property. When it comes to real estate, which real estate to buy may be a more important decision than whether to buy real estate in the first place. For this reason, generalizations on real estate often have less significance than similar broad statements about stocks and bonds. The direction of the local market or the attributes of a particular piece of property will often trump the broader trend.

So as we attempt to address the question of how much real estate to hold, it will often turn out that the answer is: it depends. While we can make certain generalizations about how real estate behaves, in many cases the evidence is weak, and the case for buying or selling real estate based on a particular economic scenario is not that clear.

The answer becomes even fuzzier when you broaden the definition of what constitutes real estate. Owning a physical property is one thing; owning a share of a REIT is another. REITs, while backed by underlying positions in real estate, can and do perform very differently than the underlying properties.

REITs are securities that trade like stocks. But whereas traditional stocks represent an ownership interest in a company, REITs represent an ownership interest in a portfolio of real estate or mortgages on real estate. They are vehicles that allow investors to pool their assets.

The REIT market both in the United States and in other countries is well established and large. In the United States, Congress created REITs in 1960 as a way to make investment in real estate more easily accessible to all investors.[1] In this sense, REITs are to real estate what mutual funds are to stocks. Mutual funds provide individual investors with a tool to easily assemble a well-diversified portfolio of stocks. REITs perform the same function for real estate. Another similarity with mutual funds is that REITs also provide the additional advantage of professional management. Just as individuals often lack the tools and information to make a selection from a universe of thousands of stocks, few investors have the resources or information to build a real estate portfolio from scratch. REITs provide this service.

As with mutual funds, REITs come in many flavors. *Equity REITs* invest in and own property. Their revenue comes from rent. *Mortgage REITs* own the mortgages on property. In effect, they loan money for mortgages to owners of real estate, or they purchase existing mortgages. Revenues come from interest. There are also *hybrid REITs* that own both property and mortgages.[2]

There are even finer distinctions within the REIT asset class. Some REITs own residential real estate while others own commercial real estate. Even within commercial real estate some REITs may further concentrate their holdings in one area, such as office buildings or shopping malls.[3]

Finally, REITs can be focused on different geographic markets. Not all REITs are U.S. centric. Many other countries have similar structures for pooling real estate investments, and the market for international REITs is substantial. While the market for U.S. REITs is by far the largest in the world at approximately $270 billion, other countries also offer large, deep markets, including Australia, $70 billion; France, $65 billion; the United Kingdom, $35 billion; Japan, $30 billion; and Canada, $20 billion.[4]

While the underlying assets of REITs are real estate, REITs trade and often behave like stocks. REITs are bought and sold like ordinary stocks, and they are often viewed as high-yield substitutes for stocks. This will be a critical distinction as we explore how to adjust your real estate holdings in the face of continuing deficits, particularly when it comes to inflation. While REITs own physical assets, often they act more like paper assets.

How Real Estate Behaves: Slow Growth

So how will REITs and physical real estate perform in the environment that the deficit is likely to produce? And, more specifically, how will they perform differently from each other?

To the extent that the deficit slows growth in the U.S. economy, it will hurt real estate, both REITs and physical real estate. As described above, real estate, whether residential or commercial, is not only owned for its capital gains potential but also for its income production. When the economy slows, there is less demand for real estate, just as there is less demand for labor or manufacturing capacity.

On the residential side, a weaker economy means that people are more cautious about buying property. It is hard to afford a house when your income is stagnant and virtually impossible when you don't have a job. A weak job market and anemic wage growth hurt people's ability to afford real estate or even pay the rent. Even for those who can still afford to buy, recessions and economic malaise shake confidence. Regardless of your income bracket, a house is often your largest investment. When economic growth slows, people are more wary of buying big-ticket items, even if they can afford them.

For commercial real estate the impact of an anemic economy is even greater. A slower economy lowers demand for everything from office to retail space. And as is the case with home buyers, a loss in confidence can be catastrophic for investors' willingness to fund grandiose commercial real estate projects. During boom times, it seems that builders can develop virtually any idea, thanks to a childlike faith in future demand. But when economic conditions turn, few industries turn down as quickly as commercial real estate. Suddenly what seemed brilliant in the midst of a boom now comes across as extravagant and unsustainable.

The recent recession provides a good illustration of how economic weakness can impact real estate performance. While the period between 2007 and 2009 was marked by sharply falling interest rates and decelerating inflation—both positives for housing—the collapse in the global economy gutted the real estate market. Everyone is well aware of what happened to home prices in the United States.

Real estate investment trusts fared no better, and in many cases the damage was even worse. Overall, the REIT market in the United States got hammered along with virtually every other asset class. In 2008, REITs in the United States were down approximately 37 percent, in line with the broader U.S. stock markets' performance. Some REITs, notably those with more defensive and less cyclical characteristics, fared a bit better. For example, REITs that specialize in medical spaces—renting to doctors—held up much better than the broader market. But for those REITs that invested in the more cyclical parts of the real estate market, the carnage was far worse. REITs that invested in commercial real estate mortgages were down an astounding 75 percent, regional malls down 60 percent, and office REITs fell more than 40 percent.[5] In this aspect, the performance of various types of REITs resembled stocks. The more economically sensitive the security, the more it was negatively impacted when economic conditions slowed and financial markets fell.

The recent experience is indicative of the longer-term relationship between real estate and economic activity. The historical pattern suggests that real estate returns are closely related to real economic activity.[6] In the case of the U.S. housing market, the evidence is fairly clear. In the post–World War II period, for every 1 percent increase in real economic growth, the U.S. housing market has appreciated an extra 0.50 percent. So leaving out local variations, in an environment in which the U.S. economy is growing at 1 to 2 percent a year rather than 3 to 4 percent a year, all else being equal, U.S. real estate returns should be about 1 percent less per year.

As discussed above, commercial real estate tends to be even more sensitive to economic conditions, and it has in the past been subject to even more dramatic boom and bust cycles. There are several reasons for this. First, demand for office space is closely tied to the labor market: the more people working, the more office space you need. Second, commercial real estate developers rely on sales of completed projects to pay off existing development loans. As such, when developers are no longer able to sell properties, they are likely to default. Defaults add to the glut of commercial real estate, pushing supply up at a time when there is little demand. Finally and somewhat related, developers are very sensitive to not only the price of money but also its availability. Property developers need to constantly roll over or refinance their debts. When credit conditions tighten and loans become harder to get, the developers find it hard to refinance, and more of them default.[7]

Just as slower economic growth was bad for stocks, a slow growth economy will have a similarly negative impact on real estate. Slower growth in the economy translates into slower rental growth. As real estate is partially valued on the income it produces, less rental income means the property is worth less. Slower economic growth will further hurt real estate prices as demand tends to track overall economic activity. When economic growth is anemic, the market for everything from homes to office buildings slows as investors become more conservative. Real estate will suffer along with stocks and commodities from a slower economy.

How Real Estate Behaves: Interest Rates

The second long-term side effect of higher deficits is higher interest rates. Higher rates hurt every asset class, and real estate is no exception. Higher rates raise mortgages, thus hurting housing affordability. When rates are lower, individuals can afford larger homes, and they tend to bid up prices. As rates rise, first-time home buyers are priced out of the market, and those who are still able to afford to buy wind up settling for smaller homes. As a result, when rates are lower, home prices tend to be higher relative to what people earn. As rates rise, home prices decline in relation to income.

The same relationships hold for REITs. Rising interest rates hurt the underlying value of a REIT's property holdings. On top of this, there is a second mechanism by which higher rates hurt REITs. As discussed in Chapter 6, higher rates are particularly painful for stocks that are viewed as bond substitutes. Generally, these types of stocks have high dividend yields, and they include utilities and telecom stocks. This group also includes REITs. As with other high-dividend-yield stocks, such as utilities, REITs possess a high degree of sensitivity to interest rate fluctuations.[8]

Looking forward, the sensitivity of REITs to interest rates is likely to be even stronger than it was in the past. This is because over the next several years the underlying properties owned by many REITs will be under pressure to refinance their debt. This is particularly true of REITs that invest in commercial real estate. Roughly $500 billion of commercial real estate debt will be coming due every year for the next several years.[9] If REITs are forced to refinance their debt at higher interest rates, this will negatively impact the bottom line and detract from earnings.

Rising rates will hurt both physical real estate and REITs. Higher interest rates will further hamper housing affordability and demand. For commercial real estate, higher rates will raise the cost of financing property, which will in turn directly detract from earnings. Whether you're considering owning a property or investing in a REIT, higher rates will hurt real estate, particularly commercial real estate, along with stocks and bonds. And in the case of REITs, the impact is likely to be doubly painful as higher rates not only impact the underlying real estate holdings but also give income-oriented investors another reason to reconsider this asset class.

How Real Estate Behaves: Inflation

So far all the news for U.S. domestic real estate has been bad. Slower growth and higher rates will not result in an imminent rebound in real estate prices. What may eventually save real estate is a bit of inflation. For while higher rates and slower growth hurt real estate, inflation does not. Rising prices generally apply to physical assets, including real estate.

Over the long term, U.S. housing has kept up with inflation. Since 1957, housing has gained approximately 7.5 percent per year, while inflation has risen by less than 4 percent on average. And even when you focus on the more recent past, which includes the 2007 to 2009 collapse in the housing market, home prices have matched inflation. Since 1990, home prices have risen by approximately 75 percent, slightly ahead of the 70 percent increase in the CPI.

Now, while real estate has kept up with inflation over the long term, there have been a few notable exceptions. Figure 8.1 tracks the inflation-adjusted value of U.S. homes beginning in 1890. The values on the vertical axis illustrate how home prices compare, after adjusting for inflation, to their level in 1890. For example, a value of 150 indicates that real home prices are 50 percent higher than they were in 1890.

Figure 8.1 **Real U.S. Home Prices, 1890 to Present**

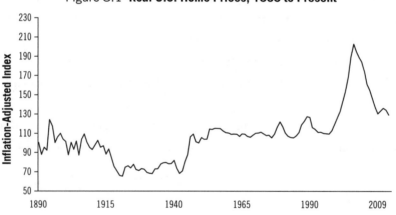

Source: Robert Shiller, Online Data, www.econ.yale.edu/~shiller/data.htm.

As Figure 8.1 illustrates, over the past 50 years, there have been three distinct periods when U.S. home prices failed to keep pace with rising prices (these periods would be indicated with a declining line). The first period was during the initial inflation spike in the early 1970s, when inflation went from 3 percent in 1972 to 12 percent by the end 1974.

The other two instances were less about housing keeping up with high inflation and more about a softening in nominal home prices. The first of these occurred after the savings and loan crisis in the early 1990s. In that instance the problem was not inflation but a weak national housing market. Home price appreciation decelerated from 9 percent a year in early 1989 to around 1 percent a year in 1991. The third instance is the period between 2007 and 2009. During this period, home prices fell on both a nominal and inflation-adjusted basis. This is the first time this has occurred in the post–World War II period.

These episodic issues, while relatively rare, illustrate a broader truth regarding the relationship between inflation and real estate. While home prices have kept up with real inflation over the long term, real home price appreciation has been inconsistent in the past. Between the 1950s and mid-1990s, real home prices were effectively stagnant. In other words, the value of your home generally held its own against inflation, but it did not provide any real or inflation-adjusted returns. Between the mid-1990s and the middle of the last decade, both nominal and inflation-adjusted prices surged. We are now in the process of reversing that surge. While home prices have done a good job of holding their value over the long term, measured in decades, they are a less consistent inflation hedge over the short to median term.

Figure 8.2 compares the annual change in the consumer price index, represented on the horizontal axis, with the annual change in home prices, represented on the vertical axis. As you can see, generally home prices rise more when inflation is higher. However, the relationship is somewhat loose. By way of comparison, while inflation explains roughly 30 percent of the annual variation in gold prices, it explains only about 15 percent of the annual variation in home prices. On an annual basis, the relationship between real estate prices and inflation, while positive, is relatively weak.

Figure 8.2 **U.S. Home Prices versus Inflation, 1890 to 2010**

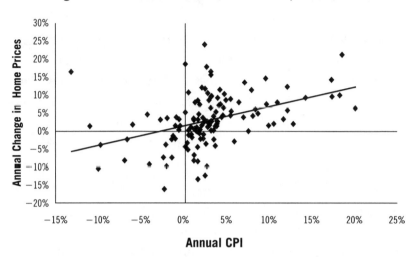

Source: Robert Shiller, Online Data, www.econ.yale.edu/~shiller/data.htm.

Why should houses be less responsive to inflation than gold? Hous-ing is a less effective hedge against inflation for the same reasons that copper and wheat are less effective: housing is good for something other than preserving purchasing power. Home prices are influenced by eco-nomic growth, interest rates, tax policy, and the availability of credit. All of those are only tangentially related to inflation. When it comes to infla-tion, housing does a decent job of tracking inflation over the long term, but on an annual basis, the relationship is weaker and less reliable than that between inflation and gold. Economic growth and changes in inter-est rates are likely to have a far larger impact on housing over the short term than changes in the CPI. When it comes to tracking inflation over the short term, gold is still the most effective hedge.

The shortcomings of real estate as an inflation hedge are even more pronounced for REITs. In fact, they are much worse. When it comes to inflation, REITs behave more like stocks than like physical assets. Histori-cally, REIT returns have actually been negatively correlated with sudden and unexpected spikes in inflation. REITs generally keep up, although they don't beat expected inflation. (In thinking about what rate of inflation is "expected," in the market, recall the discussion earlier in the book on the TIPS market. The breakeven inflation rate derived from TIPS is a good proxy for what the market thinks inflation will be in the future.) So if inflation matches the market's expectations, REITs will generally keep pace. Under this scenario REITs don't appear to be impacted by expected inflation, either positively or negatively.[10]

However, when inflation rises suddenly in a way that the market is not expecting, REITs not only fail to keep up but actually fall. An inflation spike hurts REITs just as it negatively impacts stocks. The overall results indicate that REITs do not represent an effective inflation hedge, and they may actually magnify losses during short-term spikes in inflation.

There are two related schools of thought on why REITs perform poorly as an inflation hedge. First is the hypothesis that the markets for REITs and equities are tightly integrated. The weak, and even negative, relationship between REITs and inflation may be the result of the equity component in REITs.[11] While REITs are backed by real estate, investors still think of them as more akin to stock. When the overall stock market sells off due to inflation concerns, investors don't discriminate between REITs and other publicly traded securities.

The second school of thought concerns the gap between REITs, which are, at the end of the day, companies, and the underlying real estate holdings. Just as many factors determine the performance of gold companies other than the price of gold, REITs can also trade away from the value of their underlying assets. Gold performs well as an inflation hedge, but gold stocks do not do as good a job.[12] In a similar vein, REITs may be one degree of separation too far removed from physical real estate to provide an effective hedge against inflation.

While the theory may be difficult to pin down, the empirical results are fairly clear. Real REIT returns are negatively correlated with inflation, and these results are very consistent over the long run.[13] Neither equity nor mortgage REITs are likely to offer a safe haven during inflationary periods that are not expected by investors.[14] If inflation picks up suddenly, REIT returns are unlikely to keep pace.

Where does all this leave investors? When thinking about inflation and real estate, follow a couple of guidelines. First, physical real estate does do a good job of hedging against inflation, but only over the long term. Over the short or intermediate term, housing does not necessarily track inflation. If you're looking at a time horizon of only a couple of years, stick with gold. And when it comes to REITs, while they may offer additional yield in your portfolio and provide some diversification, historically they have not proven to be an effective inflation hedge. While backed by real estate, they trade like stocks, and they often suffer along with stocks when inflation rises. Similar to the relationship between gold and gold stocks, if you're looking for an inflation hedge, you want the physical asset, not the security.

CONCLUSION

Most people have a preference for owning a home that supersedes any investment considerations. This is particularly true in the United States, where homeownership is a critical component of the national character. And at least in the past, this tendency has been rewarded. Historically, owning a home has not made you rich—although for those with good market timing, the last decade was an exception to that rule—but it has generally turned out to be a decent investment. Despite the real estate meltdown, over the long term, home prices have still kept up with inflation. When you factor in the advantages of leverage and the deductibility of interest for federal income tax purposes, homeownership has been and will likely continue to be a decent financial proposition.

Looking out over the next decade, nothing about the deficit should necessarily change this. Home prices are down considerably from their peak, and prices look reasonable, though not cheap, relative to income and rents. While a slower economy and the prospect for higher rates suggest that nominal gains in housing will be modest, first-time buyers are still getting in at a better point than they were just five years ago. While buying a home is unlikely to make you rich, this was never the reason people traditionally choose to own.

However, if you are looking to add to your real estate position for purely financial reasons, you should be cautious. The same headwinds that will impede U.S. equities will have a similar impact on U.S. real estate. Owning a house generally makes sense in most parts of the country—those who live in New York or San Francisco may want to reconsider—but you should moderate your expectations. The next decade will not resemble the last. Housing is reasonably priced, but it is not cheap, and there is little to suggest that home prices are about to take off the way they did in the last decade. Higher real interest rates and slower economic growth are not a winning recipe for home appreciation. Over the next decade, home prices are likely to keep up with inflation. However, this also implies that if inflation stays low for the next few years, as it is likely to do, don't expect much appreciation.

So what should you do? For the time being, if you already own a house, don't look to add to your real estate exposure. If you don't already own a house, there are obviously a number of considerations, both financial and nonfinancial, that you need to consider before you buy one. But keep in mind that price appreciation is likely to be slow. If you're buying a house based on the assumption that you'll enjoy big price appreciation, you may want to reconsider. For those who want to add to their real estate exposure without buying a house, follow the same advice given in Chapter 6. In that chapter you'll recall that international stocks are likely to outperform U.S. stocks over the next decade, particularly if those stocks are in emerging markets. In a similar vein, favor international rather than domestic REITs.

The time to more aggressively increase your real estate holdings is if and when inflation starts to stir. And even then, owning more real estate is likely to be an effective strategy only if you focus on the physical variety and plan to hold it for a long period of time. While real property is not as effective as gold at tracking inflation over the short term, it does a better job than most other asset classes over the longer term. Also, to the extent that you can use borrowed money to increase your exposure to real estate, you will be further improving your returns because the value of the money you have to use to pay back the loans will be less than the value of the money that you borrow. This suggests that buying a large home, a second home, or some commercial property is a good strategy in the event of higher inflation. Buying REITs is not.

CHAPTER 9

BUILDING PORTFOLIOS IN AN ERA OF FINANCIAL TURBULENCE

IN THE PREVIOUS five chapters, we have looked at each of the major asset classes one at a time. While this type of review is useful for organizing a book, it is not how people actually invest. You own a portfolio, not a stock, bond, or bar of gold.

Understanding how the deficit will affect stocks, bonds, and commodities is important, but at the end of the day what you really need to think about is how the deficit will impact your portfolio. When you open your brokerage statement every month, the first thing you look at is not how one particular security performed but whether your overall portfolio made or lost money, and how much. As we'll explore in this chapter, how your portfolio behaves is as much a function of how you combine the various assets as the individual assets themselves.

Many investors spend too much of their time considering a particular buy or sell decision—should I invest in this stock or sell that bond? While important in isolation, these decisions rarely have as large of an impact on your financial well-being as it may seem at the time. The major decisions that will impact your long-term performance generally revolve around what types of assets to own—stocks, bonds, cash, and commodities—

and in what proportions. This is known as *asset allocation*. Security selection—which particular stocks to own—has been shown to account for less than 5 percent of the overall performance of an investor's portfolio. In contrast, asset allocation has historically driven over 90 percent of performance.[1]

Over the next decade, asset allocation is likely to become even more critical. The buildup of debt in the United States and other developed economies has already caused significant economic turbulence. In a world in which economic and financial conditions—economic growth, interest rates, and inflation—are more volatile and uncertain, the choice of what kind of assets to own and in what quantities will be the primary driver of whether you make or lose money. When the overall economic environment is volatile, there tends to be a huge difference in returns between the different asset classes. Having the right proportions of stocks, bonds, and commodities is likely to have a much larger impact on your portfolio than buying one stock over another.

And while everyone will have to contend with the same financial conditions, you'll also need to consider your personal circumstances, and personality, when building a portfolio. Why you should own fewer bonds or more commodities than your neighbor is a function of several factors including wealth, risk tolerance, and the time horizon of the investment. But those individual differences notwithstanding, there are a few key principles everyone should embrace in building portfolios.

First, and the arguably the most important, spend more time thinking about what types of assets to own rather than which individual securities. In other words, place the emphasis on asset allocation rather than securities selection.

One way in which the macroeconomic environment can dramatically influence the returns on different asset classes is through inflation. We've spoken at length about inflation, which while not much of a risk over the next couple of years represents a long-term threat for investors. Even modest changes in the prevailing level of inflation can have an enormous impact on the performance of the different asset classes. Since 1950, U.S. inflation has averaged approximately 4 percent a year. In those years when inflation has been above average, U.S. stock returns net of dividends have averaged less than 2 percent a year. In contrast, in those years when inflation has been below average, stock returns have been approximately 15 percent a year. There is nearly a tenfold difference in U.S. equity market performance based simply on inflation! It is unlikely that your choice of an individual stock or mutual fund will have as large an influence on your portfolio as your choice of how much to put into stocks in the first place.

Second, when it comes to what you expect to make, consider how your investments do after accounting for inflation, or as economists like to say: think about the real, not the nominal, returns. It would be very nice to earn a steady 10 percent a year return in a year in which inflation is running at 2 percent. However, when inflation rises to 5 or 6 percent, the real, after-tax return from that nominal 10 percent return is close to zero. Money is only as good as what it will buy. By focusing on inflation-adjusted returns, you'll have a better chance of maintaining your purchasing power. When inflation rises, you'll want to have the majority of your investments in assets that will keep pace.

Finally, and this is probably the one principle most people tend to ignore, think about the potential risks of an investment, not just the return. Risk can be viewed in many ways, but one of the simplest is to think about it in terms of the range of returns you might receive on a given investment. In other words, assets that can move around a lot in a short period of time are inherently more risky. A stock that moves up or down by 10 percent a month is much more volatile than a bond that rarely moves more than 2 percent a month. If you're taking on additional risk in your portfolio, make sure you expect to earn a higher return. In investing, it costs you risk to get return. Taking on new risk, such as by adding emerging market stocks to your portfolio, makes sense if you expect to get a higher return on those stocks. It makes less sense if you believe that the return on emerging markets will be equal to those of the bond markets—why would you accept more risk for the same return?

Focusing on risk also means considering how the different parts of your portfolio move, not just in isolation but with respect to each other. Diversification does not just mean owning a mix of stocks, bonds, and commodities. Rather, and more importantly, it means owning assets that behave differently.

BUILDING PORTFOLIOS: BALANCING RISK AND REWARD

Before turning to the question of how to build portfolios in an environment defined by large, persistent deficits, it is worth thinking about how to build portfolios in the first place. Constructing a robust portfolio requires some estimate of both the returns and risks of the different components, as well as an understanding of your own circumstances—time horizon and risk appetite.

The reason portfolio construction is so critically important is that while your portfolio represents a collection of different types of assets, many of them will respond in the same way to certain financial conditions. For example, stocks and bonds will both lose value when inflation first starts to rise, while physical real estate and commodities will both perform well in that type of an environment. If you don't balance out the different types of assets, you'll be left with a portfolio that does spectacularly well in some years but is devastated in others, when economic conditions change. Given that even the most successful investors will be wrong a fair amount of the time, it is not a good practice for them to replicate the same bet in all parts of their portfolio. Very few investors are willing to tolerate that type of volatility.

To minimize the volatility, we talk about *building portfolios*. As the term implies, this is largely an engineering problem. It is a matter of balancing out two opposing forces: risk and return.

The first component in building a portfolio is to have some estimate of the return of an asset. To state the painfully obvious, the more money you expect to make and the greater the confidence you have that you will make it, the more you should invest. I would suggest that most individuals focus on *real returns*—what you are making after inflation. You want to maximize your purchasing power in real terms. This is particularly important if your own expenses tend to rise faster than the overall CPI. For example, if a large part of your disposable income goes to private school tuition or private health insurance, you can be fairly sure that your personal inflation rate is higher than the national average. Under these conditions, protecting your purchasing power is even more important because the things you spend the most money on are going up by 5 to 10 percent a year. It is important that your portfolio keeps up. If your expenses are less volatile and less subject to inflation, you may be more content with less risk and a lower rate of return.

That said, higher returns almost always entail higher risk. After returns, the second component that you need to think about is how much risk you take on when you buy a particular asset. As a general rule, the higher the risk, the higher the potential return. Investing in a small, start-up firm implies a much better chance of doubling your money in a few years than investing in a large, established multinational company. With a start-up, however, there is also a substantial chance that you could lose all your money. The spread between the potential outcomes—doubling your money versus losing your money—is one measure of the risk of the investment. In contrast to the start-up company, investing in the stock of a larger more established firm probably encompasses a smaller range of outcomes. IBM is more likely to return ±20 percent in a given year than produce returns of +100 percent to −100 percent. For an investment-grade corporate bond, the likely spread in returns for a given year is even smaller. If return is quantified as a potential outcome, think of risk as a range of outcomes: the broader the range, the higher the risk.

The relationship between risk and reward generally holds that there is no free lunch when it comes to investing. If you want to earn a higher return, you need to accept more risk. While this is true at the individual asset level, there is one important loophole when it comes to your portfolio. By assembling a basket of assets with a low correlation to each other, you can lower the risk of your portfolio while maintaining your returns In effect, you squeeze out more return for the risk you take. Diversification is best measured by the correlation between your assets. This is the third input into building a portfolio.

In order to achieve a reasonable amount of diversification in your portfolio, you need to assemble assets that behave differently. The assets in your portfolio should not all be going up or down together. In mathematical terms, this means that the correlation between the various assets in your portfolio should ideally be low, close to zero, or, even better, negative, meaning that one tends to go up while the other is falling.

To use an extreme example: A portfolio of energy stocks, bonds from energy companies, Canadian dollars, and oil futures is not diversified even though the portfolio contains a mix of stocks, bonds, cash, and commodities. All the assets are likely to rise when energy prices go up and fall when energy prices retreat. They will all do approximately the same thing at the same time, despite the fact that each of the investments belongs to a different asset class. For risk you need to consider not only the asset's volatility but also its correlation to the other parts of your portfolio. The more any one investment is correlated with other investments, the less you should own.

By assembling a broad, diversified set of assets, you accomplish two things. First, you help insulate your portfolio against the shock of a particular macroeconomic event: rising rates or a spike in unemployment.

The other advantage of diversification is that it removes the idiosyncratic risk around any single investment.

Stocks, bonds, or even commodities can move up or down by a significant amount based on news that is specific to that one asset. In the case of a stock, it may be a management change or an unsuccessful drug test for a pharmaceutical company. In the instance of commodity, a significant increase in supply—say, a bumper wheat harvest—may cause the price to crash. By owning lots of different types of assets, you lower the impact on your portfolio of a specific event or bit of bad luck. Unless you have some very good information about why a particular stock or bond is likely to do well, you're generally better off owning a broad, diversified basket of assets.

Finally, when thinking about diversification, try to include all your assets, not just the ones you typically think of as part of your portfolio. This means including your house, a small business, land, or anything else of value that you own. The reason is that often these assets will make up a significant portion of your net worth. In addition, they often tend to be *pro-cyclical*—they do better when the economy is strong. If your portfolio is full of cyclical stocks like industrials and mining companies at the same time that your home equity represents the majority of your net worth, you have in effect taken a big bet on a strong economy. In a recession, you will see a bigger decline in your net worth than if you had balanced out your home position with more defensive stocks or bonds. Diversification requires thinking of all your assets at the same time and having a general understanding of how they all respond to changing conditions such as a recession, rising interest rates, or an unexpected spike in inflation.

So far, we've spoken about building a portfolio in terms of the inputs: after-inflation returns, the volatility of an asset, and its correlation to other assets. The rules of thumb are fairly straightforward:

1. The higher the expected return, the more you should own.

2.   Favor higher returns with less risk. Even if the expected return is high, if you need to take on a lot of risk to own that asset, dial back on your bet.

3.   If two assets in your portfolio tend to do the same thing under the same economic conditions—both go down when inflation goes up—own a little less of each. You're effectively taking the same bet twice.

All of these rules apply regardless of individual circumstances. But as everyone has different investment needs and considerations, you also need to adjust your portfolio for your personal circumstances. When assembling a portfolio, there are two other and somewhat related factors to consider: *risk aversion* (or *risk tolerance*) and *time horizon*. Think of these two as constraints.

The best theoretical (no one actually knows the best portfolio because the future is always uncertain) portfolio given a set of economic assumptions might be to own 50 percent stocks, 30 percent commodities, 15 percent real estate, and 5 percent cash. However, while that portfolio may be optimal over the next decade, it is going to be very volatile on a year-to-year basis. Most of the portfolio is made up of inherently volatile assets. On top of that, they all tend to do best when the economy is strong. This means that while the portfolio might produce the highest return over a 10-year period, you will likely lose a lot of money in those years when the United States is in recession.

For many individuals, having a good night's sleep and not worrying about a 25 percent drop in their net worth is more important than earning a marginal $50,000 over a decade's time. This is what I mean by a *constraint*. Even if it is the best portfolio, your personal circumstances constrain you from investing in it. *Risk tolerance* comes down to how much volatility you can stand. This has nothing to do with financial theory or investment skill. It is simply a function of different personalities.

Some people are more comfortable with risk than others. One simple way to think about this is the following: How much money are you prepared to lose in a given year?

A second and related issue that everyone needs to consider is this: Over what *time horizon* will you need the money? Different assets have different liquidity profiles. In other words, how quickly can you convert the assets to cash, and what price will you get when you liquidate them?

Consider the decision of whether to buy a stock index fund during a market meltdown. From a long-term perspective, that might be an excellent time to buy stocks, as you'll be getting them at a discount to their typical valuations. However, if the market is in the midst of a collapse, it is highly unlikely that you'll be able to pick the exact bottom. While you may be thankful that you bought in 10 years' time, your fund is likely to go down, potentially significantly, before it begins to rebound. That may be fine if the money in the fund won't be needed for a decade's time, but it may be problematic if the money is going toward the down payment on a house you're closing on next month.

A second way to think about the importance of time in investing is to consider the odds of a loss over different investment horizons. Let's say that over the long term, the average annual stock market return is around 9 percent. While that may be true over a 20- or 30-year investment horizon, the odds of your getting exactly 9 percent in any given year are low. As you lengthen your holding period, the odds of hitting the average return go up. This is similar to flipping a coin. While you're likely to get a 50/50 split of heads and tails over hundreds of tosses, it is not uncommon to get two or three heads in a row. In a similar fashion, over a short-term horizon, even an asset that normally produces 9 percent returns will have some truly horrific years. If one of those unusual but not totally unexpected down years happens when you need your cash, you'll have to sell your investments at an inopportune time.

If you are investing money that you will need in one or two years' time, the fact that you might garner those returns over the long term will probably be of little comfort. What you care about is, will the money be there in 6, 12, or 18 months when you need it? So if a pool of money is one you'll need to access in under a year's time, you'll want to keep most of it in instruments that are likely to hold their value over the near term—money markets, certificates of deposit, short-term bond funds. As your need for near-term liquidity diminishes, for example, if you are young and considering your retirement savings, you can afford to take more risk.

What to Expect: Asset Assumptions to Build Your Portfolio

In building your own portfolio, you'll need to start with reasonable return assumptions for each of the different parts. In this section, we'll recap and outline what to expect for each of the major asset classes in the years ahead. To do so, it is useful to start with how the various asset classes have done over the long term and then adjust those estimates for how the deficit, as well as other factors like valuation, is likely to impact how stocks, bonds, and commodities perform over the next decade.

While it is difficult to have an accurate estimate of how a particular bond or stock will do over a given year, it is somewhat easier to generate an estimate for a broad asset class, like stocks, over a long period of time. While the performance of stocks, bonds, or commodities can differ considerably from year to year, long-term averages have historically been more stable. And to the extent that you have some visibility on the economic environment, something that has hopefully been provided in this book, you can formulate an even better estimate of what stocks, bonds, cash, or commodities are likely to return.

Consistent with the notion that riskier assets typically produce higher returns, over the long term, stocks outperform bonds by a substantial amount, particularly when you take inflation into account. In the past, stocks have returned roughly 5 to 6 percent a year after inflation. In contrast, long-term government bonds have typically produced half the real return: around 2 to 3 percent a year. Of course, the price for better performance is more volatility over the short run.

In keeping with the same principle—lower returns with less risk—cash typically produces the lowest returns, both nominal and inflation adjusted. Cash carries no risk, is completely liquid, and even does a reasonable job of keeping up with inflation over the long term. However, in return for having immediate access to your money, banks are able to pay a low rate of return. Because cash carries few risks—other than a bank failure, and even then the Federal Deposit Insurance Corporation (FDIC) will cover all but the largest accounts—it offers the lowest inflation-adjusted returns. Historically, cash has produced returns close to or slightly above the rate of inflation.

What about the other asset classes? Looking back over the past 40 years, high-yield bonds produce real returns that are very similar to those of stocks—roughly 5 to 6 percent a year. The return profile also looks similar for real estate and commodities. Broadly speaking, over the long term, risky assets have typically produced returns of roughly 5 to 6 percent above the rate of inflation, safer bonds produce real returns of roughly 2 to 3 percent above the rate of inflation, and cash has historically beaten inflation by just about 1 percent a year.[2]

Now, while stocks have produced real returns of 5 to 6 percent over the long term, for those whose time frame is not measured in decades, it is worth remembering that returns are significantly impacted when you buy an asset. As the stock boom in the late 1990s illustrated: A company may have fantastic prospects, but if the price of its stock is too high relative to what it is likely to earn, the stock may still be a terrible investment. The same is true for the other financial markets as well. Virtually all market crashes are preceded by sky-high valuations. Markets crash when everyone is the most bullish and willing to pay exorbitant prices to own an asset, regardless of its relative value. On the other side, the best time to buy stocks, or any asset classes, is often when sentiment is most negative, for that is when the asset will be the cheapest and any good news will help lift prices.

You don't even need wildly undervalued or overvalued markets to impact performance. Even a modest deviation from fair value can impact the long-term return profile of an asset class. For example, since 1954, the S&P 500 Index has had an average price-to-earnings ratio of approximately 16.5. In other words, the S&P 500 usually trades at 16.5 times the aggregate earnings for that index over the previous year. Historically, whether you invested when the market was above or below its long-term average has had an enormous impact on your returns over the following 12 months. In those years when the S&P 500 started the year with a P/E ratio above its long-term valuation, the index advanced 5.4 percent on average over the following year. If the index started the year with a P/E ratio that was below average, the average annual gain, without dividends, was 10.8 percent. Put differently, if you only bought U.S. stocks in those years when their valuations were below average, you doubled your return compared to years when valuations were above average.

The lesson here is to incorporate an asset class's valuation into your mental calculus on how much to invest. For stock markets, the price-to-earnings ratio is a good proxy for relative value. For bonds, look at the real interest rate, nominal rate minus inflation, for Treasuries. Historically, that rate has been around 2.5 percent. When the rate is significantly below that level, it raises the risk that bonds are overvalued. When the spread is much wider, as it was in the early 1980s, bonds are arguably undervalued. For real estate, the best metric is normally the rental yield of a property: How expensive is the house relative to the rent you would have to pay on it? In the past, a multiple of 15 has been a good, rough proxy of fair value in the housing market. If your home is costing you significantly more than 15 times the annual rent, you're probably buying at an inopportune time.

Unfortunately, there is no simple rule of thumb for commodities. Commodities don't produce income the way that stocks, bonds, and real estate produce income, so it is impossible to evaluate the cost of a commodity against the income stream that it produces. As a result, it is hard to know when commodities are over- or undervalued.

How do today's valuations stack up against the long-term averages? For stocks, U.S. stocks are close to their long-term average valuations, suggesting that while the deficit may be a drag on returns, valuations probably won't be. However, for bonds, be cautious. Not only will the deficit produce a headwind for bonds, but also right now the U.S. Treasuries' real yields are well below their long-term average. In addition to all of the other headwinds facing the government bond market, right now Treasuries look particularly overvalued.

THE DEFICIT AND RETURN ASSUMPTIONS: INTEREST RATES, GROWTH, AND INFLATION

In addition to long-term averages and valuations, investors should also consider the environment in which they are investing. In the 1980s and 1990s, we benefited from a macroeconomic landscape in which most things were getting better. Interest rates and inflation were falling, and growth was by and large consistently strong, with fewer and more shallow recessions. As outlined in the first two chapters, the federal deficit will unfortunately lead to an environment in which rates are rising, growth is slower, and inflation becomes more of a risk. This means that the returns from both bonds and domestic stocks are likely to be lower than their long-term averages.

The impact of rising real interest rates on the various asset classes is almost exclusively negative. Rising rates hurt bonds, as described in Chapter 5: the longer the duration of the bond, the worse the hit. Higher interest rates will also negatively impact stock returns, even if overall earnings are rising, as higher rates are likely to lead to lower valuations. Rising interest rates also hurt commodities, as higher rates slow the economy and lower the demand for more cyclical commodities. Higher interest rates even hurt gold. If interest rates are higher, the opportunity cost of holding gold—which produces no income—goes up. Cash is about the only asset class that benefits from rising interest rates. So a simple rule of thumb is to assume modestly lower returns than the long-term averages due to rising real interest rates.

When it comes to economic growth, a slower economy will hurt stocks, high-yield bonds, and real estate, as well as commodities.

While stocks produce average annual returns of around 5 to 6 percent a year over the long run, in years in which the economy is weak, inflation-adjusted returns are negative on average. Since 1970 weak economic growth has lead to real negative returns of around −0.70 percent a month, or −8.5 percent a year, for domestic stocks and −0.94 percent a month, or around −12 percent a year for international stocks. However, in periods when the economy is strong, real returns have averaged around 12 percent a year.[3]

Commodities and real estate respond in a similar fashion. Commodities lose an average of around 10 percent a year after inflation when the economy is weak and gain more than 12 percent a year above inflation when economic conditions are strong. The impact on real estate is slightly more muted but follows a similar pattern. Real estate returns, adjusted for inflation, are effectively zero when the economy is weak, and around 9 percent a year above inflation during periods of strong growth.[4]

For bonds, the impact of economic growth is much less pronounced. Treasury bonds and notes pay the same in good and bad times, as even during recessions investors assume the government will meet its obligations. As a result, over the past 40 years, annual real returns for government bonds have averaged around 3 percent, regardless of the economic environment.[5]

Among all the different types of bonds, not surprisingly high-yield bonds are the most sensitive to economic growth. Recall that high-yield bonds are issued by smaller, more speculative companies or by companies that are already carrying high debt loads. As a result, companies issuing high-yield debt bonds are rarely as stable as larger, more established firms issuing investment-grade bonds (this is why high-yield bonds pay more—because they are inherently riskier). Returns to high-yield bonds have been great when times are good, nearly 10 percent a year after inflation, but when the economy is struggling, the returns become negative.[6] One way to think about high-yield bonds is that even though they are technically bonds, when it comes to risk and their sensitivity to the economy, they behave more like stocks.

Interestingly, the asset class that has arguably done the best when the economy is weak is TIPS. Recall from Chapter 5 that TIPS are inflation-protected U.S. Treasuries. What differentiates TIPS from normal bonds is that the principal of the bond resets as inflation rises, making TIPS and other inflation-linked bonds more resilient to inflation. Historically, TIPS have returned around 4 to 5 percent after inflation, slightly better than nominal bonds but less than stocks and commodities. But during periods when the economy has been weak, TIPS' real returns have been particularly strong.[7] One word of caution before loading up on TIPS ahead of the next recession: While TIPS' returns have historically been strong during periods of economic weakness, because TIPS have not been around as long as other asset classes, these estimates may not be as reliable as estimates for stocks, bonds, and commodities, for which we have more data.

What about the other potential side effect of deficits: inflation? While not a near-term threat, investors with a 5- to 10-year horizon need to be concerned about the risk of higher inflation. Given the current trajectory of the deficit and the Fed's persistence in buying government bonds, the risk of inflation is likely to rise over time. And even in the absence of intentional inflation, you'll recall that higher government spending by itself will add to inflationary pressures.

When and if inflation starts to rise, how will different asset classes perform? As it turns out, inflation negatively impacts the returns of most asset classes, with the noticeable exception of commodities, which perform best when inflation is high and economic growth is strong. Even within the commodity class, some commodities are likely to struggle with inflation. Since World War II about the only commodity that has demonstrated a consistently positive relationship with inflation, regardless of the level of economic growth, is gold.[8]

With the exception of TIPS, all types of bonds do worse when inflation is high. For Treasuries, real returns are approximately 5 percent a year when inflation is low and −5 percent a year when inflation is high. For corporate bonds, the difference is even starker. Low inflation has historically lead to average annual real returns of around 7 percent a year, while periods of high inflation have witnessed annual losses of greater than 10 percent in inflation-adjusted terms.[9]

Even more than bonds, equity returns are subject to the prevailing rate of inflation. For U.S. stocks, real returns during low inflationary periods have averaged nearly 12 percent a year. Those returns fall to around 3 to 4 percent with medium inflation. In years when inflation is high, annual real returns for U.S. equities fall to around −7 to −8 percent a year. For international stocks, the pattern is very similar, although not surprisingly, they don't benefit quite as much when U.S. inflation is low.[10]

In this respect, commodities differ from stocks. While the stock market wants to see high growth and low inflation, commodity investors not only want growth but inflation on top of it. Commodities do best when the purchasing power of the dollar is falling and inflation is rising. When high growth is paired with high inflation, commodities outperform all other asset classes.[11]

While commodities do well in the near to intermediate term when inflation rises, there can be too much of a good thing. Eventually, persistently high inflation will hurt even commodity prices, or at least those commodities that are influenced by economic conditions. The reason for this is the Fed. If in an effort to prevent any further increases in inflation the Federal Reserve starts to raise interest rates, the increase in interest rates will eventually hurt even commodities. Higher real rates are a signal to the market that the Fed is trying to cool down the economy, which will eventually mean lower demand for more cyclical commodities, like copper and oil.[12] In anticipation of more sluggish demand, investors are likely to sell more cyclical commodities, explaining why higher inflation does not always provide the same benefit for the broader commodity complex as it does for precious metals, and especially gold.[13]

As you'll recall from the last chapter, the impact of inflation on real estate depends on what you actually own. Inflation will hurt REITs, which tend to trade like equities. Like stocks, REITs do best when inflation is low. Under a low inflation regime, REITs return over 12 percent a year in inflation-adjusted returns. Even with a little bit of inflation, returns drop sharply. In a medium inflation environment, REITs go from producing real returns of 12 percent a year to barely 1 percent a year. And when inflation is high, REIT returns go sharply into reverse. In a high inflation environment, REITs have lost around 11 percent a year after inflation.[14] Physical real estate does not necessarily follow the same pattern. The lesson is that, if you expect inflation, own bricks-and-mortar real estate, not REITs.

The real returns to cash also tend to decline in the immediate aftermath of a spike in inflation.[15] The good news on cash is that cash instruments such as money markets and short-term certificates of deposit do eventually catch up with inflation. Cash returns do increase in response to an inflation shock, but the response is very gradual and less than full. Over time, cash begins to recover on an inflation-adjusted basis, but this process plays out over a very long period.[16]

So putting this all together, what assumptions should you make for the different asset classes? In the near term, and in the absence of inflation, assume that U.S. bond returns are below average. In the case of Treasuries, this is due to overvaluation and the prospect of deficits pushing real rates higher. For corporate bonds it is more of a function of slower growth. If the past is any guide, the one exception to this rule is likely to be TIPS, which have historically done well in a low growth environment.

Equity returns, at least in the United States, should also be lower due to slower growth and rising rates. International equities are likely to do better. Slower growth will also hurt commodities, at least until we witness some uptick in inflation.

If and when inflation starts to rise, bonds get hurt even more, as will stocks and REITs initially. For longer-term portfolios, stocks eventually recover, and over a long period they tend to keep up with inflation. Commodities are the big beneficiary of an initial spike in inflation, with gold and precious metals getting the biggest boost.

As Volatility Rises, Diversification Becomes Harder

Even the most successful investor does not have a crystal ball. Return estimates are just that: estimates. Even when you're right about the direction of an asset, the magnitude of the returns can differ substantially from what you expect. In addition to the uncertainty of how a single asset will behave, there is the issue of understanding how the assets interrelate.

In the previous section we focused on what to expect for returns. But, as described above, returns are only half the equation. You need to also consider risk, which has two components: the volatility of the asset and the way it moves in relation to other assets.

Starting with volatility, commodities and stocks are generally more volatile than bonds, with the exception of high-yield bonds. Since 1970, stocks have been roughly 50 percent more volatile than 10-year Treasuries, while Treasury bills—that is, short-term instruments with maturities of a year or less—have had less than one-fourth the volatility of the 10-year Treasuries.[17]

The other part of evaluating risk is more difficult. Part of risk management is to understand the volatility of the assets you own. The other part is to understand how those assets interrelate. The reason the second is more difficult than the first is that the volatility of assets tends to be more stable than their correlation to each other. Most years, stocks and commodities will be more volatile than bonds. It would be a rare year for the bond market to experience wild gyrations and for the stock market to remain placid. Yet it is not at all unusual for the correlations, or co-movements, between different asset classes to change over time. In fact, it is normal for this to occur. This means that when looking for diversification and trying to build a portfolio of relatively uncorrelated assets, you need to be aware of the environment.

Just as the deficit impacts the return assumptions for different assets, it will also impact how those assets relate to each other. The growing overhang of the U.S. national debt, and the question of who will fund it, will create a more volatile economic environment. As the economy becomes more volatile, investors tend to swing from periods of abject pessimism to wild optimism. This type of market has the effect of driving correlations higher, which means it becomes more difficult to achieve diversification.

We've already had a little taste of this in 2008 and 2009. In 2008, as investors feared a global depression, they sold all risky assets—stocks, high-yield bonds, real estate, and commodities. In 2009, as optimism took hold and investors began to believe that the worst had past, they rushed to buy back all those risky assets they had dumped the year before. As a result, over the last several years a relatively diverse mix of assets—from emerging markets stocks to high-yield bonds—have been moving in tandem to a far greater extent then they typically do.

In dealing with this increase in correlation, I would again look to commodities to provide some diversification in your portfolio. While commodity returns are likely to be muted until inflation picks up, they still provide the benefit of diversification. While the correlation between stocks and commodities has risen since the financial crisis, it will probably stay low enough so that commodities still offer some necessary diversification for your portfolio. This is likely to be particularly true when inflation rises above its current low levels. Recall that stocks do best when there is low inflation and a strong economy, while commodities do best when both are high. Rising inflation will create a divergence between stocks and commodities. To the extent that you want different parts of your portfolio responding differently to varying conditions, commodities will help diversify your stock and bond holdings, specifically when it comes to inflation.

In particular, precious metals still tend to march to their own drummer. This is borne out by the last 40 years of experience. While precious metals were by no means the best-performing asset class, they were arguably the most interesting. Since the early 1970s, a portfolio of precious metals—silver, gold, and platinum—performed best during periods of high inflation. In those years when inflation was highest, precious metals had the highest compounded annual return of 20 percent.[18]

Further supporting the argument for diversification, precious metals not only did well when inflation was high but they consistently defied what the other asset classes were doing. Of the 33 years of data, there were 9 years that U.S. large-cap stocks had negative returns. During these 9 years, precious metals had the highest returns. Put differently, precious metals provided positive returns when they were most needed.[19]

PORTFOLIOS FOR THE NEXT DECADE

So given all of the above—return, risk, and correlations—what is the bottom line? What should your portfolio look like? In this section I'll describe a few different portfolios for the economic assumptions described above. The portfolios will be for both a conservative and a more aggressive investor, with both a short and long time horizon.

In most cases, the portfolios will look very different from the typical blend of 60 percent stocks, 30 percent bonds, 10 percent cash that is the default setting for many asset allocation strategies. As a general rule, assuming a world of slower economic growth, at least in the United States, higher interest rates, and at least over the long term a heightened risk of inflation, you'll want to lower your bonds, modestly lower your equities (at least the domestic variety), and increase your commodities and/or physical real estate exposure.

Start with your short-term money. Here, it doesn't make much difference if you're a conservative or aggressive investor. If you're going to need to liquidate the funds in under a year or two, most investors should have a similar portfolio, one dominated by short-term, liquid instruments. A short time horizon necessitates risk aversion.

For short-term funds your money should be mostly invested in cash (around 85 percent). The remaining percentage should be composed of a mix of inflation-linked bonds (around 10 percent) and a small portion of stocks and commodities. As the investment horizon begins to lengthen beyond a couple of years, you'll want to slowly start to increase your allocation to inflation-linked bonds, equities, and commodities, as well as real estate.[20]

How should the above portfolio change as your time horizon and willingness to tolerate risk increase? As a general rule, you'll want to raise the portion of your portfolio in riskier assets. Practically, this means increasing the allocation to equities and commodities at the expense of cash and bonds as your time horizon and/or risk tolerance increase. Within equities, favor international over domestic, and as described in Chapter 7, keep about half of your commodities exposure in precious metals, preferably gold.

Here is a basic portfolio for an average investor. The portfolio assumes that the leading indicators of inflation, described in Chapter 3—payroll growth, capacity utilization, and growth in the money supply—are still signaling little near-term risk of inflation. The portfolio also assumes a slow growth environment and slowly rising interest rates: bonds, 20 percent; stocks, 45 percent; TIPS or inflation-linked bonds, 10 percent; commodities, 10 percent; and cash, 15 percent.

As signs of inflation begin to pick up, you'll want to decrease your allocation to bonds and increase your allocation to commodities, with around half of the commodity allocation in gold. Under this scenario, the portfolio should look more like this: bonds, 15 percent; stocks, 40 percent; TIPS, 10 percent; commodities, 25 percent; and cash, 10 percent. Under this scenario, investors can also substitute physical real estate for some of their commodities position.

To the extent that an investor is particularly risk averse, he or she can substitute more cash and TIPS for commodities. While neither asset class does quite as good a job as commodities in protecting against inflation, both are much less volatile while still affording some protection against rising inflation.

For an investor with a long horizon and a more aggressive streak, the portion of risky assets in the portfolio should rise dramatically. These investors should hold the majority of their assets in equities and commodities, with the remaining portion in inflation-linked bonds. They should be looking to have roughly 50 to 60 percent of their long-term money in equities, with another 25 to 30 percent in commodities, and the remainder in TIPS or other inflation-linked bonds.[21]

And at the risk of being repetitive, keep a good portion of your commodity portfolio in precious metals. When you look at the historical data, the lesson is very clear. Precious metals can modestly improve the efficiency of your portfolio; that is, they provide better inflation-adjusted returns with less risk.[22]

KNOW YOUR TOLERANCE FOR RISK

It would seem that investment plans should be fairly consistent for people of similar circumstances. Assuming two individuals of similar age and wealth, why would you offer differing recommendations? The simple answer is that while investors all want the same thing, high returns, their willingness to pay for them differs. To get returns, you need to accept risk. This is the one immutable law of finance, and it is the one that most investors, both individuals and professionals, have the most trouble accepting. It is for this reason that investment plans need to be custom-made. While we all live through the same markets, everyone experiences them differently. Some individuals are content to ignore major swings in their net worth in the belief that everything will work out in the end, while others will sweat every brokerage statement. In implementing the advice in this book, it is important to know where you fall in that spectrum.

The recommendations above should be adjusted to fit you. Start with how aggressive you want to be. This will be a function of both personality and also of time horizon. The older you are and the closer you are to retirement, the more conservative your portfolio should look. If you have significant excess savings and the extra money is meant for an intergenerational bequest, you can also afford to be more aggressive. However, again, distinguish between the money you'll need and the money your heirs will need. Even for younger investors, differentiate between those funds you're investing in for your retirement and those you'll need for next year's tuition payments. The simple rule is this: the longer the horizon, the more aggressive you should be.

Once you've put yourself on the financial couch, consider your investment objectives. Try to maximize your long-term purchasing power. That is why I've emphasized real returns throughout this chapter. Next, you'll need to have some feeling for both return and risk for the different asset classes. In estimating return, use the following rules of thumb. First, riskier assets tend to produce higher returns over the long term, although at the cost of many a sleepless night. Second, consider the economic environment. Finally, consider the value. Investors often have a bad habit of buying assets at the top, after they have already risen. Think of a stock or bond in the same terms as any other purchase: look for the bargain. The cheaper the asset, the higher the long-term return is likely to be.

In terms of risk, just as you have some feeling for how well an asset is likely to do, have a similar mental estimate of the asset's risk. Also, have some rough idea of how the assets in your portfolio are likely to relate to each other. If you have two investments that do the same thing at the same time, own a little less of each. If there is only one takeaway you get from this chapter, it would be the following: never think about returns without also considering risk.

CHAPTER 10

IS IT TOO LATE?

L OOKING BACK, the financial crisis of 1998 appears small and almost quaint when compared to the far scarier events that unfolded a decade later. But at the time, investors were terrified. They feared that financial markets were on the verge of collapse and another Great Depression was about to unfold. That autumn, Long-Term Capital Management (LTCM), a particularly large and influential hedge fund, was in a death spiral, and only at what appeared to be the last minute did the New York Federal Reserve manage to pull together a rescue package.

What was so unsettling about the event was not that the Fed thought LTCM crucial enough to warrant a rescue but that this particular fund would need to be rescued in the first place. LTCM truly represented the best and brightest in the industry. The firm included a former head of Solomon Brothers famed bond trading desk, a couple of Nobel laureates, and a particularly impressive assortment of financial overachievers.

LTCM began trading in early 1994 and minted money during its first several years of operations. Then things started to go horribly wrong. The fund began to lose money quickly, and instead of revisiting their models and approach, the fund's traders doubled down. In other words, rather than assuming that they might be wrong, they assumed that the market was wrong. And while some of their bets would have ultimately proven profitable, they ran out of money before they could claim their winnings. As the economist John Maynard Keynes famously remarked,

"The market can remain irrational longer than you can remain solvent." LTCM forgot that.

Roger Lowenstein's bestselling book *When Genius Failed* detailed the failure of LTCM and illustrated a critical truth that all investors—both professionals and individuals—must never forget: overconfidence is death. It is not always the smartest investor that does the best, because often the most talented are the most arrogant. In order to prosper, even to survive, investors must always ask themselves one question whenever they commit money: What will I do if I'm wrong?

So now, I am going to address that question here. I have spent nine chapters painting a picture of how continuing, huge federal deficits will impact your finances and telling you what you should do about it. But what if my critical assumption is wrong? What if Washington does start to tackle our fiscal problems in a responsible way, and the deficits don't continue to balloon? As bad as the deficit and national debt are, with sufficient political will, the problem could, at least in theory, be addressed and resolved. And while this looks unlikely right now, so did the demise of LTCM in 1997.

There is historical precedent. In the past, other countries have managed to tame seemingly intractable deficits. So let's look at how they did it and at what commonalities suggest a way out for the United States. Then I'll describe what real deficit reduction in the United States would look like and how it would manifest itself in the economy. How large will the budget cuts need to be, and what form should they take in order to truly put the country back on a solid financial foundation?

Finally, I'll get to what the payoffs are and how you should change your investment approach if Washington really does get serious about fiscal reform. Real and long-term deficit reduction will lead to faster growth, lower bond yields, stronger equity markets, and arguably a lesser risk of long-term inflation. In short, many of the investment choices suggested in the previous chapters will have to be revised.

Deficit Reduction: How to Step Back from the Abyss

As dire as the U.S. fiscal situation is, there are recent examples of countries that were in a similar bind and that still somehow managed to enact meaningful and long-lasting reform. As I mentioned in the opening of this book, deficit spending is as much a political problem as an economic one. With sufficient political will, countries in the past have addressed deficits and national debts of similar magnitudes and succeeded in bringing spending back in line with revenue. But in most of the instances, a crisis was a necessary prerequisite for real reform. This suggests that even if we are ultimately able to tackle our own imbalances, things are likely to get worse before they get better.

While there are a number of examples of countries that have enacted meaningful deficit spending reform, three cases in particular are worth highlighting: Ireland, Sweden, and Canada. There are several reasons to focus on these three. First, all occurred in the recent past, meaning that they had to enact their reforms in the context of modern financial markets, rather than in the distant past when the world's economy and financial markets looked very different. Second, while all arrived at their respective financial crisis via different paths, the solutions were remarkably similar. This suggests a way out for the United States should we ever decide to take it.

Let's start with Ireland. Given Ireland's current financial travails, the country seems like a strange example of financial responsibility. The truth is Ireland's current crisis is mostly due to the government's desperate effort to bail out the banking system rather than a result of state overspending. In the decade preceding the financial crisis, Ireland was considered a financial miracle and posted the fastest growing economy in Western Europe. It achieved that growth in no small part due to its late 1980s fiscal reforms.

Before Ireland's financial miracle earned it the nickname the "Celtic Tiger," it was a fiscal basket case. Between 1980 and 1987, government debt as a share of GDP rose from 75 to 123 percent, economic growth averaged just 1.5 percent a year, and unemployment rose from 7 to 17 percent. Ireland tried to address its growing fiscal imbalances through a number of unsuccessful attempts in the early and mid-1980s. Most of these attempts involved tax increases to bring the debt under control.[1] None of these plans were successful. Things kept getting worse.

Then, between 1987 and 1989 a new government put a more successful plan in place. The new approach followed a general election in which the previous coalition government was replaced—a theme we'll see repeated in each of the three examples. While the new incoming government did not have a working majority, a number of factors forced its hand and led to real fiscal reform. First, the government's ability to raise new financing was threatened by a loss of market confidence. The debt had become so high and the deficits so large that the country was losing its ability to finance its debt through new bond issuance. It also became evident that taxes were already so high that the economy could not tolerate further tax increases.[2]

Ireland solved its budget dilemma through across-the-board cuts to government expenditures. These cuts were implemented throughout all government departments, but the cuts were particularly large in health care, social security benefits, and state pensions. Education was the only major area of public expenditure that was "ring fenced." Ultimately, the Irish government slashed its payroll by 1.5 percent of GDP. The cuts resulted in a 7 percent reduction in public sector employment between 1986 and 1989.[3]

Following these changes, there was a dramatic improvement in the government's finances. The budget deficit was reduced from 10.6 percent of GDP in 1986 to 2.6 percent in 1989. Debt fell from 122 percent of GDP to 93 percent. The drop in debt coincided with a surge in growth, with the annual GDP growth averaging 5.5 percent in the subsequent years. This period marked the start of Ireland's Celtic Tiger period.[4]

A more recent example of deficit reduction occurred in Sweden during the mid-1990s. As in the United States, the problem in Sweden began with the bursting of a real estate bubble, in 1989 and 1990, which in turn caused a banking crisis. Again, in a similar dynamic to the one the United States is now facing, the efforts to clean up the aftermath of the banking crisis caused an explosion in the deficit and national debt. By 1993, Sweden was running a deficit of over 11 percent of GDP.[5]

Similar to Ireland, Sweden's fiscal reform was preceded by a change of government and trouble in its bond market. In the months preceding the election, Swedish bond yields surged relative to Germany's—German government bonds are generally considered the safest in Europe— suggesting a loss of confidence in Sweden's fiscal health.

Once in power the new government cut total public expenditures as a proportion of GDP by 16 percentage points from their peak in 1993. Roughly half of this adjustment came from reducing state benefits and sharply tightening eligibility requirements. The other half of the spending reductions came from reducing government consumption. This worked brilliantly. The budget went from a deficit of 11.2 percent of GDP in 1993 to a surplus of 1.2 percent in 1998, while GDP growth averaged a healthy 3.5 percent a year during this adjustment.[6] Again, once the drag of the deficit was removed, economic growth rebounded smartly.

The final recent example is Canada. Canadian budget difficulties began in the late 1980s, the result of a steady increase in unfunded government expenditures (sound familiar?). The budget deficit rose from 4.6 percent of GDP in 1989 to 9.1 percent in 1992. In common with Ireland, there were a number of unsuccessful attempts to bring the deficit under control by increasing tax revenues.[7]

Once again, the successful fix followed a change in government. The Canadian Liberal Party won a strong majority in the federal election of

1993. The Liberal Party defeated the Conservative Party on an explicit platform of addressing Canada's fiscal issues, and it actually provided a surprising degree of detail on how it would implement these changes. In the four years from 1993 to 1997, the budget swung from a deficit of 8.7 percent of GDP to a surplus of 0.2 percent of GDP, government debt was brought under control, and GDP's growth averaged 3.4 percent per year. The deficit was tamed primarily through cuts to primary current expenditures, including a significant reduction in the size of the public sector.[8]

While each of these three countries got to its respective crisis via a different route, the ultimate exit strategies were remarkably similar. In each case, successful reform began with a new government. In some instances the government explicitly ran on a platform of deficit reduction, as in Canada. In other cases the reforms were driven by market forces, as was the case in Ireland. In a more recent example, a similar dynamic appears to be playing out in the United Kingdom. In 2010, the new Conservative/Liberal Democrat Coalition, which defeated the existing Labor government, embarked on one of the most ambitious fiscal retrenchments in decades.

It appears that genuine fiscal reform is more likely when there is a change in leadership. In contrast, studies have shown that the likelihood of major budgetary reform falls in the run-up to an election.[9] Parties that are in power apparently rarely run on a platform of serious fiscal reform.

It may simply be the case that there is only so much honesty that the populace will tolerate. In the past, it would seem that the necessary but nevertheless painful cuts to government spending were possible only once a new government was safely in power. Perhaps a government, any government, needs the dual advantages of a new mandate and several years of breathing space before an election in order to make the necessary cuts, cuts that under normal conditions would be intolerable to voters. Another explanation is that given the amount of political capital that these changes required, only a fresh government, with little or no political baggage, was in a position to enact the necessary reforms.

Second, in all of the above cases the largest part of the fiscal consolidations occurred through reductions in public expenditures.[10] Tax hikes played a relatively small role. Each of the respective governments made deep cuts to public spending, specifically entitlement spending, and the size of the government payroll. In the absence of these cuts, there was little lasting success in reforming budgets. This is important as the historical evidence suggests that trying to tackle budget deficits primarily through tax increases does not work. Large tax increases tend to slow economic growth, which in turn slows government revenue and makes the deficit even higher. This is particularly true in the United States, where there is significant evidence that there is an upper limit on how much revenue the government can generate through taxes. Historically, in the United States this upper limit has been around 20 percent of GDP. This means that regardless of the tax rate, U.S. tax revenue seems to hit an upper limit of about one-fifth of the total economy. Tax hikes aiming to raise revenue above that threshold don't work because individuals and companies adapt their behaviors in ways that lower their tax liabilities.

Finally, it is worth noting that to a greater or lesser extent, market discipline also played a part in each case, via a rise in bond spreads, a more general increase in bond yields, or via a sovereign downgrade.[11] Each country needed a crisis to propel it to get sufficiently serious to make the difficult choices and implement the necessary reforms.

WHAT WILL A CREDIBLE U.S. PLAN LOOK LIKE?

As much as economists like to think of themselves as scientists, economics is not a hard science like physics. Ask 10 physicists to describe the relationship between mass and energy, and everyone will quote Einstein's famous $E = mc^2$. In contrast, economics is ultimately based on human behavior, which unlike the behavior of the planets, is inherently unpredictable and fickle.

So it is not surprising that when it comes to outlining the right way to reform government and balance the budget, there are a variety of opinions. Some of these differences are based on the ideology of the economist, and others are due to legitimate ambiguities in the historical examples. Still, there are some issues around which a general, often grudging, consensus tends to form. As the examples cited above illustrate, there is a fairly clear path to fiscal rectitude.

Before going through the specifics of how to reform the U.S. budget, however, it is worth highlighting the goal of any reform. What should be the proper measure of success? Obviously, deficits need to come down as a percentage of GDP. This can occur through smaller deficits and/or faster growth—happily the former normally induces the latter. The other key goal is to stabilize the national debt. The national debt will be a drain on future resources because all that debt needs to be repaid. So besides shrinking the year-to-year deficits, any deficit reform needs to also stabilize the national debt, preferably at a level below the 90 percent of GDP threshold, which has historically been the point at which real trouble begins.

Stabilizing the national debt requires not only smaller deficits but also greater economic growth and lowered interest rates. Based on interest rates, economic growth, and the size of the debt, you can easily calculate how big a surplus you need to keep the debt from getting any larger relative to GDP. In order to stabilize the debt-to-GDP ratio, a country's *primary budget balance*, which is the budget excluding interest payments on the debt, must be equal to or greater than $d \times (r - g)$, where d is the debt-to-GDP ratio, r is the interest rate on government debt, and g is the growth rate of the economy.[12]

Put in a less mathematical context, the faster the economy is growing, the easier it is to stabilize the debt. That is because a faster economy means a larger GDP, so a country can have a larger debt and still maintain a stable debt-to-GDP ratio. Faster economic growth also translates into higher tax revenues, which obviously make it easier to balance the budget. And lower interest rates will reduce the cost of carrying the debt. The simple point is: It will be easier to stabilize our debts when they are smaller, the economy is growing faster, and interest rates are low. The above formula also implies that the greater the debt level, the larger the primary surplus needed to stabilize the debt.

As an example of this dynamic, if the average interest rate paid on debt is 1 percent higher than the economy's growth rate, so $r - g = 1$ percent, then the required surplus gradually rises as the debt level rises. At a 50 percent debt-to-GDP ratio, the government would need to run a primary surplus of 0.5 percent to keep the debt-to-GDP ratio stable. In real life, the actual primary surplus needed would probably be a bit higher. Recall that higher debt levels can mean higher interest rates and slower economic growth. So as the debt grows, the government needs higher and higher primary surpluses.[13] The longer we wait, the bigger the debt will be, the more draconian the spending cuts will need to be, and the more difficult it will be to stabilize our national debt.

Even the Congressional Budget Office (CBO) acknowledges this. If you assume a very optimistic budget picture, one in which taxes go up on schedule and spending cuts actually happen, a permanent cut in spending or increase in revenue equal to about 1 percent of the GDP would stabilize the debt-to-GDP ratio over the next 25 years. Under a more realistic scenario, one in which tax cuts are extended and spending cuts don't always materialize, we would need to immediately eliminate spending or raise taxes equal to about 5 percent of GDP to stabilize the debt. And that assumes the very unlikely scenario that these actions would happen today. If the reforms are delayed, the cuts or tax hikes would need to be significantly greater to achieve the same objective.[14]

So, what needs to be done to get our fiscal house in order? First, we need a plan that is decisive, not gradual. Modern examples of successful budget reform all involved a "Big Bang" approach, rather than incremental changes. Second, as highlighted above, the reform should be led by spending cuts that reduce the size and scope of government obligations, rather than by large tax hikes. Finally, in the case of the United States, there is little disagreement that in order to address its long-term spending imbalances, medical spending needs to be reformed and the pace of health-care inflation slowed.

The first critical element in addressing the budget deficit is that the changes need to be decisive. Economic growth fares best when fiscal corrections are unequivocal, and faster economic growth will make it easier to bring our debt burden under control. There are several reasons for this. First, when fiscal imbalances are severe, people and businesses rationally assume that future spending will have to be cut or taxes will have to rise. As a result, individuals and corporations adjust their spending in advance. If the deficit is less threatening and individuals are less worried about future tax hikes, this can boost private spending. Second, when the fix is based significantly on spending cuts, this may help to loosen monetary conditions, either by reducing the cost of long-term debt or by reducing the exchange rate (recall that a cheaper dollar makes our exports more competitive). Finally, by cutting public sector employment, we lower the overall demand for workers. This has the added benefit of reducing labor costs, which in turn makes private companies more competitive.[15]

Large deficits make businesses, along with individuals, nervous. If government spending is too high relative to income, businesses rationally assume that at some point government will try to raise new income in the form of taxes. As a result, companies are more cautious when it comes to hiring and investing. It is, after all, more difficult to make a new investment or to hire new workers when a company is unsure what the tax bill will be next year. Conversely, when governments provide credible evidence that they are addressing their fiscal imbalances, investors grow more confident about the future and less scared that their taxes will have to rise to pay for the deficit. Companies are then more willing to hire more workers and invest in new plants and factories.

The second critical element is that any plan, like those of Ireland, Sweden, and Canada, needs to be disproportionately tilted toward spending cuts. Deficit reduction that is primarily financed by spending cuts is more likely to lead to a surge in net business investment, which ultimately helps spur economic growth.[16] Tax increases, on the other hand, cause both individuals and companies to rein in their spending, thus providing a break on overall economic growth.

In the case of the United States, budget reform must address government medical spending in the form of Medicare and Medicaid. Fiscal retrenchment needs to focus on Medicare and Medicaid for the same reason Willy Sutton used to rob banks—because that's where the money is. While Social Security, at least as it is currently structured, is also problematic over the long term, it is federal health-care spending that poses the greatest risk to fiscal solvency. The projected growth of Medicare and Medicaid is perhaps the single most important cause of the growing imbalance between projected revenues and expenditures. Under the projections using the current administration's assumptions, cutting the annual growth rate of health-care spending by 1.5 percentage points of GDP for 10 years would reduce the long-term fiscal gap by 1.5 percent of GDP. The same reduction for 30 years would reduce the gap by almost 4 percent of GDP.[17]

While addressing federal medical spending is a necessary precondition to addressing the deficit, it will not be easy. We have never succeeded in cutting health-care spending, but furthermore, since 1970, the average annual per enrollee growth rate for Medicare has been 9.6 percent![18]

And for those who naturally wonder, didn't we already address runaway health-care spending with health-care reform in 2010: there are good reasons to be skeptical that we've truly tackled this issue. While the bill originally purported to extend health-care coverage and still shave $138 billion off of the federal deficit, there is considerable doubt about those numbers. A former director of the Congressional Budget Office, Douglas Holtz-Eakin, suggests that the true cost of the 2010 reform act is to *add* $562 billion to the cumulative deficit over the next decade.[19] If he is right, that suggests that the cumulative increase in debt between the official estimate and reality would add another $700 billion to the national debt by 2020.

How can two estimates for the same budget item be nearly $1 trillion different from each other? The answer lies in the plausibility of the assumptions written into the legislation. First, the official budget estimates frontload the revenue from extra taxes, but it backloads the extra spending. New taxes start immediately, but new spending does not kick in until later. The result is that 10 years of revenue are compared to 6 years of spending. Second, Congress conveniently omitted the extra $144 billion of annual spending it will need to operate the new programs. Third, the bill counts approximately $50 billion in anticipated higher Social Security taxes to offset the higher health-care spending. These higher contributions are expected to come from higher wages as employers shift from paying health-care insurance to paying higher wages. But if employees make higher contributions, they will eventually be owed higher benefits. So the extra money raised is already spoken for. Only in the surreal world of government budget math do we get to spend the same money twice. Fourth, and the most disingenuous part of the process, the legislation proposes to trim nearly half a trillion dollars from Medicare spending to finance insurance subsidies. Similar cuts have been proposed in the past, but they have never materialized.[20]

A workable plan for the United States will not look that different from the ones enacted by Ireland, Sweden, and Canada. If the United States is ever to solve its fiscal problems, it will need to do it decisively. That means that the necessary fiscal reforms need to be enacted in one shot rather than in several. A piecemeal approach is not likely to succeed. In terms of the composition of the plan, most of the savings need to come from reduced government spending and reduced entitlement spending. And finally, the spending cuts will have to include significant modifications and cuts to the big entitlement programs—namely, Social Security,

Medicaid, and particularly Medicare. Unfortunately, we are still a long way from any of this taking place.

The truth is, the United States is pretty far down the path, heading toward a debt crisis. And while the vast resources and underlying vitality of the U.S. economy have made this a long time in coming, we should not be complacent in thinking that real damage has not been done. Even under the most optimistic estimates provided, closing the U.S. fiscal gap will require a permanent reduction in noninterest spending of around 25 percent or a permanent revenue increase of more than 30 percent. These are big, and arguably politically impossible, numbers. If the spending cuts and tax increases aren't made across the board and are more narrowly focused, they will have to be even more draconian. A 56.6 percent increase in income taxes, for example, would be needed![21] Not exactly a winning campaign slogan.

IMPROBABLE, BUT NOT IMPOSSIBLE

The only encouragement comes from the fact that other countries have somehow managed to pull it off, and others are making a good-faith effort even under the current fragile economy. The United Kingdom's efforts are the best real-time example of a large, developed economy attempting significant budgetary reform. The United Kingdom has been able to implement these reforms despite the fact that its annual deficits are modestly higher as a percentage of its GDP; the annual deficits are around 11.5 percent in the United Kingdom versus 10 percent in the United States for 2010. Furthermore, the United Kingdom does not have the advantage of having its pound sterling serve as the world's currency. Yet, despite these obstacles, following the 2010 election and the formation of the Tory/Liberal Democrat Coalition, the government is at least making a stab at serious fiscal reform. This follows the pattern seen in the previous examples. The Conservatives effectively ran on a platform that the existing fiscal situation was unsustainable.

While the full program has yet to be enacted, the plan follows the formula outlined above. It is decisive and aggressive, and it relies primarily on spending cuts rather than tax increases. If all goes according to plan, the deficit will fall from 11 percent of GDP in 2009 and 2010 to 2.1 percent of GDP in 2014 and 2015. The *structural deficit*, which is calculated to strip out the effects of the economic cycles, will drop from 8.7 percent of GDP to 0.8 percent, with the vast majority of the adjustment coming from spending cuts. Outside of the national health services (NHS), which will for now be spared the pain of any budgetary cuts, the departments responsible for other public services face cuts of 25 percent by 2014 and 2015.[22]

All of this will be very painful, and it may not all come off as planned. But while there will be bumps along the road, there have already been some early rewards. The government has already gained some credibility with investors: interest rates started to fall soon after the plan was announced.[23]

So there is some hope. Even today, in a world of slow economic growth, some countries are summoning the necessary political will. But again, it is interesting to see that the recent example has followed the pattern of Ireland, Sweden, and Canada. The reforms came after an election and after a change of government. Given our electoral calendar, this suggests that meaningful deficit reform could theoretically begin in 2013, or not until 2017. By that point, we probably will be looking at a crisis.

THE ECONOMIC PAYOFFS OF REAL REFORM

So for the sake of argument, let's say in two or six years, the United States follows in the footsteps of Ireland, Sweden, Canada, and the United Kingdom. Somehow we manage to summon the will to own up to our problems and propose real solutions. What will happen next?

At first, fiscal reform will be painful. As government spending pulls back, there will be some drag on economic growth. This can be mitigated to some extent by easier monetary policy, although the Fed may not have much scope to cut interest rates if they are still close to their current level, effectively zero. Slower growth will also probably cut into corporate earnings. Economic growth will likely remain anemic until the private sector—both individuals and companies—starts to develop confidence and resume spending and investing.

The good news is that in an environment of slower growth and less government spending, inflation becomes less of a risk. Recall that inflation tends to correlate with government spending. Unless private consumption and investment immediately rally, lower demand from the government will mean lower overall demand and less inflationary pressure.

Like any tough medicine, it will take a while for the beneficial effects of deficit reduction to be felt. But if other economies that have followed a similar path are any guide, there are real long-term benefits that will significantly change some of the gloomy prognostications from earlier in the book.

As the government shrinks and the threat of new taxes starts to fade, economic growth eventually accelerates. As a result, businesses spend more, and new investment helps to drive a recovery. Private consumption and business investment more than make up for the drop in government spending, especially if taxes remain stable and people are less fearful of future deficit-driven tax increases. In short, a virtuous cycle ensues.

Alongside better economic growth, financial markets also perform well in the wake of a dramatic cut in government expenditures. To start with, both nominal and real bond yields fall as investors become less concerned with the government's finances. The benefits are not confined to bonds. Stocks also tend to rally. Faster economic growth translates into stronger corporate earnings, and lower interest rates mean higher earnings multiples. As a result, stocks tend to rally strongly following significant fiscal reform. In the aftermath of deficit reduction, equity markets in that country also outperform other countries by a large margin. Historically, developed countries that enact meaningful deficit reduction outperform their peers by a significant margin, 64 percent, in the three-year period following the fiscal reform.[24]

So the long-term payoff for real fiscal reform is significant. It includes a more robust economy, lower bond yields, and a strong stock market. Lowering or at least stabilizing the national debt will also lower the risk that a future government decides to monetize the debt. As such, the risk of a big spike in inflation will also be reduced. All considered, a pretty good deal if the United States can ever pull it off.

How to Shift Your Portfolio

The investment strategy outlined over the previous chapters was predicated on an environment of slow growth, high real and nominal interest rates, and a growing risk of high inflation over the long term. And while a smaller deficit does not remove all the world's problems—recessions can still occur, and we had some pretty nasty inflation in the 1970s before the deficit ever got as bad as it is now—it does suggest a brighter economic picture and fewer risks. Both of these argue for a more aggressive and less defensive asset allocation and investment strategy.

Addressing the deficit is likely to be a positive influence on most financial markets in another respect as well. Any successful fiscal reform is likely to go hand in hand with addressing some of the nation's other long-term challenges, including an overly complex tax code that favors consumption over investment and runaway health-care inflation. In conjunction with reducing the deficit, you will also need to address at least two of the other principal challenges facing the United States. The result will be a more dynamic economy and a better environment for taking risk.

Removing, or at least mitigating, one of the biggest risks to the U.S. economy should have a big impact on how you position your investments. When and if we start to see the policy responses described above, you'll want to make the following shifts to your portfolio. Start with less cash, more high-yield bonds, more stocks (particularly U.S. stocks), and less gold.

INTEREST RATES, BONDS, AND CASH

In all the previous recommendations, the assumption is that the deficit and debt problems will not be seriously addressed anytime soon. As a result, in terms of your cash and fixed-income exposure, I have recommended that you should increase your cash holdings, reduce your exposure to bonds, lower the duration of your bond portfolio, and avoid U.S. Treasuries. Interestingly, many of these recommendations remain broadly the same even in the case of real deficit reform. What really changes under deficit reform are which bonds you hold and the extent to which you lower your bond duration.

The recommendation on cash is the big change. Holding a lot of cash in your portfolio makes sense in a rising rate environment because cash actually performs decently in the event of inflation. The other argument for holding more cash is that it is a source of stability during volatile times. However, if rates are more stable, inflation is less of a threat, and if a financial crisis is less likely, there is no investment reason to hold a big cash position. In a world in which the deficit threat is mitigated, the cash holdings in your long-term portfolio should be minimal.

One strategy to stick with, even in the face of real deficit reform, is to lower your bond allocation from the traditional 30 percent recommendation. As of this writing, investors are too infatuated with bonds. Flows into bond funds resemble the type of excessive enthusiasm that investors had for stocks in the late 1990s. Patterns suggest that bonds are overvalued. Lower your bond positions regardless of what happens in Washington. However, in the event of real reform, you won't need to cut your recommendation as aggressively as recommended in Chapter 5.

Under a controlled-deficit scenario, investors who are still decades away from retirement should probably look to have roughly a quarter of their investable assets in bonds. Given the recent historically low level of U.S. interest rates, even without large deficits, interest rates are likely to rise, albeit less so, over the long term. Once the U.S. consumer sector repairs its balance sheet and corporations stop stuffing money under their collective mattress, the demand for capital will resume and rates will rise. But the rise will be more modest and less of a long-term threat in a world where the government is not forced to borrow over $1 trillion a year to finance its deficit. This means that while a long-term bond bull market is still unlikely, the bear market in bonds is likely to be less severe and interest rates will not rise as far as they might have otherwise. I would still advocate avoiding long-dated bonds—that is, bonds with maturities of 10 years or more. But to the extent that the yield curve is steep and investors can gain some extra yield by owning 5- to 7-year bonds rather than 2- or 3-year bonds, the risk will be much less in the absence of large deficits.

And as for the types of bonds: Buying a 10-year Treasury at 3 percent still makes little sense to me. Even if inflation remains muted and the Fed does its job, in a normal economy we are likely to see inflation in the 2 to 3 percent range. Assuming tax rates stay where they were the previous decade, that still means that after paying your federal taxes, your after-tax yield on a long duration asset is barely 2 percent in a world where inflation is likely to be at least that high. Buying Treasuries in the 3 percent range makes sense only in a world where you expect long-term deflation, where any income is a good thing. In a more normal environment, this is not a good way to build wealth—deficit or no deficit. Stick with munis, corporate bonds, and foreign sovereign bonds—unless Treasury yields get back to above 5 percent.

In particular, in the face of deficit reform, investors should allocate a higher portion of their bond portfolio to high-yield corporate bonds. Following meaningful deficit reform, the historical pattern suggests a period of high growth and low inflation. Under these economic conditions, high-yield bonds are the second-best-performing asset class after equities because a high growth environment helps support corporate cash flows and lowers the default risk on these securities.

STOCKS: A NEW BULL MARKET?

Long-term bull markets normally start with a catalyst. In the early 1980s it was a growing conviction that the Fed was finally winning the fight against inflation. Real deficit reform could be the catalyst for another secular bull market. So in the event that the government really does slash spending, you should buy more stocks, particularly those of U.S. companies.

Earlier, I made a distinction between a cyclical bull market and a secular one. Cyclical bull markets can happen even when the long-term direction of the market is down. Over the past decade, there have been some fantastic years to invest in stocks, particularly 2003 and 2009. Yet anyone who invested in the U.S. stock market in 2000 has probably still not broken even. That is because we are in a secular bear market. In contrast, the period between 1982 and 2000 was a great time to own equities. There was still the occasional bear market, and there were a few crashes, but had you bought stocks at the lows in 1982 and slept for the next 18 years, you would have been deliriously happy when you awoke. Arguably, meaningful deficit reduction could kick off another positive cycle. Through deficit reduction we are likely to see an economy defined by faster economic growth, which will in turn lead to faster corporate earnings, lower real interest rates, and less of a risk of inflation. All of these will be unambiguously good for equities.

In Chapter 2 a case was made for why debt can drag down growth and hurt most domestic companies. This relationship also works in reverse. Faster economic growth translates into more robust corporate earnings. Lower interest rates will enable companies to borrow more cheaply because they won't have to compete with the federal government for access to capital. Lower rates are also likely to lead to higher earnings multiples. So not only will earnings grow faster, thanks to a more robust economy, but investors are also more likely to pay more for each dollar of earnings. Finally, lowering the national debt removes a huge potential risk from the market. An ever-growing national debt implies a greater chance of a financial crisis over the long term. It might be an unexpected spike in inflation if the government appears to be monetizing the debt. It could also be a plunge in the dollar as foreign investors start to step away from dollar-denominated assets. Investors don't like uncertainty, and removing these potential sources of financial instability will also be good for stocks.

Recall from Chapter 7 that stocks were by far the best-performing asset class when economic growth was high and inflation was low. This is exactly the type of environment that countries typically enjoy in the wake of real fiscal reform. Under this scenario, you want to overweight or increase your allocation to equities. Rather than looking at a 40 to 50 percent position in stocks, younger more aggressive investors should probably be looking at 60 to 65 percent in stocks.

Furthermore, if the route to fiscal redemption comes via a crisis in faith, investors are likely to get an even better opportunity to load up on equities. Just as the inflation crisis of the 1970s and 1980s led to the abandonment of equities, a debt crisis will probably lead to a similar aversion to stocks. In 1982, investors were so unwilling to invest in equities that you could buy large, stable U.S. companies for seven to eight times earnings—a quarter of the valuation on those same stocks in 2000. If the precedent to fiscal reform is the fear of fiscal collapse, investors are likely to get another such buying opportunity. Once you start to see the real reform steps outlined above, buy.

As for what to buy, investors still want to favor emerging markets as the arguments for overweighting these stocks regardless of the U.S. deficit. But, as for your allocation to developed countries, put more of an emphasis on the United States. Following significant fiscal reform, U.S. stocks are likely to outperform other developed markets. This means owning more U.S. stocks, and fewer of other developed countries like Europe, Japan, Canada, or Australia. Finally, favor more cyclical companies that will benefit from faster economic growth. These include technology, industrial, and consumer discretionary stocks. (Consumer discretionary stocks are companies that sell things to consumers that they don't necessarily need. They would include stocks in department stores or restaurants.)

Commodities: Keep the Copper, Lose the Gold

Deficit or no deficit, you still want to keep roughly 10 percent of your assets in commodities. Even in a regime characterized by high growth but low inflation, commodities do all right. While they probably won't do as well as stocks or high-yield corporate bonds, historically they have still beaten cash, Treasuries, and investment-grade bonds in these environments.

As outlined in the previous chapter, from diversification to faster demand from emerging markets, there are good reasons to have a significant commodity position, regardless of the fiscal health of the United States. Furthermore, if we do have stronger economic growth as a result of reforms in our deficit spending practices, this will support more cyclically oriented commodities—industrial metals and energy—as faster economic growth equates with more demand. So favor a commodity fund or index with a heavy allocation to oil, copper, and other industrial metals. These will benefit the most from a robust economy.

What should change is your allocation to gold. Chapter 7 outlined gold's many virtues. It protects purchasing power and hedges your portfolio against inflation. It is a safe haven in a financial crisis. And finally, it is an alternative currency. In a world in which investors are concerned that money may not be worth the paper it's written on, gold becomes an attractive way to store wealth.

The flip side to that argument is that gold produces no income, and unlike copper or energy, it serves no useful purpose. Demand for gold does not suddenly spike because the economy is strong, unless economic growth is starting to lead to inflation. In a more stable world with stronger growth and a lower overall risk of a crisis, there are fewer reasons to own gold. And as the return to other asset classes—everything from high-yield bonds to U.S. stocks—rises, the opportunity cost of owning gold also rises. You give up potential returns to own an asset that produces no income and no growth.

If the government does tackle its deficit spending, you should lower your allocation to gold. In Chapter 7 I advocated a position of 5 to 10 percent to gold, depending on how imminent the inflation risk is. Lower government spending mitigates the risk of inflation, as inflation has historically been higher when governments are spending more. A smaller national debt will also lower the risk, as there will be less of a temptation to monetize the debt or otherwise encourage inflation. All else being equal, lower deficits should lower the risk of inflation.

If gold is an insurance policy against inflation, the circumstances I described above will mean that you'll need less insurance. Assuming you no longer need the same level of inflation protection, investors can probably lower their allocation to gold from 5 to 10 percent to 2 to 3 percent.

So what you are left with is a portfolio somewhat different from the one described in Chapter 9. If deficit spending remains unchecked and the national debt continues to pile up, you will want a more defensive portfolio: 10 to 15 percent cash, 15 to 25 percent bonds, 40 to 55 percent stocks, and as much as 20 percent in commodities and gold. In contrast, in the wake of meaningful deficit reform, things are likely to look a lot better. Once it is clear that we are on this path, get more aggressive. Under this scenario a more appropriate portfolio would entail less cash, 5 to 10 percent; a slightly higher allocation to bonds, 20 to 25 percent with an emphasis on high yield; a much higher allocation to stocks, 60 percent; and an allocation to commodities of around 10 percent, but tilted toward energy and industrial metals and away from gold.

CONCLUSION

Back in the summer of 2010, when I was in the middle of working on this book, an interesting news story appeared. The article was about the deficit commission that had recently been assembled to address the United States' long-term fiscal future, no small undertaking. In setting up the commission to tackle this broad problem, the administration had to provide a budget. The budget would be used to pay for staff, office space, travel expenses, and so on. By way of comparison, there were a number of other commissions operating at the same time. One commission was addressing the BP oil spill. That commission had a budget of $15 million. There was another commission that had been convened to investigate Wall Street and the financial meltdown. It got a budget of $8 million. The budget commission—charged with reengineering $3.5 trillion of annual spending, $14 trillion of national debt, and tens of trillions in unfunded liabilities—received a budget of $500,000, less money than the government had recently spent on a study to expand a congressional underground garage.[25] If you want one anecdote to sum up the challenge we face and the extent to which the United States is still in denial, this is a pretty good choice.

Whether and when we address the deficit is ultimately a political choice. Unfortunately, recent evidence is not encouraging. In late 2010, two events illustrated that while the deficit lends itself to good political rhetoric, and occasionally theater, there are few easy or politically viable solutions. First, the president's deficit commission was unable to muster enough votes to support its own recommendations; leaving the plan more or less dead on arrival. Second, Congress was able to add another

$900 billion to the deficit through the extension of various tax cuts and unemployment insurance, but it was unable to summon the same spirit of bipartisanship to offer any plans on longer-term fiscal reform. This follows the pattern of recent years. The political compromises that are reached all tend to increase the deficit, never reduce it. As has been repeated throughout this book, despite all the economic jargon, the deficit is a political issue that will ultimately manifest itself as an economic problem, and eventually a crisis.

Thirty-five years ago in one of the seminal books on the hyperinflation that plagued Weimar Germany, Adam Fergusson framed the issue of inflation as a political one. His language is just as relevant for the related issue of the deficit:

> How can one gauge the political significance of inflation, or judge the circumstances in which inflation in an industrialized democracy takes root and becomes uncontrollable, unless its course is chartered side by side with the political events of the moment?[26]

The deficit can be addressed, the national debt stabilized and even reduced. But this can happen only when the United States owns up to its problem and enacts fiscal reform with teeth, not gimmicks. In the absence of this, the problems will continue to mount. And while it is fun and to some extent fair to blame our politicians, the truth is that most of the country is still in denial. A recent poll, taken shortly after the president's commission announced its findings, illustrates the disconnect. While Americans acknowledge that the deficit is "dangerously out of control," they want to address it only under two conditions: minimize the pain and make the rich pay. The public would like Congress to fix the deficit, but kindly avoid touching Medicare, Medicaid, Social Security, cuts to major domestic or defense programs, farm subsidies, and tax breaks like the mortgage-interest deduction.[27] In short, we are nowhere near addressing this problem.

For investors trying to make sense of how all of this will eventually play out, the question comes down to: Is the United States on a course to emulate Rome or Canada? Admittedly, a strange comparison, but the simple fact is that Rome's eventual demise had a large economic component, and the policies that the Romans used to address their imbalances—such as debasing the currency—further exacerbated their problems and contributed to the ultimate decline of that society.

On the other hand, other nations have faced up to the implications of unsustainable policies, changed course, and reaped the benefits. Ireland, Sweden, and Canada all demonstrate that this can be done with sufficient political will. Interestingly, real cuts and a sustainable plan seem to occur only when all other options have been exhausted.

Ironically, this fact will work against the United States, and it is one reason I believe that things will get worse before they get better. If a crisis is needed to precipitate real reform, it will be slower in coming for the United States than it was for Canada or Sweden. The United States is still the world's largest and richest economy. Most economic transactions are denominated in dollars. And despite all the aforementioned problems, the United States is still viewed as a safe haven when the rest of the world appears to be crashing down. In early 2010 when investors woke up to the budgetary problems of Greece, Spain, and other southern European countries, the dollar and U.S. Treasuries rallied. While we were and still are facing our own imbalances, for most investors buying a U.S. Treasury and owning a U.S. dollar seemed safer than the other choices. As a result, the United States will get away with an irresponsible fiscal policy and unsustainable spending longer than any other country. Investors will give it more latitude, which it may ultimately use to its detriment. When the financial crisis finally does hit, government spending, deficits, and the national debt are likely to all be much larger than they are today.

In the absence of reform, one day investors will wake up to the reality that the United States is no longer the safest place to put their money. What precipitates the crisis is hard to say. It may begin with a weak government bond auction or some particularly aggressive budgetary gimmick. But on the current trajectory, it will eventually happen.

And while there are no certainties in investing, investors need to prepare for the most likely scenario and environment. Today, that future includes an increasing likelihood of slow growth, higher interest rates, a weak U.S. stock market, and a significant chance of inflation over the long term. Not every change has to happen immediately, but investors should have a playbook on hand on what to watch for and what to do as events unfold. As with any potential crisis, it is better to have a plan ready before it hits.

NOTES

INTRODUCTION

1. Sara Murray, "Obstacle to Deficit Cutting: A Nation on Entitlements," *Wall Street Journal*, September 14, 2010.

CHAPTER 1

1. Amaud Mares, *Ask Not Whether Governments Will Default, but How*, Morgan Stanley, August 25, 2010, p. 3.

2. Congressional Budget Office (CBO), Long Range Fiscal Brief, No. 1, Government Printing Office (GPO), Washington, D.C., June 14, 2002; revised July 3, 2002.

3. Bruce Bartlett, "How Excessive Government Killed Ancient Rome," Cato Institute, *Cato Journal*, vol. 14, no. 2, fall 1994.

4. Joseph M. Miller, Daan Joubert, and Marion Butler, "Grand Super Cycle National Bankruptcies Part IV: Fall of the Roman Empire." Accessed at www .freebuck.com/articles/elliott/030209bankruptcies1.htm on September 8, 2009.

5. Office of Management and Budget, *Economic and Budget Analysis*, p. 21. Accessed at www.whitehouse.gov/omb/budget/Overview/ on January 31, 2010.

6. Congressional Budget Office (CBO), "Cost Estimation for Pending Health Care Legislation," Congressional Budget Office Director's Blog. Accessed at www.cboblog.cbo.gov/?p=546 in an entry posted on Sunday, March 21, 2010.

7. John Steel Gordon, "A Short History of the National Debt," *Wall Street Journal*, February 18, 2009.

8. Ibid.

9. Douglas Elmendorf, "CBO Testimony: The Long-Term Budget Outlook," before the Senate Committee on the Budget, July 16, 2009, p. 1.

10. Census Bureau, U.S. Population Projections. Accessed at www.census.gov /population/www/projections/summarytables.html on February 10, 2010.

11. Ibid.

12. Elmendorf, "CBO Testimony," p. 16.

13. Ibid.

CHAPTER 2

1. Peter R. Orszag, *The Budget Deficit: Does It Matter?* paper presented at the City Club of Cleveland, July 16, 2004.

2. Douglas Elmendorf, "CBO Testimony: The Long-Term Budget Outlook," before the Senate Committee on the Budget, July 16, 2009, p. 21.

3. Orszag, *The Budget Deficit.*

4. Ari Aisen and David Hauner, *Budget Deficits and Interest Rates: A Fresh Perspective,* working paper, International Monetary Fund (IMF), February 2008.

5. Bruce Bartlett, "How Excessive Government Killed Ancient Rome," Cato Institute, *Cato Journal,* vol. 14, no. 2, fall 1994.

CHAPTER 4

1. www.federalreserve.gov/pubs/arms/arms_english.htm. Accessed on May 4, 2010.

2. Ibid.

3. Ibid.

4. Sewell Chan, "Fed Ends Its Purchasing of Mortgage Securities," *New York Times,* March 31, 2010.

5. Ibid.

6. www.federalreserve.gov/pubs/arms/arms_english.htm. Accessed on May 4, 2010.

7. Ibid.

8. www.fdic.gov/EDIE/fdic_info.html. Accessed on May 3, 2010.

CHAPTER 5

1. Wikipedia. Accessed on May 14, 2010.

2. Ibid.

3. George Strickland, Josh Gonze, Christopher Ihlefeld, and Christopher Ryan, *Strategies for Building Real Wealth,* Thornburg Investment Management, June 2, 2010.

4. Ibid.

5. Anna Prior, "Comparing ETFs and Index Funds," *Wall Street Journal*, August 2, 2010, p. R5.

6. Ibid.

7. BlackRock Individual Investor, Point of View with Peter Hayes, "On New Playing Field, Munis Still Swinging Strong," May 2010, p. 3.

8. Ibid., p. 2.

9. Ibid.

10. Amaud Mares, *Ask Not Whether Governments Will Default, but How?* Morgan Stanley Research, August 25, 2010, p. 3.

11. Ibid.

12. PIMCO, Global Bond Basics, www.pimco.com/Left/NAV/Bond+Basics /2007/Global+Bond+Basics12-07.htm. Accessed on May 21, 2010.

13. *Emerging Market Debt: Becoming a Mainstream Asset Class*, BlackRock, March 2008, p. 2.

14. Ibid., p. 3.

15. Alexander P. Attie and Shaun K Roache, *Inflation Hedging for Long-Term Investors*, working paper, International Monetary Fund (IMF), June 2010.

16. *Inflation-Linked Bonds Primer*, BlackRock, October 2009, p. 1.

17. Ibid.

18. Fred Weinberger and Brian Weinstein, "TIPS to Hedge Inflation: Problems with TIPS," *Currents Quarterly News from BlackRock*, May 2010, p. 12.

19. Ibid.

20. Ibid.

21. Bureau of Labor Statistics (BLS), "How the CPI Measures Price Change of Owner's Equivalent Rent of Primary Residence and Rent of Primary Residence," www.bls.gov/cpi/cpifacnewrent.pdf, p. 1. Accessed on May 21, 2010.

CHAPTER 6

1. Jan Hatzius, Ed McKelvey, Alec Philips, Sven Jari Stehn, and Andrew Tilton, *No Rush for the Exit*, Global Economics Paper No. 200, Goldman Sachs, June 30, 2010, p. 9.

2. Ben Broadbent and Kevin Daly, *Limiting the Fall-Out from Fiscal Adjustment*, Global Economics Paper No. 195, Goldman Sachs, April 14, 2010, p. 7.

3. Alexander P. Attie and Shaun K. Roache, *Inflation Hedging for Long-Term Investors*, working paper, International Monetary Fund (IMF), April 1, 2009, p. 8.

4. Ibid., p. 23.

5. International Monetary Fund (IMF), World Economic and Financial Survey, "Navigating the Fiscal Challenges Ahead," *Fiscal Monitor*, May 14, 2010, p. 21.

6. CIA World Factbook Country Comparison, Public Debt, www.cia.gov/library/publications/the-world-factbook/rankorder/2186rank.html. Accessed on July 19, 2010.

7. *Myths and Realities of Global Equities, Six Reasons to Rethink Your Approach to Global Investing*, BlackRock, June 2010, p. 7.

8. Russ Koesterich, *The ETF Strategist: Balancing Risk and Reward for Superior Returns*, Portfolio Books, 2008, p. 65.

9. Norbert Michel, Ph.D., and Ralph Rector, Ph.D., *Dividend Policy and the 2003 Tax Cut: Preliminary Evidence,* published on October 25, 2004. Accessed at www.heritage.org/Research/Reports/2004/10/Dividend-Policy-and-the-2003-Tax-Cut-Preliminary-Evidence, on July 9, 2010

10. Minder Cheng and Ananth Madhaven, *The Dynamics of Leveraged and Inverse Exchange-Traded Funds*, Barclays Global Investors, April 8, 2009, p. 2.

11. BarclayHedge, Alternative Databases, Barclay Equity Market Neutral Index, www.barclayhedge.com/research/indices/ghs/Equity_Market_Neutral_Index.html. Accessed on July 19, 2010.

12. Ibid.

13. Koesterich, *The ETF Strategist*, p. 192.

CHAPTER 7

1. Alexander P. Attie and Shaun K. Roache, *Inflation Hedging for Long-Term Investors*, working paper, International Monetary Fund (IMF), April 1, 2009, p. 9.

2. Ibid., p. 15.

3. U.S. Energy Information Administration, "Highlights," *International Energy Outlook 2010*, release date May 25, 2010, www.eia.doe.gov/oiaf/ieo/highlights.html. Accessed on August 6, 2010.

4. Anna Stablum and Millie Munshi, "Copper Shortages Loom as Codelco Sees Limits on Mines," Bloomberg, July 6, 2010.

5. Rhodri Thomas, *Energy Report, World Energy Book: Unconventional Hydrocarbons: A Hidden Opportunity, Petroleum Economist,* January 15, 2010, www.petroleum-economist.com/default.asp?Page=14&PUB=279&SID=700775&ISS=24502. Accessed on August 2, 2010.

6. Ibbotson Associates, *Portfolio Diversification with Gold, Silver, and Platinum,* study prepared for the Bullion Management Group, Inc., by Thomas M. Idzorek, CFA, June 1, 2005, Executive Summary.

7. Ibid.

8. Scotiamocatta, Precious Metals Forecast 2010 Silver, October 2009.

CHAPTER 8

1. www.reit.com/AboutREITs/AllAboutREITs.aspx. Accessed on August 28, 2010.
2. Ibid.
3. Ibid.
4. *Global Real Estate Trust Investment Report 2010, Against All Odds,* Ernst & Young, p. 11.
5. Janet Morrissey, "REIT Returns Fell 37.3 Percent in 2008," *Investment News,* January 7, 2009, www.investmentnews.com/article/20090107 /REG/901079980. Accessed on September 2, 2010.
6. Bahram Adrangi, Arjun Chatrath, and Kambiz Raffiee, "REIT Investments and Hedging against Inflation," *Journal of Real Estate Portfolio Management,* vol. 10, no. 2, 2004, p. 7.
7. John D. Greenlee, Associate Director, Division of Banking Supervision and Regulation, "Residential and Commercial Real Estate," before the House of Representatives Subcommittee on Domestic Policy, Committee on Oversight and Government Reform, Atlanta, Georgia, November 2009. Accessed at www.federalreserve.gov/newsevents/testimony/greenlee20091102a.htm. Reprinted in Youguo Liang and James R. Webb, *Journal of Real Estate Research,* p. 1.
8. Youguo Liang and James R. Webb, "Pricing Interest-Rate Risk for Mortgage REITS," *Journal of Real Estate Research,* vol. 10, no. 4, 1995.
9. Greenlee, "Residential and Commercial Real Estate."
10. Adrangi, Chatrath, and Raffiee, "REIT Investments and Hedging against Inflation," p. 1.
11. Ibid.
12. Ibid.
13. Ibid.
14. Ibid, p. 10.

CHAPTER 9

1. Gary Brinston, Brian D. Singer, and Gilbert L. Beebower, "Determinants of Portfolio Performance II, an Update," *Financial Analysts Journal,* May–June 1991.
2. *Role of Asset Classes in Strategic Asset Allocation,* Asset Allocation Staff, Calpers Investment Office, Appendix 1, March 15, 2010.
3. *Asset Returns under Economic Regions: January 1970 to December 2009,* Calpers Investment Office, Appendix 1, March 2010.
4. Ibid.

5. Ibid.

6. Ibid.

7. Ibid.

8. Alexander P. Attie and Shaun K. Roache, *Inflation Hedging for Long-Term Investors,* working paper, International Monetary Fund (IMF), April 1, 2009, p. 23.

9. *Asset Returns under Economic Regions: January 1970 to December 2009.*

10. Ibid.

11. Grace Gu and Phil Green, *Dynamic Asset Allocation under Different Phases in Business Cycles,* BlackRock, July 29, 2009, p. 7.

12. Attie and Roache, *Inflation Hedging for Long-Term Investors*

13. Ibid.

14. *Asset Returns under Economic Regions: January 1970 to December 2009.*

15. Attie and Roache, *Inflation Hedging for Long-Term Investors,* p. 14.

16. Ibid., p. 23.

17. *Real Returns Risk and Correlations (1970 to 1998),* Barclays Capital Equity Gilt Study, 2010.

18. Ibbotson Associates, *Portfolio Diversification with Gold, Silver, and Platinum,* study prepared for the Bullion Management Group, Inc., by Thomas M. Idzorek, CFA, June 1, 2005, p. 2.

19. Ibid.

20. M. Briere and O. Signori, *Inflation-Hedging Portfolios in Different Inflation Regimes,* University Libre de Bruxelles Solvay Brussels School of Economics and Management, Credit Agricole Asset Management, August 24, 2009, p. 18.

21. Ibid., p. 20.

22. Ibbotson Associates, *Portfolio Diversification with Gold, Silver, and Platinum.*

CHAPTER 10

1. Ben Broadbent and Kevin Daly, *Limiting the Fall-Out from Fiscal Adjustment,* Global Economics Paper No. 195, Goldman Sachs, April 14, 2010, p. 16.

2. Ibid.

3. Ibid., p. 17.

4. Ibid.

5. Ibid., p. 18.

6. Ibid., p. 19.

7. Ibid.

8. Ibid., p. 20.

9. Ibid.

10. Ibid.

11. Ibid.

12. Jan Hatzius, Ed McKelvey, Alec Philips, Andrew Tilton, Sven Jari Stehn, David Kelley, and Maria Acosta-Cruz, "Assessing the Sustainability of Government Debt," *U.S. Economic Analyst,* issue no. 10/15, April 16, 2010, Goldman Sachs Global ECS Research, p. 2.

13. Ibid.

14. Congressional Budget Office (CBO), Economic and Budget Issue Brief: Federal Debt and the Risk of a Fiscal Crisis, Current Path, July 27, 2010, p. 2.

15. Broadbent and Daly, *Limiting the Fall-Out from Fiscal Adjustment,* p. 4.

16. Ibid.

17. Alan J. Auerback and William G. Gale, "The Economic Crisis and the Fiscal Crisis: 2009 and Beyond—an Update," Brookings Institution, June 2009, p. 4.

18. Christina Boccuti and Marilyn Moon, "Comparing Medicare and Private Insurers: Growth Rates in Spending over Three Decades," www.content .healthaffairs.org/content/22/2/230.full. Accessed on August 15, 2010.

19. Douglas Holtz-Eakin, "The Real Arithmetic of Healthcare Reform," op-ed, *New York Times,* March 20, 2010, www.nytimes.com/2010/03/21 /opinion/21holtz-eakin.html.

20. Ibid.

21. Auerback and Gale, "The Economic Crisis and the Fiscal Crisis," p. 16.

22. "The Unlikely Revolutionary," *Economist,* August 14, 2010, p. 19.

23. Ibid., p. 20.

24. Broadbent and Daly, *Limiting the Fall-Out from Fiscal Adjustment,* p. 5.

25. Brian Faler, Bloomberg News, June 25, 2010.

26. Adam Fergusson, *When Money Dies: The Nightmare of Deficit Spending, Devaluation, and Hyperinflation in Weimar Germany,* Public Affairs, New York, 1975, p. x.

27. Heidi Przybyla and Mike Dorning, "Americans in Poll Want Deficit Cut with Entitlements Secured," Bloomberg News, December 9, 2010, p. 1.

INDEX

ABOUT THE AUTHOR

Russ Koesterich is iShares chief investment strategist and global head of investment strategy for BlackRock Scientific Active Equities. He previously served as senior portfolio manager in the U.S. Market Neutral Group for Barclays Global Investors. Koesterich is the author of *The ETF Strategist*.